UNDERSTANDING THE
DALAI LAMA
A SIMPLE SMILING MONK

Edited by Rajiv Mehrotra

HAY HOUSE

Australia • Canada • Hong Kong • India
South Africa • United Kingdom • United States

Published and distributed in the United Kingdom by:
Hay House UK Ltd, 292B Kensal Rd, London W10 5BE. Tel.: (44) 20 8962 1230; Fax: (44) 20 8962 1239. www.hayhouse.co.uk

Published and distributed in the United States of America by:
Hay House, Inc., PO Box 5100, Carlsbad, CA 92018-5100. Tel.: (1) 760 431 7695 or (800) 654 5126; Fax: (1) 760 431 6948 or (800) 650 5115. www.hayhouse.com

Published and distributed in Australia by:
Hay House Australia Ltd, 18/36 Ralph St, Alexandria NSW 2015. Tel.: (61) 2 9669 4299; Fax: (61) 2 9669 4144. www.hayhouse.com.au

Published and distributed in the Republic of South Africa by:
Hay House SA (Pty), Ltd, PO Box 990, Witkoppen 2068. Tel./Fax: (27) 11 467 8904. www.hayhouse.co.za

Published and distributed in India by:
Hay House Publishers India, Muskaan Complex, Plot No.3, B-2, Vasant Kunj, New Delhi – 110 070. Tel.: (91) 11 4176 1620; Fax: (91) 11 4176 1630. www.hayhouse.co.in

Distributed in Canada by:
Raincoast, 9050 Shaughnessy St, Vancouver, BC V6P 6E5. Tel.: (1) 604 323 7100; Fax: (1) 604 323 2600

A catalogue record for this book is available from the British Library.

Previously published by Penguin Books, 2006, ISBN 978-0-14310-129-1.

ISBN 978-1-84850-037-2

Printed and bound in Great Britain by TJ International, Padstow, Cornwall.

To

The long life of my Guru, Gyalwa Rinpoche

His Holiness The Dalai Lama

The memory of my mother, Shanti Mehrotra

and for

My father, H.N. Mehrotra

Sarada Gopinath

And my best friend, fellow traveller

And wife, Meenakshi Gopinath

Contents

Preface

'Don't be nervous,' I said. 'He's the most human person you could ever hope to meet.'

She gave me a shocked glance. 'He's a living Buddha!' she protested.

'Well, isn't it the same thing?' I asked her.

The Foundation for Universal Responsibility is honoured and delighted to present *Understanding the Dalai Lama*. To Tibetans, the Dalai Lama is known as Yeshi Norbu, the precious Wish-Fulfilling Gem, the reincarnation, Avalokiteshwara, of the Buddha aspect of compassion. To others, he is known by his Mongol title—the Dalai Lama or Ocean of Wisdom. To the more initiated, he is quite simply His Holiness. His own description is Tenzin Gyatso, a simple Buddhist monk.

So what describes him best? The contributions in this book provide some answers to this question. This compilation of personal narratives as well as scholarly interactions brings out facets of an extraordinary life. Each contribution represents a personal response to the charisma of a supremely integrated personality, and together they reveal that he remains, in spite of all his achievements and all the accolades, self-effacing and intensely human. We can never completely know and understand the many dimensions of a human being, less so when that human form is a manifestation of the Buddha—the epitome of human striving. In attempting to answer the impossible, the book thus remains incomplete and inadequate. Yet, in a decision perhaps born of the vanity and blessings of being led by a great master, the Foundation felt it owed it to history and to the millions around the world whose lives the Dalai Lama has touched, more often through his ideas than his physical person, that we offer these contemporary insights into his personality and work by those who have met him and in most cases are well acquainted with him.

The Dalai Lama remains one of the most accessible public figures and has come to represent a singular if idealistic response to the individual and collective needs of our times. He evokes a range of views, analyses and descriptions, so similar and yet diverse, as he impacts the world in varied ways and dimensions. As with all truly great and inspiring leaders, his life is his message and philosophy. His Holiness represents a progressive and logical continuum of a mind that has evolved through lifetimes and the institution of the Dalai Lama, of whom he is the fourteenth reincarnation.

As one of His Holiness's personal, if most unworthy, disciples, I feel twice blessed and privileged to have helped bring together this collection of essays, to be able to write these words and in a small way help make available this collection of contemporary insights into a living Buddha. I dedicate any merit gained to the benefit of all sentient beings and acknowledge total responsibility for any errors in the book.

New Delhi   Rajiv Mehrotra
September 2004   Secretary/Trustee
                              Foundation for Universal Responsibility

Introduction

Rajiv Mehrotra

Tenzin Gyatso is heir to a religious tradition that began in India more than 2500 years ago when, seated under a tree, a young Indian prince, from deep meditation, attained decisive knowledge of the human condition and the unshakeable certainty that he was released from its suffering. He had become the Buddha, the Enlightened One. The core of the Buddhist path is the recognition that life is an endless round of suffering, disease, death and rebirth—a cycle caused by a desire bred of ignorance and of an innate misconception of reality.

Liberation or enlightenment occurs when, through a training of the mind, the mind itself is transcended. There is then an experience of the innate nature of reality, the recognition that all matter exists only in the manner of an illusion and in an ultimate void. Some beings who have attained enlightenment, and thus liberation from rebirth, opt for reincarnation voluntarily out of compassion for others, in order to teach and serve humanity. They are called bodhisattvas. The Dalai Lamas are bodhisattvas, Avalokiteshwara, a reincarnation of the patron saint of Tibet.

Buddhism, from its earliest forms, included the finest moral philosophy encompassing vast mind development and pioneer psychology. As it travelled the globe it evolved into religion, advanced philosophy, mysticism, metaphysics and the triple yogas—the paths of reason, devotion and action. It was not enough to be told to be moral and ethical. Buddhism became an adventure in 'how'.

Spreading 2000 miles from China in the east to Afghanistan in the west, with India, the home of much of its culture, in the south, Tibet is a severe Himalayan plateau 15,000 feet above sea level. Tibetans were confronted by natural grandeurs so cruel that it brought an intense awareness of the contrasting splendours and terrors of the Universe. Their palliatives were a few pleasant plains and a spiritual quest. It was a remote, secret Shangri-la so deeply inspired by the Buddhist cosmic view that it pursued its religion in splendid isolation with an unusual fervour. Hunting and killing ceased because it meant an arbitrary interruption in that being's own evolution. Armies disbanded and their soldiers became monks. Traditional kings were replaced by religious rule. The essential peace-loving nature of their religion encouraged a simplicity and quiet pragmatism in the people. Famine was unknown, disease rare.

'Unfortunately, some monasteries, institutions, became like landlords. The general public's practice of Buddha dharma declined. Though there was a great deal of devotion, there was little actual education,' the Dalai Lama acknowledges. The social structure became feudal. Most Tibetans were peasants paying taxes to the great monastic and noble estates. One in four Tibetans was a monk or nun and constituted its de facto ruling class. Naturally warm-hearted, with an innate sense of order and humour, the various classes had been immutably defined for centuries. Inside the cloisters flourished a rich culture and tradition.

In 1933 the Great Thirteenth Dalai Lama passed on to the Honourable Fields. Two years later, Tibet's regent journeyed to its sacred lake seeking a vision of the one who would be the new leader returned in a new body. In the waters, he was shown a monastery, a house nearby and a baby.

Other omens directed the search party to the northeast,

to the monastery and the house of the vision. There a two-and-a-half-year-old boy approached and recognized the disguised lamas, calling them by name. He spoke in the dialect of the capital, Lhasa, over 1000 miles away. He identified as his own the rosaries, walking stick and hand drum of the Thirteenth Dalai Lama. On the child's body were the marks distinguishing the Dalai Lamas, including the large ears, tiger stripe-like streaks on the legs and the conch shell print on the palm. There was no doubt that this was indeed the holy one himself: the Fourteenth Dalai Lama of Tibet. Talking of his reincarnation he humbly says, 'The original Dalai Lamas, the first, second, third, these were no doubt the reincarnations of Avalokiteshwara. I believe I am a blessed one, but my own spiritual level is not high. I am still practising.'

On a bright October morning in 1939, the now four-year-old boy entered the great city of Lhasa in a brilliant procession, where thousands lined the yellow and white route cheering and waving. The philosopher–king born of peasant parents began his long arduous training while a regent held temporary power. Surrounded by tutors and attendants he lived in splendid but disciplined isolation. He was soon recognized as an exceptional student. As most of Lhasa watched, His Holiness the Fourteenth Dalai Lama won his Doctorate of Buddhist Philosophy degree with honours, in public debates, at the age of twenty-four.

Meanwhile, China had begun to assert a claim on Tibet contending that the Tibetan nation was part of the Chinese motherland because the Tibetans, descended from the Mongolians, were part of the five races comprising the Chinese. On New Year's Day in 1950, when he was barely sixteen years old, Tenzin Gyatso's education in real politics began. The newly-declared People's Republic of China announced its intentions to 'liberate' Tibet. As its armies marched into a nation physically and temperamentally unprepared for war, at the urging of the state oracle and his people, His Holiness assumed formal temporal power of

Tibet as the Fourteenth Dalai Lama, to steer the country through its darkest hour.

On 17 March 1959, after nine years of fruitless attempts at compromise with the Chinese, as atrocities against the Tibetans grew, on a night of firing, shelling and popular revolt in Lhasa, the Dalai Lama, guarded by Tibetan guerillas, slowly began his long, dangerous escape into India. Over the next few weeks an estimated 87,000 Tibetans were killed and 25,000 imprisoned. A hundred thousand followed him into exile.

The 1960 report of the International Commission of Jurists recognized Tibet's status as a fully sovereign state. China was found guilty of genocide—'the gravest crime of which any nation can be accused; the intent to destroy, in whole or in part, a national ethnic, racial or religious group'. Yet the Dalai Lama believes:

> As a Buddhist, the basic factor or cause of all these tragedies is one's own previous karma. The external factors are the Chinese forces but the basic cause is one's own previous bad karma. Although personally that enemy is harming you, forget that so-called enemy. Look at him as a human being just like you or me who also wants happiness. With that reason you can develop genuine sympathy or compassion.

At the end of the 'cultural' revolution the new Chinese order revealed that forty-five of Tibet's 6000 monasteries had survived. The number is soon to be increased to fifty-three. Of the more than 500,000 monks and nuns, 1300 survived in Tibet. These numbers may increase; however, a socialist education is today a prerequisite for permission to enter the monkhood.

On the afternoon of 31 March 1959, the Dalai Lama entered exile, seeking political asylum in India. This initially embarrassed the Indian government, for though India and Tibet shared a long religious and cultural history, Prime Minister Nehru was obliged to take into account the then recent delicate rapprochement between India and China. However, humanity triumphed over politics and asylum was granted. The Dalai Lama became an honoured guest in the land of Buddha's birth. But even though there was profound sympathy and substantial material support for the refugees, there was little political backing worldwide. Tibet's isolation had given it no experience of international diplomacy and few friends.

The Dalai Lama found residence in Dharamsala, a day's travel from the capital, New Delhi. A residential area of less than two acres, given out of graciousness by a foreign government, was now the Dalai Lama's physical domain. He was shorn of the external symbols that attested to his power and authority in Tibet. It was a call to Tenzin Gyatso to build a much vaster empire sourced on an inner kingdom— for the Dalai Lama the cultivation of inner peace and a refined integrity are the ultimate weapons that an individual can use to make a difference in this seemingly mad world.

For more than four decades now he has lived in exile, while Chinese oppression in Tibet has continued, as has the systematic decimation of its culture and heritage. He has remained a transient on a refugee's passport, dependent on the generosity of foreigners.

The Nobel Prize for Peace awarded to him in December 1989 became a formal global acknowledgement of his personal spiritual striving and the goal that he personifies, of liberating Tibet from Chinese oppression. In awarding the Nobel Prize to a religious leader the Nobel Committee identified three specific elements of his philosophy: non-violence, the inter-relatedness of social and individual human rights, and the critical need in our generation to confront the threat of a global environmental disaster. It is significant that the ecological issue has been put on the agenda of the Nobel Peace Prize by a spiritual leader. He combines rationality, humanism and religious tradition as foundations for moral responses to the great challenges of our century. Nor did the Nobel Committee shirk from identifying the

Dalai Lama as the 'political and spiritual leader' of the Tibetan people and his struggle for the 'liberation' of Tibet, despite strong Chinese protests.

Tibet today is at once a tragedy and a triumph, a stark example of modern totalitarianism fighting to a draw against an unwilling traditional society. A number of delegations from the Dalai Lama first visited Tibet in the 1980s, evoking powerful emotions amongst Tibetans in Tibet. Following the death of Mao, in 1976, delicate and potentially substantive contacts were first established between the Dalai Lama and Beijing. This was followed by a virtually decade-long impasse following the student protests at Tiananmen Square in May 1989 created by, in the words of the Chinese government, counter-revolutionaries, capitalist agents and enemies of the people. Protests and demonstrations continued in Tibet. Martial law was in force for over a year and only supervised tourist groups were allowed into Lhasa. The Chinese government repeatedly, rhetorically, continued to accuse the Dalai Lama of instigating anti-Chinese and anti-national sentiments. There has been increasing Chinese nervousness over growing popular global support for the Dalai Lama and international pressure to resolve the Tibetan question, even if usually under the guise of drawing attention to human rights issues in Tibet.

In recent years the Chinese have adopted a more subtle strategy to overcome Tibet. They have used attractive incentives to create a massive influx of Chinese into the harsh terrain of Tibet. In the Kokonor region in northeast Tibet, for example, where the Dalai Lama was born, there are now an estimated 3.5 million Chinese as against 500,000 Tibetans.

The Dalai Lama has always been open to dialogue through direct contact and visits to Beijing by his representatives. While these have been described as a confidence-building step, it seems that the Tibetan position draws more on the decade-old proposal of a Five-point Peace Plan set out by the Dalai Lama. He believes:

The Tibetan problem is the problem of six million human souls, not that of the Dalai Lama Institution. The Dalai Lama is not so important, the important thing is that the nation must remain. In future, it will remain. Happiness and the right of the nation are very important. The Institution of the Dalai Lama...that will come and go, that depends on the actual circumstances. If people feel that there should be another Dalai Lama, then I will appear. As my own incarnation I will be there. As long as suffering of the sentient being is there, I will serve as much as I can, this is my determination. This is not something extraordinary. This is the way of thinking of all persons who sincerely practice the Buddha's teaching. I may be reborn as an American, as a Canadian, as a Tibetan, as an Indian, I don't know.

The Dalai Lama has proposed the transformation of Tibet into a zone of peace, a respect for fundamental human rights, an abandonment of China's population transfer, the protection of Tibet's environment and the commencement of earnest negotiations. This was followed by an offer, made before the European Parliament, renouncing Tibetan independence and any political role for himself in the Tibet of the future. But the Dalai Lama has also warned that if there is no concrete response from the Chinese in the near future he will be obliged to reconsider his position.

*

Exiled in India, the Dalai Lama plunged into frenetic activity serving as leader and shock absorber to a traumatized people uprooted from their natural habitat to the heat and dust of India. Drawing upon a philosophy that provided important insights into the permanent nature of change and flux, of how 'becoming' is a vital aspect of 'being', the Tibetan refugees not only survived change but flourished.

While the world prepared to put Tibet back on the

shelves of myth and legend, the Dalai Lama and his people were driven by a different perception of reality. Religion was their well spring and it had top priority. Preserving it as it had evolved, and perpetuating Tibetan religion and culture became an essential strategy in exile to counter Chinese attempts to decimate it. The Tibetan identity could not be allowed to die. For every major monastery destroyed in Tibet, a new, if smaller, one was built in India, continuing the same lineage and practices as in Tibet. Children, the hope of any exiled people, continued to be ordained as monks and senior lamas now began to reincarnate in exile. His Holiness has observed, 'Because I am outside Tibet, the pure form of Tibetan culture has survived. Now today, strangely, the true Tibetan culture or community is found outside Tibet, not inside.'

The major challenge was rehabilitation. The refugees arrived with few assets and little immunity to the many diseases unknown in Tibet's dry atmosphere but prevalent in subtropical India. Slowly the survivors began to weave a small economic miracle. Their former feudal lives were quickly relinquished. The barren land was equitably distributed and a marketing and purchasing collective established. Tibetan medicine, Tibetan arts and crafts and Tibetan education were encouraged. The Tibetans in exile have carved out one of the most successful stories of the rehabilitation of a people—of vigorously maintaining their own identities yet harmonizing with their new environment to remain welcome by their hosts. By the 1990s forty-four Tibetan settlements linked by commercial, political and religious ties housing almost all the 100,000 exiles looked to Dharamsala as their headquarters.

One of the first tasks the Dalai Lama undertook in India was the establishment of an education system that would inculcate traditional Tibetan values and culture while imparting instruction in modern ways. The first Tibetan schools were for orphans, but soon a network of schools accommodated all children. Many of them have subsequently

gone through Indian universities and now serve in the
Government in Exile. The Dalai Lama's keen personal
interest in the modernization of a medieval social system
has been rewarded with the emergence of a new generation
of Tibetans fiercely loyal to their cause, the first children to
see maps of the world and hear about people other than
their own.

The Dalai Lama, while still in Tibet, had recognized the
disadvantages and the injustices of the old ways. Always
drawn towards the lowest strata in society, the Dalai Lama
now included them in a power-sharing scheme with their
former rulers.

> We have a draft constitution that is based on the
> basic principles of the democratic system. Buddhist
> practice, especially the monk-system, is really a
> democratic system, so in a draft constitution I have
> mentioned 'according to principles of Buddhist
> teaching we are making a democratic constitution'.
> So we are trying to make as much as we can while
> we are exiled in a different country. Now in the
> future, as I often mention, I regard myself as a free
> spokesman of the Tibetan people so that . . . the
> final decision will be taken by people inside Tibet.

The text of the constitution draws heavily on the
International Declaration of Human Rights, but is uniquely
Tibetan; the preamble refers to the principle of justice,
equality and democracy laid down by Lord Buddha. Today,
the Dalai Lama is the head of the government, assisted by
a directly elected Kalon Tripa or de facto prime minister
and his cabinet. A parliament consisting of deputies is
chosen by popular mandate from amongst the exiled
community. An annual general meeting enables the public
questioning of individual departments. Article 36, Section
(e) of the draft constitution provides for the suspension of
the Dalai Lama's executive functions by a two-thirds majority
of the assembly.

The Dalai Lama has personally laid the foundation for his administration in exile. A cabinet, a liaison bureau with the Indian government and a civil service was established early in 1959. Though no country has recognized the Dalai Lama's Government in Exile, he has representatives in several countries including the US, Britain, Switzerland, France, South Africa, Taiwan and Japan, often working as centres of Tibetan culture rather than his political nominees. Together they have managed to keep the Tibetan issue on the international agenda.

*

Buddhist monk, spiritual leader, political head, compassionate human being—these are just some of the facets of the Dalai Lama's persona. Each of these facets is discussed in the contributions in this book.

For six million of his followers, he is Holy Lord, Gentle Glory, Eloquent, Compassionate, Learned, Defender of the Faith, Ocean of Wisdom—His Holiness, the Fourteenth Dalai Lama of Tibet. He represents the past as well as future history of Tibet. Tibetologist Jeffrey Hopkins served as His Holiness's official interpreter for more than a decade and gives a syllable by syllable translation in English of the Dalai Lama's full name.

Matthieu Ricard, a monk himself, notes in his profile how 'he [the Dalai Lama] always describes himself as a simple Buddhist monk, but to various writers he has been the God King of Tibet; to the Chinese, a 'splittist'; to most politicians, the true head of Tibet; to dharma students everywhere, a great teacher; and to the world at large, a Nobel Laureate, a great statesman, the leading advocate of non-violence and peace, the voice of Buddhism and, in general, our best hope for the future.'

Pico Iyer suggests it is not just what he says that gives meaning to all that makes him unique but also because 'the heart of the man . . . exists in silence'. It is not a severe

silence but one that ever brims with joy and the infectious
laughter that frequently spills over, disarming and moving
us all a step closer to our real selves.

Describing him as 'a very human being' writer Mary
Craig emphasizes that he is a 'uniquely luminous person
who can make you want to laugh aloud for the sheer joy of
being alive...who can hoot with mirth'. In an unexpectedly
extended afternoon she got to spend with His Holiness, she
saw several Dalai Lamas: one of them pedalling a brand-
new exercise bike, gifted to him by a Swiss lady, with the
enthusiasm of a small child! What this writer has learnt to
value most is His Holiness's genuine humility and refusal, in
spite of everything, to hate the Chinese. Ever looking for
insights and understanding the Dalai Lama began to study
Marxism in order to find common ground with the Chinese.

> I think in Buddhism there is much emphasis on love
> and compassion. In Marxism somehow the basis of
> the class struggle is hatred. Also, of course, Buddhism
> is not only thinking of this life but the next. But
> both believe that the individual is capable of taking
> control of his own destiny, there is no belief in a
> creator in either. I believe that the two can co-exist.

Psychologist and author Daniel Goleman observes that
the roots of empathy are latent in compassion. He suggests
that empathy and ethics are closely linked and empathy
underlies many facets of moral judgement and actions. The
Dalai Lama's secular philosophy of Universal Responsibility,
bred of a profound insight of our interdependence, has had
an enormous impact. Goleman continues: 'Science and
technology have brought immense control over nature, but
power without wisdom is dangerous. We need to balance
our modern capabilities with an ancient wisdom . . . The
Dalai Lama has said, also, that just because these times are
so dire, it is a great honour to be alive now, at this moment,
on this planet. It is we who bear the responsibility, who face
the challenge, who must take care of the planet, not just for
ourselves, but for the future of our children'.

How would the Dalai Lama have the world remember him? 'Just as a human being, perhaps as a human being who smiles?' the Dalai Lama tells Ela Gandhi, granddaughter of the Mahatma, while discussing Tibet with her. Describing him as a 'simple smiling monk', she says 'his power comes from a life of ethics, the force of truth. In Tibetan he speaks with a range, depth, inspiration, humour and sincerity that inspires insight and motivates.'

For the Tibetans whose cause he represents, he has led the struggle for a free Tibet and the survival of its ancient heritage. Researcher Senthil Ram observes how 'from exile the Dalai Lama pursued various landmark reforms: on the one hand to democratize the Tibetan polity and on the other to non-violently handle the conflict with China'. Dalip Mehta, a former Indian diplomat, notes, 'He has succeeded in keeping alive the aspirations and hopes of the Tibetan people, and in preserving Tibet's unique culture. He has achieved the delicate task of adhering to his principles, and at the same time not jeopardizing the interests of his adopted homeland. And he has ensured that the Tibetan diaspora, not just in India, but elsewhere in the world, has developed and progressed in the modern world, even while remaining rooted in their traditions. In his quest for "freedom in exile" in India, the Dalai Lama has perhaps achieved far more than he would have if destiny had not forced him to flee Tibet.'

It is altogether too early to make any judgements about what his intellectual legacy will be but as Thubten Jinpa, the translator and interpreter for His Holiness, observes, 'His life mirrors the wider picture of classical Tibetan culture's encounter with modernity'. The Dalai Lama's exile has perforce meant that he has reached out to a much larger world, and the world has been extraordinarily receptive to his personality and message.

Robert Thurman, one of The Dalai Lama's first western students, writes: 'His Holiness is a giant of spiritual development—a living exemplar of the best qualities of a

Buddhist monk, an inspired practitioner and teacher of the ethical, religious and philosophical paths of the bodhisattva, and an elegant and energetic wielder of the vajra sceptre of the Tantric adept.'

A constant theme of the Dalai Lama's teaching is that the essence of a Buddhist's life lies in a person's own efforts to purify his mind. By replacing its coarse deluded states such as anger, attachment and ignorance with patience, wisdom and equanimity, a lasting internal happiness can be achieved, independent of external conditions.

> Without training you cannot utilize even your little finger properly. Once you train your mind properly even a small finger can do big things. It seems very difficult sometimes, almost impossible, but through gradual training, step by step, you can do these things. So that is one of the good qualities of human consciousness; frequently it is a trouble maker, but if you train properly it will be very nice, very useful, like a real jewel.

To a mind thus cultivated, the precision and logic of modern science and technology holds out a strong attraction. This has been a passion since childhood, when the adolescent Dalai Lama took apart watches, film projectors and Tibet's three cars; today he is an expert at and enjoys tinkering with mechanical things. Journalist Swati Chopra writes 'Science grows from a spirit of discovery and I know that Buddhism, and certainly the Dalai Lama, have always been interested in leading explorations into the area beyond the circumference of doctrinal beliefs.' The Dalai Lama himself believes:

> Scientific research is very important. The general Buddhist attitude is that we must accept reason. If we cannot believe a certain thing by reason as a fact or something then we must accept the fact rather than the certain thing described in the scripture. For

example, the Buddha himself says you must accept certain things through your own investigations, your own use and logic and reason, not out of faith.

The Dalai Lama in word and deed seeks to demonstrate how ethics and noble principles have been obscured by the shadow of self interest, particularly in the political sphere. The instruments of our political culture have destroyed the ideals and concepts meant to further human welfare. He questions the popular assumption that religion and ethics have no place in politics and that religious persons should seclude themselves as hermits. Ethics is as crucial to a politician as to a religious practitioner. Such human qualities as morality, compassion, decency and wisdom have been the foundations of all great civilizations. He says:

> We [must] try to develop a real human feeling. No matter what the differences to ideology or distance, all are human beings, all have to live together on this planet. On this level [there should be] more contact, more exchanges. Even disagreements are human, so the human [dimension] is still there. On that basis we should make an understanding, that way you can achieve mutual trust. Then you can talk.

The Dalai Lama's role as a pre-eminent Buddhist monk is today almost universally acknowledged amongst the different schools of Buddhism. While the battle between Marxist or more lately western materialism and Buddhist spiritualism in China, between the power of the gun and the power of wisdom and compassion continues to simmer, the Dalai Lama himself reaches out to a world increasingly responsive to his personality, teaching and message, if not to his political cause. In our increasingly fragmented world the Dalai Lama has sought dialogues with other faiths. Brother Wayne Teasdale feels 'His Holiness's commitment to inter-religious dialogue, which is really a dialogue of life itself, is

not a stiff, formal activity as it often is in academic forums.'
He adds, 'Basically, what I discern in his example is a highly
developed humanism rooted in spiritual practice and extended
to all sentient beings.'

His emphasis on the inter-connectedness of all things
has helped generate a new sensitivity to the significance of
our environment and the real potential for a truly secular
inter-religious dialogue. The Dalai Lama has not sought one
common faith for all people. He has instead reached out to
the common ground of all religions in the quest for happiness.
The Dalai Lama himself says:

> Major religions of the world carry more or less the
> same teachings, same messages. I always look for
> what is the real purpose of these different teachings,
> different philosophies. I find all are meant for entire
> humanity. All focus or aim at the same
> aim...meantime because there are so many mental
> dispositions among humans, one religion may not be
> suitable for everyone. Under the circumstances, the
> one thing we should keep in our mind is closer
> relations and closer understandings. [This] will
> develop mutual respect.

> Small, small differences between this church or that
> church or this faith or that faith, are very minor.
> Always the main goal, the supreme thing, is very
> important. Forget these small things; try to make
> common effort for the bigger goal.

> I feel the ultimate aim is society's nirvana—my
> definition is completely peaceful, harmony, no hatred
> for each other. Even if there is some disagreement,
> solve it by human understanding. [There should be]
> no racial problem, no ideology problem. Ideology is
> a private business. If someone believes in a certain
> ideology, the best means for him to achieve happiness,
> it is his right to pursue that thing; other persons

have the right to a different ideology or a different faith, if they think that is suitable, they can follow that. [Each should] not interfere with the other, understand that both are human beings, members of the human family. Both want happiness, and do not want suffering. Both have the right to be happy. Under these circumstances, they remain as brothers and sisters. Now that is my dream.

His disarming personality demonstrates the joy and laughter in the journey. Buddhism, never a missionary religion, is revealed on his smiling face.

In the finely balanced mixture of spirituality and politics, the transcendental and the everyday, personal contemplation and altruistic action, what room is there left for the man, the monk? He constantly surprises, questions, or overturns old habits, shifts entrenched certainties. In the middle of a solemn Nobel lecture he can pause, wave to a familiar face in the audience and resume as if nothing had happened, he can shed tears touched by the work of Baba Amte, break out into infectious laughter at his inability to express himself in English, or admit 'I don't know' when he doesn't have an answer to the innumerable questions he confronts. The Dalai Lama carries his erudition and insights with an easy, comfortable grace.

Tenzin Gyatso is, then, more than a mere Buddhist monk or the spiritual and temporal leader of the displaced Tibetan people. His message of compassion, altruism and peace have made him a statesman for our troubled times. His Holiness has been widely received and applauded at many capitals around the world by politicians, who, anxious not to offend the Chinese, often greet him merely as a great spiritual leader, paying discreet lip-service to his political cause.

But Tibet's cause is never far from the pilgrim's thoughts. Today there is renewed hope; the Nobel Peace Prize reflects a measure of consensus in international public opinion in support of both the Dalai Lama's cause and the strategy he embodies. Forty-odd years later the US Congress, the European Parliament and numerous groups across the political spectrum have articulated their concern over human rights violations, the threat to the environment in Tibet and the future of its people.

The Dalai Lama believes that it is only by building up a collective merit of good karma through overcoming each individual's own delusions can the situation resolve itself favourably. Each day's teachings conclude with prayers for their brethren, both friend and oppressor, who still suffer, followed by a dedication of the merit gained to the speedy end of their suffering. In the words of the Tibetan prayer:

> By their rough actions masses of cruel ones are bringing down ruin on themselves and on others. They are drunk with demonic delusions. Forge the glorious unity of friendship among them, these objects of compassion, and with love and mercy help them acquire the Wisdom Eye to see what is right and what is wrong.

The cultivation of altruism remains the essential and pivotal goal of Buddhist practice and the essence of the Dalai Lama's own practice.

> The essential teaching of Buddha Dharma is bodhichitta—the firm determination to achieve Buddhahood for the benefit of others, that is on the basis of Karuna and Maitreya. I am developing that mind for the last thirty years and somehow I am gaining experience. The other one is wisdom, which is Sunyata. By learning to understand what is Sunyata, I am gaining experience.

The Buddha's teaching is a call to all human beings to engage with life and overcome one's desires and difficulties, not to run away from an imperfect world. The Dalai Lama, in his various personas and in his daily practice, is an extraordinary example of leading an ordinary life based on the Buddha's teachings, and in doing so has become more God than man.

The Dalai Lama's Roles and Teachings

Robert A.F. Thurman

The Institution

The reincarnation lineage of the Dalai Lama is traced back to a Brahmin boy who met Shakyamuni Buddha near the tree of enlightenment at Bodhgaya and offered him a crystal rosary. Many incarnations are mentioned in the history of the lineage in India, up until the first Tibetan incarnation, the ordained lay Buddhist teacher Dromtonpa (1004–1064 CE), who was the Bengali master Atisha's foremost disciple and the founder of Rateng monastery and the Kadam order.

The evolutionary theory of karma has existed from Buddhism's beginnings, and the concept of conscious, voluntary reincarnation (as contrasted with involuntary, instinct-driven rebirth) developed quite early. The Buddha himself is presented as popularizing the principle in his Jataka and Avadana stories that illustrate the multi-life continuum perspective. Throughout history, small children in Buddhist cultures routinely astounded parents, relatives, and neighbours by announcing that they were in fact merely the rebirth of such and such deceased person known to everybody. It is thus interesting that only in Tibet, as far as we know, did formal reincarnation lineages become institutionalized as a way of preserving traditions of leadership and authority in primarily religious settings, but also eventually in the political arena.

This clearly was connected to the scale of monasticization that occurred in Tibet, unparalleled in any other country on earth under the aegis of any religion. Monastics being vocationally celibate, blood lineage eventually became too weak a consideration in choosing leaders, and was replaced by a commonly accepted notion of individual spiritual evolution in continuing reincarnations. Beginning as an institutional factor in the 13th century, by the 17th century reincarnation pedigree had become the dominant consideration in Tibetans' choosing their leaders.

His Holiness the Victor Karmapa was the first of such formal reincarnations, as far as we know. His first incarnation, Dusum Kyenpa (1110–1193) wrote a letter before he passed away in which he predicted his reincarnation in specific circumstances, a prediction realized ten years after his death with the birth of the Second Karmapa Lama, Karma Pakshi (1203–1283), who soon asked to be taken back to his monastery at Tsurpu to continue his teachings. The Karmapa reincarnations have continued to develop their institution and perform great service to the people of Tibet and now the whole world. The current Seventeenth Victor Karmapa, Orgyen Trinley Dorje (1982–), has recently escaped from Chinese-occupied Tibet and is living in Dharamsala near the Dalai Lama, showing every promise of becoming another major teacher of the Dharma.

The second important reincarnation institution was that of the Dalai Lamas. It began formally with the birth of Gendun Gyatso in 1475, who soon declared himself the reincarnation of the famous Gendun Drubpa (1391–1474), and expressed the wish to return to his disciples at the Tashi Lhunpo monastery, which he had built during the last twenty-five years of his previous life. He was accepted as the true reincarnation by his parents, tutors and attendants, and was taken back in glory to the monastery. However, the ruling abbots of that large monastic university were clearly reluctant to formalize his recognition by handing the young boy the head position. So at a certain point in his studies, he took advantage of this blessing in disguise, escaped from his duties of office and spent a number of years in intermittent retreat with the great teacher of the Kalachakra Tantra, Khedrup Norzang Gyatso.

During this time, the young reincarnation, Gendun Gyatso, built the important monastery of Chokorgyal in the sacred area near the Ode Gungyel mountain, where Tsong Khapa (1357–1419), his spiritual grandfather, had taken his own six-year retreat in the 1390s, and he made a special bond with the fierce protector goddess Shri Devi, whose sacred soul lake lay hidden nearby. Eventually Gendun Gyatso's reincarnation status was established beyond question as the main teacher of the Gelukpa order, his main seat located in the Ganden Palace at Drepung monastery as well as in Tashi Lhunpo.

The third reincarnation was Sonam Gyatso (1543–1588), who was invited to northeast Tibet to the encampment of Altan Khan, a major Mongolian ruler. On this occasion a major step was taken in converting the Mongols to Buddhism, building on the changes they had undergone when Kublai Khan ruled in China three hundred years earlier. During the festive atmosphere of this transformative event, the Mongol Khan dubbed Sonam Gyatso the 'Oceanic' ('Dalai') Lama, ('gyatso' is 'ocean' in Tibetan) and he became known as the 'Third' in acknowledgement of his conscious connection to Gendun Drubpa and Gendun Gyatso. Sonam Gyatso did the great work of teaching and monastery founding among the Mongols and the Amdo people in northeast Tibet, but still had no direct political responsibility in central Tibet.

The Fourth Dalai Lama was Yonten Gyatso (1589–1617), who was not Tibetan but was reincarnated among the Mongolians, as a grandson of Altan Khan himself. He immeasurably strengthened the bond between the Mongolians and the Tibetans, returning while still quite young to central Tibet and his seat at Drepung monastery.

It was the Fifth Dalai Lama, Losang Gyatso (1617–

1682), who presided over the momentous changes of the 17th century that were to produce Tibet's modern form of society. During the mid-16th century, there had been intermittent conflict between the secular rulers of southern Tibet and those of central Tibet, which some historians have attributed to sectarian conflict between the Karmapa Lamas and their followers and the Gelukpa Lamas and their followers. But it is more accurate to recognize this to be the result of a conflict between the secular warlord rulers of feudal Tibet and the continually increasing monastic institutions and spiritual leaders of all the Buddhist orders.

In all Buddhist (and Christian) societies throughout history, monasticism and militarism have opposed each other as institutional competitors for land, resources, manpower and womanpower. Whenever and wherever monasticism dominated, militarism was weakened. Whenever warlords or a single emperor dominated and increased their militaristic activities, monastic institutions were purged, their resources confiscated, and their monks turned into warriors. The 15th and 16th centuries in Tibet saw a vast increase in monasticism, reaching a point by 1600 where aristocratic rulers saw their authority and resources dwindle to what they considered danger point. Their basic opponent was not a sect or leader, but the whole new 'mass-monastic' (a term I use for this unique Tibetan social development) social system itself.

The most powerful secular leader of the time was the King of Tsang, and of course he had to use an important religious leader for legitimacy in the eyes of a people more and more interested in spiritual pursuits and less and less interested in feudal power struggles. He chose Karmapa Lama, His Holiness Choying Gyatso (1604–1674), who was young and just growing up at the time. The King of Tsang proclaimed himself the lama's disciple in order to sanctify his aggressive intention to maintain his secular power, and then set about trying to break the hold of mass monasticism on the Tibetans.

The Dalai Lama institution, which had up to that point declined to enter the political arena, devoting itself to the continuous expansion of the monastic universities and their demilitarized lifestyle, reached out for its defence to its Mongolian patrons, who came into Tibet and defeated the warlord coalition. Then, in 1642, the Fifth Dalai Lama took an unprecedented step: he assumed political responsibility for the whole country, demilitarized and bureaucratized the secular warlords, defeudalized the ownership of land and the networks of relationships between people at all levels, and formalized mass monasticism as the official social system of Tibet, what is called the 'Dharma–state-coordination' system (*Chos-srid zung-'brel*).

This unprecedented arrangement is not to be confused with the 'church–state unity' which led to intensive religious persecution in Europe and so was remedied in America by the constitutional 'separation of church and state'. 'Dharma' means 'teaching', the Buddha teaching of personal liberation and scientific enlightenment, not 'religion', 'church', or even 'religious belief', and so Dharma–state-coordination intends that the central purpose of the national life is the evolutionary education of all citizens, more like 'university–state unity' than 'church–state-unity.'

Furthermore, Buddhists are not monotheistic, so the ruler is not thought to represent an inscrutable, omnipotent, authoritarian god, but rather to be himself a selfless, intercessionary angel of a bodhisattva. The monastic ruler as a Buddhist monk holds solemn vows of gentleness, poverty, chastity, honesty. Hence he is dedicated to the principles of nonviolence, economic minimalism, support of the freedom and education of individuals, and selfless service. He thus was preferred by the Tibetan people at this time over a warlord king with his armies, coercive demand for labour service and self-aggrandizing ambitions for his dynastic progeny. This new Tibetan society was unique on the planet then and still is now, and therefore terms like 'feudal', 'theocratic', even 'traditional' or 'pre-modern', are not accurate in describing it.

The Fifth Dalai Lama embarked on the building of the Potala, symbol of the new Ganden Palace government, and a remarkable fusion of royal palace, monastic establishment, Tantric mandala and celestial paradise. He patronized the building of more monasteries for all the orders, not only the Gelukpa order, the leadership of which he abdicated to the senior abbot of Ganden monastery in order to represent all people of all religious orders. He gave the former warlord families bureaucratic ranks and salaries for service to the government, after depriving most of them of their feudal rights over their own lands and peasants—most importantly the right to maintain a private army. He gave land and sustenance not only to all Buddhist orders, he protected the followers of the Bon religion, gave land to the Muslim residents of Lhasa to build mosques and allowed them to worship freely, and gave his permission and support to Christian missionary activities. Reaching out from Tibet, he made a pact to keep the peace in Inner Asia with the newly triumphant Manchu rulers of China (1644–1911) and discouraged the Mongols from rebuilding their empire, inspiring them effectively to pursue the demilitarized Buddhist lifestyle that Tibet was adopting.

The Great Fifth died in 1682, but his regent concealed his death for over a decade, owing to a long delay in official recognition of the secretly discovered reincarnation, who was kept incognito with his family in a prison-like atmosphere. Owing, perhaps, to his oppressive upbringing, the Sixth Dalai Lama turned away from his monastic avocation and refused his state responsibilities. This caused considerable consternation among his Mongolian and Tibetan followers, led to his deposition and deportation, a dangerous civil conflict, and eventual Manchu intervention in the affairs of Tibet. After some time, the Seventh Dalai Lama restored the institution somewhat, focussing on spiritual teaching empowering his Cabinet and laying the foundation for a national assembly.

From the Eighth through the Twelfth Dalai Lamas,

Tibet remained stable and peaceful, though static in governance, with the main innovations in many fields being developed in eastern Tibet and Mongolia, far from the complacent conservatism of the central authorities. The Manchu rulers of China also became less supportive of Tibet once the Mongol threat was reduced due to the pacifying effect of Buddhism, and the era of European imperialism brought the British and the Russians, for whom Buddhism was a complete enigma, into play around Tibet.

The Thirteenth Dalai Lama (1876–1933) was the first Dalai Lama to assume the full power of his office since the Seventh. His life's work was to respond to the pressures on Tibet from the decaying Manchu empire, Tsarist Russia, the British raj, the Nationalist Chinese, and finally the Russian and Chinese communists. He tried to develop Tibet economically so that it could stand up to industrial militarism. He declared formal independence from the protected relationship Tibet had enjoyed with the Manchu empire, tried to develop a national defence force, and even made gestures towards joining the League of Nations and introducing Tibetan civilization to the world. Though he was supported in this by the leaders of the British raj in India, the British home government's realpolitik policy in dealing with the Manchus and then the Chinese nationalists caused London to frustrate his every effort to gain official recognition for Tibet from the nations of the world.

From within, too, his own conservative monastic leadership frustrated his efforts to create a modernized secular school system, build up a viable defence force, and develop even a modest industrial infrastructure. After hearing detailed reports of the fate of Mongolian Buddhists at the hands of Russian communists in the early 1930s, he made statements to the effect that he was going to pass away a decade ahead of schedule in order to reincarnate and grow up soon enough to help Tibet when it would be submerged under the Red Tide of Communism which he predicted would emerge from China. He passed away in 1933.

The Fourteenth Dalai Lama is well known and has already earned the title 'Great Fourteenth' due to his profound inner development and his magnificent works of teaching, writing, political leadership and social engagement. He has resolutely proclaimed his intention to abdicate from the political responsibilities of the Dalai Lama institution once a dialogue is resumed with a less imperialistic and more pragmatic Chinese government that makes it possible for the fate of Tibet to be resolved in a just and reasonable way.

He has firmly rejected in conversation my proposal for a 'constitutional lamarchy', and so it is clear he considers that his duty will change once the occupation and exile has ended and a viable Tibetan democracy has begun to function in a free Tibet. I still wonder if there is a way to continue the noble experiment begun by the Great Fifth, and create a 'spiritual democracy' rather than just conform to the American and Indian pattern of secular democracy, wherein the god Mammon tends to take over. This 'spiritual democracy' would obviously not elevate any particular religion, order, or sect as the 'state–church', yet it would educate the people to adopt a higher level of ethics, a higher level of spiritual education both in mind and in science, and would help balance the material and the spiritual for the people of the new Tibet.

Tibet could then assume its rightful role in the world as a centre for nonviolence studies, for methodologies to implement social justice, environmentalist methodology, scientific yet natural healing arts, and spiritual education and development. The Dalai Lama institution, perhaps, according to the wishes of the Great Fourteenth, could become relatively free of political responsibilities and flourish as a source of spiritual teaching for the larger world. Future Dalai Lamas would follow in his footsteps and appeal to followers of all religions, not only Buddhists, and inspire them to curb the dangerous tendencies towards religious intolerance and ideological fanaticism, and promote the beneficial elements of their venerable faiths.

The Great Fourteenth: Personal Development

I will recount some aspects of my early meetings with the Great Fourteenth over the last thirty-eight years. This might be helpful to sketch his personal development because I am one of the few non-Tibetans who has known His Holiness continuously over such a long period.

His Holiness is a giant of spiritual development—a living exemplar of the best qualities of a Buddhist monk, an inspired practitioner and teacher of the ethical, religious and philosophical paths of the bodhisattva, and an elegant and energetic wielder of the vajra sceptre of the Tantric adept. He is also, of course, a conscious reincarnation of Avalokiteshwara, the bodhisattva of universal compassion. As such, it might seem that his great attainments and vast deeds in this lifetime have spontaneously emerged from his practice in previous lives, as if he had done nothing special to develop himself during this life.

If we think that way, we might feel he is so far beyond our capacity that though we might enjoy his presence, learn from his teaching and feel great devotion to him, it would be hard to emulate him. This would not please His Holiness at all. In relying on a *kalyanamitra* (*dge bai bshes gnyen or geshe*), a Buddhist spiritual friend, propitiation through devotion and service through actions are important, but it is far more important to actualize his teachings by putting them into practice in our own lives. An important point often made about Shakyamuni Buddha is that he was not some sort of primal divinity, a Buddha from the beginning. He was human like us, even an animal, in many previous lives. He struggled with passions and flaws, misunderstandings and inabilities, just as we do. Yet he practised the Dharma and finally overcame all inadequacies, and ultimately became the shining, perfect Buddha who showed us the way to freedom, love and happiness.

When I first met His Holiness in a personal audience, he was a young man of twenty-nine years. We met in the audience room at his hotel in Sarnath, India, where he was the guest of honour at the 1964 Congress of World Fellowship of Buddhists. I remember a feeling of tense guardedness about him, a sense of his being from far away and high above, and that he was not quite relaxed in his surroundings. I also remember his friendliness towards me, especially when he heard me speak in clear Tibetan, which I could already manage to some degree. I was presented to him as a beginning student of Buddhism (around two years into it by then with my first spiritual friend, the Mongolian geshe, Ngawang Wangyal) who wanted to study under his tutelage and if possible become a Buddhist monk. He said that I should come and see him again in Dharamsala after the conference was over and he would see how my studies should proceed. Then he swept out into the autumn sunshine to go to the dais set up near the great stupa of the Buddha's first teaching to give his speech at the conference.

I don't remember the speech very well as he gave it through an interpreter and it sounded strained and formal. His Holiness had a hard task before him. In those years, he was beginning to introduce Tibetan Buddhism to an international Buddhist audience that regarded (unfortunately, many of them still do) Tibetan Buddhism as 'Lamaism', a provincial corruption of real Buddhism, where they thought the real thing was Theravada or Mahayana. Only the relatively few Shingon Buddhists of Japan really respected Buddhist Tantra, and even they were a bit intimidated by the Unexcelled Yoga Tantras, the forte of the Tibetan Buddhists. But there is no doubt that even then His Holiness, in person, commanded great respect and his combination of being a simple Buddhist monk as well as a sincere and dedicated spokesperson for his suffering people was effective in moving people's hearts slowly but surely.

During the next year I remained largely unaware (at twenty-three I was blissfully unaware of a lot of things, even though I was all fired up to get enlightened!) of my great good fortune in meeting His Holiness regularly, almost every week, to discuss my studies and progress, as well as quite a few other things, as it turned out. His Holiness at that time lived above Macleodganj, in Svarg ashram. When we would meet, our conversations followed an invariable pattern. First, His Holiness would listen briefly to my recital of what I had been learning from my regular teachers (he had assigned me to his senior tutor Kyabjey Ling Rinpoche and to the abbot of Namgyel monastery). Then I would address a few questions to him, especially on my favourite topic of that time, the Madhyamika philosophy of voidness and relativity. His Holiness would always have a few good points to make, counter-questions and observations, but then he would refer me to my assigned teachers and embark on asking me questions about the many things he was keenly interested in. He would ask about Darwin and Freud, Einstein and Thomas Jefferson, life in the Americas and in Europe. I would answer as best I could, coining new words in Tibetan for some concepts—the subconscious, the id, relativity, natural selection—and using English terms in other cases.

Trying to explain complex subjects to His Holiness's brilliant and eagerly inquiring mind was quite a challenge, and it caused me to re-think many of my own ideas. I am afraid I disappointed His Holiness on subjects connected with the hard sciences, since I had been an English major and a would-be poet with strong philosophical and psychological leanings. But we had a fine time, often annoying his tutors and secretaries by spending too much time talking, perhaps taking time away from His Holiness's other duties. His Holiness seemed slightly stressed to me, lonely and a little sad, though basically energetic and cheery. I was so intent on Buddhist philosophy and contemplation, and I knew so little about Tibet and the sufferings of his people at the hands of the Chinese communists, that I could not really understand his situation. And I had very little idea what a tremendous blessing those meetings were for me.

Eventually I was ordained, and some time after that

returned to the US to live in the monastery in New Jersey. As the 1960s heated up with war protests and civil rights movement, I was drawn back into society through peers, and by early 1967 had resigned my monkhood and returned to lay life. I am afraid His Holiness was strongly disappointed with me for quite a while after that.

I returned to my university and went on to graduate school in Buddhist Studies, reaching the dissertation stage in 1970. Again I came to see His Holiness in Dharamsala, who by then had moved down into more adequate quarters near the newly constructed central cathedral.

My dissertation topic was a translation and study of Jey Lama Tsong Khapa's *Essence of True Eloquence* (*Drang Nges Legs Bshad Snying po*), which Geshe Wangyal unexpectedly directed me to undertake just as I was departing for India. This turned out to be His Holiness's favourite philosophical work, and in fact I discovered among my hastily packed books a modern printing of that very text he had presciently given to me back in 1965. When I reached his presence, it only took a few moments to break the awkwardness of a departed monk returning as a married layman with two children. He generously blessed my wife and family, and gave us serious admonitions to keep our relationship stable and healthy. Once he had discovered what I was working on for my dissertation (I blamed Geshe Wangyal for launching me on such a difficult work), he assigned me to a teacher, as before, and then invited me to a series of discussions with him on this text and the philosophical issues it addresses.

During this second series of conversations during 1971, I noticed an astonishing change in His Holiness that was very inspiring. He had come alive philosophically. No longer did he refer questions to other teachers. He had many points to make about Tsong Khapa's treatise, considered his most difficult. He cited many passages by heart, he was lucid and lyrical in explaining the deep impact and extensive ramifications of the fine points, especially the critical differences between the dialecticist and the dogmaticist approaches to the famous Madhyamika central way. Forgetting for a moment that he was the Dalai Lama and so should know it all naturally anyway, it was breathtaking to observe the powerful philosophical insight that shone through his infectious enthusiasm. Our talks that year were so exciting that he decided to work with me to bring out a book on the central way in English, a project we started on. Unfortunately, I didn't get the manuscript till the last minute and couldn't complete the translation myself as I had to get back to America for a teaching job, and another translator took over.

I spent the next eight years in the sword-dance of over-achievement that is required to get tenure as a university professor. I had no opportunity to visit Dharamsala, and His Holiness kept being denied a visa to the US as part of the over-solicitousness for Chinese feelings mandated by Kissinger's China policy. In 1979 I got tenure and His Holiness got his first visa, thanks to Cyrus Vance. I had a year's sabbatical in India with the whole family. That fall, I was lucky enough to host His Holiness at Amherst and Harvard on his first trip, and then travel on the same flight with him back to India to continue the sabbatical in Delhi and Dharamsala.

When His Holiness arrived in New York on that trip, I couldn't believe the further change he seemed to have undergone. I remember having an early morning dream-vision of him that day, as if he were a giant Kalachakra Buddha-couple, standing atop the Waldorf-Astoria, shining gloriously in that deity's particular luminescent pastel hues, the energy attracting a swarm of pin-stripe-suited bees of diplomats, politicians, business persons, princes of the church and other assorted bigwigs. During that entire trip and the following year I couldn't get over the rich power of his charismatic energy. He had always had the charisma of office—now he had ten times more charisma of person. Obviously he had been studying and practising the Unexcelled Yoga Tantras, especially the Kalachakra Wheel of Time.

During that winter in India, we had our third series of conversations. His Holiness was now forty-four years of age, having completed twenty years in exile. The period during the 1970s (when Chinese pressure on governments restricted his world travel) had been put to good use—his sustained series of retreats, capping his thirty years of intense study of all levels of Buddha's teaching, brought him to a manifest fruition. One would like to believe that a Dalai Lama naturally has all knowledge, ability and compassion. However, I can testify that there was a clear appearance of massive development through tremendous focused intelligence and untiring effort.

In these meetings we discussed every topic under the sun. My interest was the Tantras, and His Holiness had many profound and helpful things to say. His Holiness still seemed interested in everything, especially history, politics, sociology, ethics, and what I might call the psychology of compassion. Our dialogues were hard to publish, since he made me talk too much, answering his penetrating questions, rather than talking more himself. What he had to say was much more interesting to everyone but himself.

In the twenty-three years since then, His Holiness has written many books, dialogued with many thinkers and authors, given innumerable teachings and speeches. The constant progress I observed during those first seventeen years still continues apace, still advancing by quantum leaps. Especially since around the time he won the Nobel Prize in 1989, his general talks—on kindness, the common human religion, nonviolence, disarmament, science, ecology and the environment, and comparative religion—are better, more moving, more lucid, and more powerful in understanding and passion. I can honestly say that I have never found a single one of his speeches to be mere repetition canned like a politician's message. Though he has some main themes, each time he brings something new and fresh to them, such as another example from his ongoing readings and conversations, or a point made in a more compelling way. So it seems that his reincarnation continuum makes possible an endless advancement, growth and enrichment of his skill in liberative arts.

The Great Fourteenth: Roles and Teachings

'A simple Buddhist monk' or 'just a simple Buddhist monk!'— His Holiness often uses these phrases, and people usually smile and think he is being too modest, striking a pose of studied humility, and earnestly contradicting his enormous charisma, radiant good humour and flashing intelligence. Doth he protest too much? In the remarkable interview with Spalding Gray he reveals just how much he really means it.

Gray asks him if he ever has erotic dreams, is ever tempted by worldly desires, which Gray protests are the very stuff of his own life. The Dalai Lama responds quite thoughtfully, revealing that such imagery can emerge in the dreamtime, but he guards against losing control to it by remembering that he is a Buddhist monk and retreating to the fortress of his renunciation. He goes on to mention that sometimes he dreams of aggression, finds himself in confrontations with knives or guns, but again reflects on his deepest identity as a simple Buddhist monk, and withdraws from the patterns of hostility. Even in his dreams he never thinks 'I am the Dalai Lama!' This is truly remarkable.

The Dalai Lama does have multiple identities. He is a human being, of course, a male, the descendant of farmers, herdsmen and strong working women of the province of Amdo in far northeastern Tibet, born right on the border with Mongolia to the north, China to the east and Turkestan to the northwest. He is a Tibetan, his family naturally speaking a thick eastern dialect, is also familiar with central Tibetan and even conversant from childhood with the provincial Chinese of the Seeling district. Though she had no idea he was the Dalai Lama, his mother dreamed of his incarnation as coming to her from the southwest in the form of a bright blue dragon, escorted by two playful green snow lions! He often says that green is his favourite colour.

His next identity is that of a Buddhist monk, a person who has taken and maintains vows of personal nonviolence, poverty, celibacy and spiritual honesty, and who spends most of his waking energy in the pursuit of a perfect enlightenment believed to last for all time, to satisfy the self with unimaginable fullness, and to benefit countless other beings with selfless compassion. Simplicity is a cardinal virtue of a monk: it minimizes his distractions and maximizes his using his most essential vital energies in evolutionary development. As a monk he works on dissolving habitual egotism, including rigidity of his human, sexual and national identities. As a monk, he lives close to the bone and strives to be a universal being.

He also constantly creates—he calls it 'shaping his motivation'—his working identity as a bodhisattva, a messianically driven being who has dedicated all his lives to the attainment of perfect enlightenment, complete wisdom and inexhaustible compassion, in order to be able to help all other beings find freedom from suffering. Though others consider him the incarnation of Avalokiteshwara, the quintessentially divine bodhisattva of compassion—and he certainly seems to have grown into manifesting that august personage—he clearly does not hold on to such a self-image. He does say his religion is the common human religion of kindness, of love, of compassion, of universal responsibility. He once was asked whom he thought of on the planet as his spiritual peers. He thought a moment, and then answered with unmistakable sincerity, as if he had just rediscovered this fact afresh, that 'actually every person in the world is my spiritual peer!' As the *Transcendent Wisdom Sutras* declare again and again, he who thinks to himself, 'I am a bodhisattva', that one is not a bodhisattva. Only one who sees no bodhisattva, who sees no being, that one is a bodhisattva with true compassion for all beings.

He daily labours to lead his people and fulfil his responsibility to preserve and rule his nation—the Tibetan nation that has been under a genocidal pressure for over half a century, in such mortal danger that Tibetans should be on the endangered humans list. He is a statesman, a politician, a diplomat, a personnel manager, a chief executive officer. He maintains these duties in exile as a refugee.

He is a committed scholar and a prolific writer, researching deeply the philosophical, psychological and religious literature of his sophisticated civilization as well as exploring the modern sciences and literatures. He studies incessantly with a variety of tutors, and teaches extensively, both advanced students in the Tibetan Buddhist monastic community and the entire Tibetan populace, as well as an ever-growing public of spiritual seekers around the world. He speaks to all with clarity and sincerity, with a good sense of humour and an unfailing optimism.

He is also an accomplished vajra master, teacher of the esoteric ritual and contemplative traditions that his people consider the crown jewels of the Indian Buddhist tradition they inherited and have done so much to preserve, refine and extend. His precise knowledge of the architecture of the sacred mandala environment, of the details of elaborate ritual arts and procedures, his graceful gestures, magnificent chanting, and eloquent elucidation of the profound and poignant significance of the advanced contemplative practices leave even his veteran disciples amazed.

And finally, he is a peacemaker for the world, a Nobel Laureate, an inspirer of world leaders both political and religious who have been fortunate enough to encounter him, encouraging them not to settle for the harmful by-products of blind institutional momentum but to take responsibility for the poor and the oppressed, to use good sense and goodwill to solve the problems that beset our world, and not to give in to despair and cynicism and hide behind their powers and privileges. He is ready to be a good friend to everyone, even those who have harmed him or others, and patiently offers the alternative of constructive dialogue as a balm for violence and prejudice.

In his philosophical and ethical thought, His Holiness has powerfully emerged as a world leader with a compelling vision for a viable planetary community. Calling for a spiritual and ethical revolution, he is even a bit ahead of his time, a fact exquisitely ironic for those who assume he speaks from an 'underdeveloped' civilization outside of the progressive modern stream.

His central thesis is that human nature itself mandates kindness and love, altruism being the key to happiness. Compassion is not just sentimentality, but rather an intelligent and effective method of living the good life and attaining real happiness: it is not only a spiritual good, it is a biological necessity for human beings. This fact of nature dictates an ethic of compassion and universal responsibility on the social level. The duress of the postmodern planetary crisis requires a spiritual and ethical response as a survival necessity. His main idea is that, given broad adoption of a more spiritual outlook and more ethical actions, the planet can continue to be liveable in the coming centuries, things can go well for humanity in the future.

The second major theme His Holiness articulates in speeches and writings is that spirituality is broader than any specific form of religiosity and is essential for individual happiness and for keeping the world livable. He discourages an agenda of making anyone a Buddhist, and condemns all competition among religious institutions. In keeping with this, he argues that ethical principles are more universal than specific religious prescriptions. He elevates nonviolence as essential to overcoming the man-made disasters of conflict and wars, and always calls for dialogue to resolve tensions. He insists that such idealism is not as unrealistic as some modern secular theories of psyche and society have made it out to be.

His prophetic voice has begun to emerge with a powerful critique of material progress and soulless mechanical technology. In *Ethics for the New Millennium*, he says:

Although I never imagined that material wealth alone could ever overcome suffering, still, looking towards the developed world from Tibet, a country then as now very poor in this respect, I must admit that I thought it must go further towards doing so than is the case. I expected that, with physical suffering much reduced, as it is for the majority living in the industrially developed countries, happiness would be much easier to achieve . . . [but] the extraordinary advancements of science and technology have achieved little more than linear, numerical improvement . . . progress has meant hardly more than greater numbers of opulent houses in more cities, with more cars driving between them. Certainly there has been a reduction in some types of suffering including certain illnesses. But there has been no overall reduction.

Further, in his passionate call for a spiritual and ethical revolution, he argues adamantly for universal disarmament, sketching a series of systematic steps towards the total prevention of wars and war industries, likening war to a bonfire on which people are heaped like logs, and poignantly recalling his own visits to Auschwitz and Hiroshima. In a tradition as old as the great Buddhist teacher Nagarjuna (2nd century CE), he courageously denounces excess in luxurious living as leading to extreme gaps between the rich and poor, and makes a clear appeal for altruism and universal responsibility in economic policy. He is practical and optimistic about globalization, but not the imbalanced globalization that makes the rich richer and the poor poorer.

In spirituality, he follows the Indian emperor Ashoka (3rd century BCE) in calling for religions to focus on personal practice over institutional aggrandizement, tolerant pluralism over bigoted exclusivism. He insists on the priority of spirituality and ethics in personal practice over doctrinal purity and ritual formalism. He shows a willingness to dispense with religion altogether if it only adds to the burdens people struggle with. He acknowledges the benefit of religion sincerely applied, and makes the ingenious suggestion that to singularity in personal faith should be added pluralism in social practice.

In sum, were world leaders to take the teachings of this Nobel Laureate more seriously, we could be sure that this 21st century would not be a repeat of the war-torn, holocaust-ridden 20th century, but would be a century of peace, reconciliation, environmental restoration, economic sufficiency and spiritual progress for all humankind, with the added benefit of increased kindness to animals. The amazing thing is that in spite of the recent turn to violence, with terrorism and wars on terrorism superseding progress towards peace on many fronts, His Holiness remains unperturbed in his faith in human nature, undaunted in his call for nonviolence and dialogue, and positive in his outlook.

This refusal to give in to despair has an even greater power of example when we remember that it comes from the leader of Tibet, a nation and a people that has suffered so much genocide, mass destruction and ongoing oppression. Thus he embodies his intelligent teachings of non-retaliation, peace, understanding and dialogue, and truly makes the idealistic seem realistic, reveals the optimal as the practical!

May he continue on without interruption as long as he feels comfortable! May his deep wish for the liberation of his special charges, the noble people of Tibet, soon be miraculously fulfilled, to the astonishment of all! And may his inexhaustible compassionate effort for all peoples, including the Chinese, also come to fruition, as he becomes the Dalai Lama who serves as an Oceanic Teacher for the whole world, leading its nations back to harmony with nature, and justice and peace with each other, and its individuals to freedom, wisdom and happiness for themselves and all other beings.

In Search of the Panchen Lama

Isabel Hilton

I felt a quiet sense of achievement as the jeep rounded the final bend and the little village of Takster came into view. It clung to the side of a sunlit mountain, 9000 feet above sea level in what is now called Qinghai, the Tibetan province of Amdo. It was here that His Holiness was born. It was not a place the Chinese authorities wanted people to visit. But from the first occasion on which I had met the Dalai Lama—in Dharamsala in 1994—his extraordinary life had intrigued me. That meeting had set my own life on a different and unexpected track. Now I was determined to see the place where the Dalai Lama's story—in this incarnation at least—had begun.

There had been no encouragement in Xining, the provincial capital of Qinghai, to pursue this idea, despite the fact that the village figured in the official Chinese language guidebook to Qinghai. The birthplace of the Dalai Lama was, I read, 'a remote and beautiful village', and was listed as a tourist attraction, along with the bird sanctuary at Kokonor Lake, the great Tibetan monastery of Kumbum and the birthplace of the Tenth Panchen Lama (which was rendered equally difficult to visit). I carried the guidebook around like a talisman, my protection against the suspicious local officials who seemed to be under instructions to discourage anyone from trying to reach it.

The exact status of Takster was a small indicator of the

difficulties the Chinese government faced in trying to maintain a coherent account of their policies in Tibet. On the one hand, Beijing argued that Tibet, along with the rest of the People's Republic, enjoyed religious freedom and that the Tibetan people are happy under Chinese rule—contented members of the motherland's cheerful family of nations.

But on the other hand, the persistence of the allegiance and affection that Tibetans felt towards their exiled spiritual leader was an embarrassment to Beijing and sat uneasily with China's long-running campaign of vilification against the Dalai Lama. The leader of Tibetan Buddhism, according to Beijing, is an enemy of the state, a 'splittist' and, most bizarre of all, a man of doubtful spiritual credentials. To have his birthplace become a place of pilgrimage, as it would surely do if access to it was unimpeded, would be deeply embarrassing to Beijing. All this gives the Dalai Lama's birthplace a somewhat ambiguous status as an official tourist attraction. The solution is to list the village in the guidebooks, but to ensure that it is never 'convenient' for anyone actually to reach it. None of the coach parties that tramp through the showcase monasteries of Qinghai— feeding both the local economy and the illusion that Buddhism is thriving under benevolent government protection—make the trip to Takster. If you want to get there, you have to go alone.

I had been staying in Xining, once a walled city at one end of the great camel route west, now, after decades of modernization and 'improvement', a dreary, dusty town from which any past romance had been erased. On the streets of Xining it is evident that Qinghai is still home to that mosaic of border peoples—Tibetan, Mongolian, Golok, Tu and others—who have been brought under Chinese rule since the 19th century. But today, most of the passers-by are Han Chinese whose migration here is one element in the policy of assimilation. Once, this part of Qinghai marked the eastern edge of cultural and ethnic Tibet. It is the Tibetan province of Amdo, and both the Fourteenth Dalai

Lama and the Tenth Panchen Lama were born in the vicinity. Several centuries ago, Tsong Khapa, the great reformer of Tibetan Buddhism and the founder of the Gelugpa school, was also born here, at a place commemorated in Kumbum monastery.

Today, the Tibetans appear as a minority in Qinghai, of no more importance than the others in a province that is assuming the monotone grey cultural aspect imposed by the People's Republic. Follow the religious trail, though, and Qinghai seems like a palimpsest: just beneath the surface, obscured but not erased, the map of Tibetan culture begins to show through.

When I first met the Dalai Lama I had no idea that the encounter would send my life off in a different direction—or that, several years later, I would be dodging local Chinese scrutiny to make this sentimental pilgrimage to his birthplace. It was not that I had suffered a sudden religious conversion. I had gone to Dharamsala in February 1994 simply to interview him for a BBC television documentary on the life and death of the German activist Petra Kelly. I had studied in China in the 1970s but had never been to Tibet, and, though I had once attended one of His Holiness's lectures in London, I was not in search of a new faith—either religious or political.

Perhaps it was coincidence then, that, on that visit to Dharamsala, I would get so involved in a Tibetan story that I gave up other pursuits to explore it. The story was the search for the late Panchen Lama's incarnation—a subject that presented itself to me with such force that, the Petra Kelly documentary completed, I decided to follow the process through to its conclusion. I took leave from my job and began to plan a book and a film. Telling the story, though, was conditional on the confidence and help of the Dalai Lama. To my great relief, he agreed to help and was to prove true to the commitment.

It was a delicate proposition: the process was secret and needed to be for many reasons. But having agreed to the proposal, the Dalai Lama was more than frank. As the process unfolded, I realized that as well as following the twists and turns of the Panchen Lama process, I was also being afforded an opportunity to watch the Dalai Lama's conduct of an issue that was to test to the limit the slender diplomatic resources of his Government in Exile and to pose a problem of leadership that would have enormous implications for the future.

The work meant many visits to Dharamsala and many interviews. There were meetings elsewhere—in Switzerland and Germany, in London—all squeezed out of an impossible schedule. For me, it was an eye-opening experience, watching one man deal with competing problems: the requirements of his religious followers, his political responsibilities towards Tibetans inside and outside Tibet, the diplomatic complexities of trying to maintain a dialogue with Beijing, the burden of satisfying not only his Tibetan following but the heterodox expectations of a worldwide audience. All this, as I soon realized, with remarkably little in the way of administrative back-up.

It was a burden that I was aware we were adding to by imposing the tiresome requirements of filming, and I would not have been surprised if he had grown exasperated. But if he did, he disguised it, and when a conversation resumed after an interval of several weeks, he always began, with uncanny precision, at exactly the point at which we had left off on the last occasion.

The subject of our discussions was often harrowing. It turned out to be a difficult year: the Chinese government had sanctioned a search for the Panchen Lama to be led by Chadrel Rinpoche, the head of Tashilhunpo monastery in Shigatse. But Beijing would not admit the Dalai Lama's participation and were determined to use the process to reaffirm their claim to historical as well as actual supremacy. Chadrel was trying to juggle the competing demands of his religious conscience and his political masters: he wanted the Dalai Lama to make the final identification, but hoped that this would pass unnoticed until the Chinese government had given its approval to the boy. He also wanted the Eleventh Panchen Lama to be brought up at Tashilhunpo.

The Dalai Lama, he told me, thought that was only fair: after all, in recent history the Panchen Lama had lived in Tibet while the Dalai Lama lived in exile. And whilst many in the exile community would be disappointed, he was conscious of his responsibility to the Panchen Lama's many followers in Tibet. In late January 1995, the boy was identified from a smuggled list and in Dharamsala the Dalai Lama had no choice but to wait for the process in Tibet to run its course.

It was an agonizing few months: Chadrel had been summoned to Beijing and all efforts to contact him came to nothing. Months went by with no news, bar the rumour that a lottery was to be held. Finally, the Dalai Lama decided to announce, in June, that the Panchen Lama's reincarnation had been identified. It precipitated a crisis both in Beijing and in Tibet. Gedhun Choekyi Nyima disappeared, Chadrel was arrested and Beijing began to coerce the Tibetan religious establishment into accepting a different candidate whose name would be drawn from the object that Beijing had decided symbolized the Qing emperors' sovereignty—the Golden Urn.

It was hardly a happy or a successful outcome and I am often asked whether the Dalai Lama should have made that announcement when he did. At the time, I argued against it, since Beijing's reaction was all too predictable. Today, though, I think he had little alternative but to make the announcement. If he had not, there was an imminent danger that a lottery ceremony would be held in Tibet and a different name announced. There was nothing the Dalai Lama could do to prevent it, and to be seen as reacting to the news from Beijing—especially if the wrong candidate was selected—would have been unconvincing.

For many of his followers, the realization that the Dalai Lama's candidate was still in Tibet—and at the mercy of

Beijing's fury—came as a shock. Ideally, the boy would have been spirited out of the country to be unveiled in exile. But reality was less kind. I had begun to realize how narrow the Dalai Lama's room for manoeuvre was, and to appreciate how skilfully he operates, despite its constraints. Like the Pope, the Dalai Lama commands no military divisions. All he has is his moral and spiritual authority, the devotion of his followers, and whatever influence he can conjure from his position as a religious leader. This, of course, is not a negligible hand to play, but nor is it one that carries any guarantees of political success in the short term.

By late October of 1995, the process was nearing its end: months of coercion had left religious leaders in Tibet with little alternative but to bow to Beijing's pressure and a meeting was in preparation that would bring that stage of the process to a conclusion. I was in Qinghai, researching the life of the Tenth Panchen Lama and trying, for more personal reasons, to visit Takster. As the months had gone by, I had become steadily more intrigued by the extraordinary life the Dalai Lama had led—a life that had begun in traditions that had hardly changed since the 18th century but was to lead to exile and a remarkable adaptation to the demands of the late 20th century. Not only had the Dalai Lama survived as a political and spiritual leader, he had become a globally recognizable figure and a tireless voice for his people's cause. It can hardly have been the future imagined by the search parties that made their way to Takster in the mid-1930s, looking for a house with oddly shaped guttering that matched the vision revealed in Lhamo Latso lake.

I took a rattling public bus that headed south from Xining towards Ping An, a crossroads town that figured as the nearest point of departure to Takster.

In the marketplace, the taxi drivers looked at me bemused, and shook their heads. 'You need a jeep,' they said. The jeep driver also shook his head. He did not mind taking the job, he said, but he didn't know where it was.

An old man among the crowd of curious bystanders that had begun to gather chimed in. He knew where it was, he said. In return for a lift, he would show me.

It was a beautiful autumn day as we drove out of Ping An on a metalled road that ran along a river valley. The valley bottom was lush, fertile ground, mostly bare in this autumn season—freshly ploughed brown earth in tiny terraced fields lined with close-planted silver birch and poplar trees. On either side the hills rose steeply, the higher slopes weathered bare to the deep red rock. We sped through mud-brick villages, scatterings of houses with the decorated gateways and strings of prayer flags that mark Tibetan homes.

We dropped the old man at one of the villages, and following the route he indicated left the valley bottom and began to climb, now glimpsing the austere and compelling beauty of the snow-capped mountains that rose behind the gentler hills. Finally, we struck out on a muddy dirt road that climbed precipitously into the mountains. Two hours later, we reached the village.

As I climbed out of the jeep, a knot of people stared at me as though I had descended from Mars. The Dalai Lama's house? I inquired. They gestured up a steep path to a whitewashed house at the top of the village. I climbed the path and, skirting an unfriendly but fortunately tethered dog, stepped through a decorated doorway into the paved courtyard.

The house had been freshly painted and a flagpole stood in the centre of the courtyard, flanked by two incense burners. It was silent and deserted. I climbed a wooden staircase to the first floor and stood on the flat roof, admiring the breathtaking view. When I turned back, I was startled to see that a man had appeared noiselessly behind me. He was about fifty and was looking at me warily.

'Who are you?' he asked.

'I'm from England,' I said, hoping no further explanation would be demanded. 'I have come to see where the Dalai Lama was born.'

'Did you come by yourself?' he said, looking round anxiously for clues as to my status in the official range of permitted visitors. I reassured him that I was alone.

He seemed puzzled, but on the whole pleasantly surprised. He was, he said, the caretaker. I guessed that he was weighing up whether he should send me packing or show me round. After a pause, he added quietly, 'I am related to the Dalai Lama.' I asked if he had met his illustrious relative. He had, he said, in Dharamsala, the Dalai Lama's exile home. He smiled sadly at the memory.

The house was empty but well tended. 'It has been rebuilt,' said my guide. 'It was completely destroyed in the Cultural Revolution.' The caretaker told me that he had once lived next door, but his house, too, had been destroyed in the Cultural Revolution. 'It used to be like this one,' he said, 'but they pulled it down, flattened it completely.' He showed me some roofless mud walls, the remains of his former home. The government, though, had paid for the Dalai Lama's family house to be rebuilt in a brief period of relaxation of official hostilities towards His Holiness in the late 1970s. 'They knocked it down,' said the caretaker. 'Then they rebuilt it.'

I imagined the Red Guards rampaging through the now peaceful courtyard, the caretaker himself, captive of the mob, paraded with a dunce's cap before being put to some humiliating labour. As though to dispel bad memories, he took up his keys and began to unlock the rooms. Inside were simple shrines to the members of what, in other circumstances, would have been the ruling family of Tibet. He pointed to the Tibetan inscription on a large framed photograph of the Dalai Lama. 'He wrote it himself,' he said and translated it for me. 'Though I am far away,' it said, 'and cannot be with you, the people of Hung Nai are always in my heart.' In front of the photograph, white *katags* had been laid.

As we walked through the house, I admired the freshly painted decoration on the roof beams. 'It's very beautiful,'

I said to my melancholy guide.

'Do you think so?' he replied. 'I don't. It's not beautiful enough for the Dalai Lama. If he was here, it would be so much more beautiful.'

He was a man full of sadness, unable to speak openly of the lost world in which kinship with the Dalai Lama would have marked him out for honour rather than political disgrace and humiliation. Now he was the teacher in the local school. There were fifteen children, he told me, and he had to teach them in Chinese.

I asked if he remembered the Dalai Lama. 'I wasn't born when he left,' he replied, 'but I remember him coming to visit. I was a classmate of Ngari Rinpoche.'

I knew Ngari Rinpoche, the Dalai Lama's younger brother who now runs a guesthouse in Dharamsala. I tried to imagine him in this remote village where, but for the vagaries of reincarnation, he, too, might have lived out his days.

'You know you are supposed to get permission to come here,' the caretaker said, as we sat over a cup of butter tea. 'I told the driver,' he continued, 'that *they* will be angry if they find out.' There was no need to elaborate and my driver smiled anxiously.

'Do many people come here?' I asked.

'Not many,' the caretaker replied.

'Do many foreigners come here?'

He laughed and shook his head. My driver was beginning to fidget, perhaps turning over the possible consequences of this visit in his mind.

I rose to leave. 'Do you think the Dalai Lama will ever come back?' the caretaker asked me.

I said, as gently as I could, that I didn't know, but it seemed complicated. A mist had descended on the village as we had been chatting and he apologized for the unfriendly weather. 'When it's clear,' he said, 'you can see how beautiful the Dalai Lama's birthplace really is.'

'It's very peaceful,' I said.

He pulled a face. 'The mountains are too high,' he replied, 'and the road is too long.'

I climbed into the jeep and looked back for a final farewell. The caretaker was standing sadly in front of the house. As the jeep pulled out of the village, a row of impassive figures, hands in pockets, appeared on top of the high bank that overlooked the road. They watched, silhouetted against the sky, as we began the long slithering journey down the mud road and back to Ping An. I wondered how many of them had been there in the Cultural Revolution, foot soldiers in the mob that had tried to erase the traces of the Dalai Lama's birthplace. In my pocket there was a handful of the bright red earth, scooped up in a last-minute impulse. I thought of taking it to Dharamsala the next time I went and offering it to His Holiness, but I never did: it was not, I thought on reflection, the kind of nostalgia that he indulged in.

When I returned to Beijing, two weeks later, the Panchen Lama crisis was reaching a climax. Tibet's religious leaders were locked up in a hotel in Beijing to give the appearance of approval to the Golden Urn ceremony that would take place in Lhasa within a few days. I was only an observer of this process, yet it was impossible to avoid the emotions it aroused: to witness the coercion of a community of faith by a political force that held its beliefs and traditions in contempt made me both angry and sad. It was also clear that the process was a rehearsal for the moment when a new Dalai Lama would be sought.

According to a report from the Chinese news agency Xinhua, Raidi, the chairman of the Standing Committee of the TAR People's Congress, told a group of Hong Kong reporters: 'After the passing of the Fourteenth Dalai Lama we will find the reincarnated child, according to historical conventions and religious rituals that were formed hundreds of years ago.'

These traditions, which underwent frequent revisions during the search for the Panchen Lama, will conclude, as the search for the Panchen Lama did, with Beijing's insistence on the use of the Golden Urn lottery. There is little that Tibetans can do to prevent such an outcome if Beijing remains determined to impose it. But my own conclusion at the end of this painful story was that the appearance of victory can be deceptive. Beijing can force a religious leader on a people, but even the might of the PLA cannot make people believe what they do not choose to.

Mao's millenarian communism is already dead and his successors have ditched all of his most treasured beliefs, with the exception of his resentful nationalism and his vocation for conquest. For the Dalai Lama, the search for the Panchen Lama is one of many episodes that could be read as defeat—events to which he must respond with compassion, regardless of personal emotions.

But if I were to try to sum up what I had learned from observing the Panchen Lama process, it would be an appreciation of the long view. Buddhism has already outlived communism and endured, despite the appalling suffering of so many of its practitioners in the last five decades. The Fourteenth Dalai Lama has said that he may be the last. If he contemplates the end of the institution of the Dalai Lama with equanimity, perhaps it is in part because the experience of the last five decades has demonstrated that political ideologies may come and go, but the teachings that have been at the centre of his life as a spiritual practitioner and teacher have survived.

Writing with His Holiness

Alexander Norman

Although some of the greatest names in English literature began their careers writing in other's names, ghost-writing is generally regarded as a rather disreputable discipline. Indeed, many would argue that the term 'discipline' is over-dignified for a genre popularly associated with film-pop- and sport-star autobiographies.

Actually, many if not most political memoirs are ghost-written too. Those of Ronald Reagan, Margaret Thatcher and, further back, Golda Meir spring to mind. Yet there is some justice in this negative view. On the one hand the subject of the star memoir is often rendered improbably articulate simply as a means to cull money out of credulous readers. On the other, even in the case of such a distinguished name as that of Sir Thomas More, writing in the name of his friend and patron Henry VIII, it cannot be denied that the two were collaborating in an act of literary legerdemain.

Within the Tibetan Buddhist literary tradition, there is only one attested example of passages of autobiography having been written by someone other than the actual author (in Heruka's sequence of Milarepa's poems). There are, however, people who argue that the whole body of Mahayana literature is no more than pseudepigrapha— writings misattributed to the Buddha and others for the purpose of establishing their authority. And it is a fact that His Holiness the Dalai Lama's first autobiography, *My*

Land and My People was ghost-written by a well-known English writer, the late David Howarth, and not, as has been suggested, actually penned by the Dalai Lama himself.

Nevertheless, the great majority of the abundant autobiographical writings of Tibetan masters are entirely authentic, even if we do allow for a degree of tidying and editing by close disciples. It is, therefore, with some hesitation that I speak about His Holiness from the perspective of someone who has ghost-written two of his books. It will entail making some confessions.

The first of these is that I could not claim to be a close disciple. I am not a Buddhist. Besides, no true disciple would take a fee for his services. As a professional writer, my relationship with His Holiness is inevitably tainted with self-interest. Secondly, I do not speak Tibetan—the *sine qua non* for any real understanding of Tibetan life and thought according to Professor Michael Aris—let alone that I am no more than functionally literate in Tibetan. Finally, my formal qualifications for undertaking the two projects are almost non-existent. My literary background, such as it is, is journalistic, not academic.

Together, these factors would seem to offer quite good reasons for hesitation. Yet I am highly conscious of my great good fortune, and of the privilege I have enjoyed working so closely with the Dalai Lama over an extended period. Given that I have had an opportunity that many might envy, I take it as duty to tell a bit about the work, as well as to say something about what I have learned from it concerning His Holiness.

My first meeting with the Dalai Lama occurred during March 1988, when I travelled to Dharamsala to interview him on behalf of the *Spectator*, the English political journal. The very first impression I had on entering the audience chamber was that His Holiness was not there. I remember being slightly disconcerted when, apparently out of nowhere, he came up to greet me. My second impression was of his strong physical presence. Here was no ethereal holy man, no airy sprite. Here was someone who, in another life, might have made a useful rugby player—out on the wing perhaps. And his ready laughter—so vigorous (yet far from dissolute) as it welled up, so startling (yet so full of conviction) in its final soprano flourish—he reminded me of an earthy cherub, such as a more naturalistic Raphael might have painted.

Such are my memories of the first of a great many meetings during the sixteen years that have since elapsed. (I once calculated that *Freedom in Exile* occupied around 150 hours spent, one-on-one, with His Holiness over a period of eighteen months, albeit with interpreters present. Actually there were generally four of us. *Ethics for the New Millennium* took about the same, but over a longer period.)

Nine months after that first meeting, I was back in Dharamsala to begin work on the autobiography. How this came about is unimportant here. Suffice it to say that from my perspective it was more a matter of good luck than good judgement. There followed three of the most heady and exciting months of my working life.

It has been observed that merely to meet the Dalai Lama is to be swept up in a romance almost impossible not to succumb to. I make no claim to being an exception to this rule. In some ways it is even more difficult now to remain level-headed than it was all those years ago. Although by the end of the 1980s, Macleodganj was just beginning its transformation from senescent ex-colonial hill station to today's international tourist destination, it still retained an air of genteel charm. There was little traffic and only a handful of hotels and teahouses. There was but one public telephone offering international calls. E-mail, satellite television and the rest lay safely in the future.

Nothing but the growing stature of the Dalai Lama offered any indication of the revolution to come. And if as a visitor in those days you were a westerner, you found yourself a member of an enchanted community, and were valued, it seemed, just for being yourself. Often you would be greeted by Tibetans—so many of them monks, it was true—with a nod, almost a little bow, and a smile. All this has changed. And though the majority of Tibetans are friendly as ever, the sheer weight of visitors over the years has made them somewhat more discriminating than earlier. Yet the Dalai Lama's private compound has altered little over the intervening years. The contrast between 'the world' and this sanctuary is thus greater than ever.

To enter, you are first frisked and vetted by the guards at the gate. Glancing back, you may note to your sneaking satisfaction the faces of one or two onlookers betraying a look of curiosity mixed with envy. (How beautiful is life for the Elect!) But once inside, registering the air of unhurried order, of discipline and high purpose, you dismiss the thought as unworthy. Ushered into a waiting room just inside the gate, you have some time to collect yourself.

A few minutes later, a young official, smartly turned out in traditional Tibetan *chuba* worn over grey flannels and well-polished shoes, leads you across the courtyard and up a flight of steps. To your right, on a lower level, you half-notice a neat group of buildings forming three sides of a square around an area of lawn. In the middle stands a monk conversing with another official. You climb a second short flight leading into a well-proportioned building of colonial pattern. This, you gather, is His Holiness's audience chamber.

You now enter what is obviously an ante-room, the windows of which look onto a veranda festooned with baskets of perennial pinks. Flowerpots stand stacked against the outer wall. Looking round the room, you become aware of an array of display cabinets crowded variously with Tibetan religious statuary and a collection of awards and citations honouring the Dalai Lama.

Next, you notice the silence. It seems so studied as somehow to drown out the exuberant, day-long chatter of birds outside. Perhaps it is broken by the crash and flurry of a monkey bursting along the branches of a tree to land on top of a building. Then a call goes up from one of the

Indian bodyguards and you hear a stone skittering across its corrugated iron roof. Then a pause; then the birds again. But again their song is caught up in the silence.

Suddenly a door opens. You hear laughter as an Indian family, showily dressed, passes through the room on their way out, the children chattering excitedly. And now it is your turn to meet the earthly manifestation of the god of compassion! The god of love! To spend an hour alone in his company! Two! Four! A day! Who would not be swept off their feet?

Well, of course, not everyone feels quite this way, or at least it is only that part of them which hopes for spontaneous enlightenment that does. Naturally, the cynics say it is all a façade while the realists clutch doubt to their breasts.

Whatever my own feelings, there was never much scope for them getting out of hand. Notwithstanding the informality of our meetings, it was always clear that His Holiness's aim was to impart the necessary information as quickly as possible. We had little small talk.

For my benefit, the interviews for *Freedom in Exile* were conducted largely in English, though His Holiness would frequently lapse into Tibetan for minutes at a time. In that event, either Kasur (then Kalon) Tenzin Geyche Tethong, or Tendzin Choegyal, both of whom attended the majority of sessions as interpreters, would translate. If appropriate, the other would then add to or qualify the initial rendering in English. (And indeed His Holiness might himself then comment further in English.) Both of them had been educated in English public schools in India, so their grasp of the language was complete—added to which, for the same reason, their use of it was charmingly seasoned with the idiom of the late colonial era.

So far as method is concerned, my approach to gathering material for the autobiography was to treat the whole exercise as a single extended interview. I would familiarize myself with the broad outline of the various episodes of His Holiness's life, but only with a view to coming up with questions that would prompt. To have been provocative would have skewed the narrative. The critical point was that the telling should come entirely from him. My primary role at this stage was thus to act as amanuensis. When the raw material was down on paper (having been both transcribed from tapes and worked up from notes taken down simultaneously) the plan was to knead the resulting text into prose which retained, as far as possible, His Holiness's own distinctive vocabulary and turns of phrase.

The Dalai Lama's English, as anyone who has heard it will testify, is impressionistic, one might even say *pointilliste*. On account of this, the work of reduction, of converting the material from digital to analogue, so to speak, was by far the most challenging part of the undertaking. Always my intention was to infiltrate as few additional words as it seemed possible to get away with. (Even so, I now consider that I allowed myself rather too much licence. For a start there should have been much more sparing use of the first person singular. The use of adjectives is also a bit wanton in places.)

Thinking back to that time, I recall the very first occasion on which we sat down to discuss the autobiography. His Holiness began by asking me whether I considered that another book about him was really worthwhile? At least three biographies had been published recently. I was naturally somewhat taken aback at this as his own office had already signed a publisher's contract. I replied that since this was to be his autobiography, it would be a very different order of book to anything that had been written since *My Land and My People*. Evidently this was sufficiently reassuring as I was summoned back the next day for the first dedicated interview.

From the beginning, His Holiness was cooperative in every way, to say nothing of his affability. It quickly became evident that he has a well-developed sense of the ridiculous. A particular source of amused incredulity was the extravagant lengths to which ceremonial was taken in the Tibet of his youth. It was clear, too, that he is supremely patient with others, and ready to see their point of view.

What was not in evidence, however, was anything to corroborate some of the more startling claims made about him. Some say he is omniscient, others that as a highly realized spiritual master he is able to read people's minds. There are, of course, those who will say that great spiritual masters reveal their true nature to others only according to the capacity of the individual. (This idea, very current in Tibetan Buddhism, is strikingly reminiscent of the Docetists who, during the 2nd century AD, argued that Christ could not in any ultimate sense have been 'God made flesh'. They argued that what people would have apprehended had they seen Jesus would have differed according to their spiritual capacity.) Perhaps they are right. Nonetheless, I must say that, save perhaps for one incident, my impressions of His Holiness as our acquaintance grew were nothing out of the ordinary.

Because the majority of interviews were fitted to His Holiness's schedule on an ad hoc basis, I was on occasion able to catch glimpses of his private life. One thing that concerned me at first was the fact that he did not appear to socialize much with friends. Like its Christian counterpart, Tibetan Buddhist monasticism may be ascetic in some respects but the importance of recreation and conviviality is not ignored. Yet it struck me that His Holiness seemed to have almost no leisure time. He does not spend days out with his family as most monks do. There are no long relaxed meals with members of his private office. Of course he will chat to his staff. He is close to one of his surviving brothers. He receives various older members of his entourage from time to time. But none of this appeared to add up to much more than the occasional pleasant conversation. I wondered whether he did not sometimes feel rather cut off and lonely. Yet one could not hope to meet anyone more outgoing or more at ease with himself.

What I began to see was that the Dalai Lama is a man

of prayer before all else. This is the most important part of his work. In a sense, much of his active (as opposed to his contemplative) life is recreation. Meeting people from all walks of life, travelling, talking to journalists and reporters, this is where he socializes and enjoys himself. And as soon as these activities are over—sometimes as soon as he can extricate himself (people do tend to ask the same questions a lot of the time)—he resumes his central practice, the practice of prayer (*gom* in Tibetan, literally 'familiarization' but generally translated as meditation).

Thus, when abroad, he is not like most people who return to their hotel after a long day and, flinging themselves down on the bed, switch on the television, raid the minibar and call up room service. Instead, his first priority is meditation. Indeed, whether at home or abroad, much of his waking day is spent this way. When he arrives at his office, generally at 8 a.m., he will have spent three hours in prayer and *lectio divina*, studying scripture. There was even a period, while we were finalizing the manuscript of *Freedom in Exile*, when he would rise at 3 a.m. in order to finish some special devotions by the time we began work. (Normally he gets up at a more leisurely 4 a.m.)

The one slightly unusual experience I recall from this time occurred on a trip to Ahmedabad. His Holiness had suggested I come too so that when he had any spare time he could fit in an interview. On one occasion I was shown into his room whilst he was still meditating cross-legged on the bed. I remember being struck by how small he suddenly looked, tiny even, like an animated altar statue. At the same time I sensed an immense power—which evaporated only when he ceased his prayer some moments later. It was a fleeting impression only and easy to overlook. Yet, set in the context of a conversation I had later with a friend who is a deacon of the Catholic church, it is perhaps worthy of mention. One day the priest, whom this friend assisted, had received the stigmata of Christ. As the deacon entered the room, he was thrown to the ground by what he described as an immense power. I have sometimes wondered whether what I sensed as the Dalai Lama's 'spiritual energy' might not have been a pale, perhaps more controlled, manifestation of the same power?

A more concrete insight into His Holiness's character came on another occasion when, after a press conference in his hotel suite, I happened on him straightening up the chairs that had just been vacated—not, I think, out of fastidiousness, but just because it needed to be done. Yet there were any number of people on hand he could have directed to the task. No doubt there are other figures of world renown who straighten chairs. But they are surely in a minority. Fewer still would actually interrupt an interview on camera to see to the welfare of a young bird that had fallen from its nest, as I saw happen on another occasion. And I doubt whether any others at all are ever to be found sitting at a window in their private quarters sorrowing over the dumb stupidity of a cloud of insects tumbling past on a current of warm air.

Having completed the necessary interviews for *Freedom in Exile*, I spent a year preparing a draft manuscript. This I took out to Dharamsala during the spring of 1989. There it was read and vetted by various members of the Dalai Lama's staff. I felt at that point that probably 90 per cent of the work was done, that the changes required by these readers would bring it up to 98 per cent and that a final session or two with His Holiness would bring it up to the required standard. How wrong I was.

After taking delivery of a longish, but not particularly challenging, list of corrections and suggested alterations, I was called to see His Holiness. He wanted to know how I had got on, whether I had experienced any particular difficulties, and whether it was true that we already had publishers in a dozen countries? It was true, I replied. This, it seemed, both pleased and surprised him a little. As to the work itself, I'd got on fine, but yes, I had one or two further queries. I forget now what they were, but I explained their substance to him. I seem to remember him nodding and then remaining silent for a few moments. We were alone. 'Tomorrow then. Eight o'clock,' he said, brightening: 'Come here and bring the book.'

The next day I returned as instructed. 'So,' he began, 'read it.' I was stupefied. 'Yes, go on. Read it to me.'

The following two weeks passed in something of a frenzy. Each day I went up to His Holiness's residence to go through the manuscript, in the company of Tenzin Geyche Tethong and Tendzin Choegyal, as before, for eight, nine, even, on one or two occasions, for ten hours at a stretch. Every sentence was considered, each phrase scrutinized, and single words subjected to lengthy inquisition. Sometimes I would be drawn into quite heated debates over the use of particular terms. Often I would concede, but occasionally I refused to yield. Whenever this happened, my judgement was accepted. One instance (though not actually a contentious one) occurred in connection with my desire to use the word 'mendacious' in a particular context. Although His Holiness was unfamiliar with the term, I felt it was especially appropriate at that point and he allowed it. (I wish I could find it now, to see whether it still seems right.)

When finally we came to the end, I walked away with alterations, additions, corrections and sundry emendations accounting for a third of the manuscript. Hardly a page was not covered with scrawl. That was not the very end of the process, however. Just before the book went to press—three months late and barely six weeks before publication—it was checked again by Tenzin Geyche and by Geshe Thupten Jinpa, the latter reading it from a specifically Buddhist perspective.

The work sessions with His Holiness for *Ethics for the New Millennium* followed broadly the same pattern. This book was published in the UK under the somewhat fey title (my fault) *Ancient Wisdom, Modern World*—it should really have been called just *Ethics*, everywhere. It was altogether a much more difficult enterprise, however. The book is half the length of *Freedom in Exile*, yet it took more than three times as long to write. As with the autobiography, there were the initial material-gathering sessions, followed by an extended period when we went through the manuscript as a team.

One difference in our method was that, to save His Holiness's time, rather than have his every utterance translated into English then and there, he would sometimes explain a point to Thupten Jinpa (who collaborated on the project throughout), which the latter would then pass on to me when we came to transcribe the tapes later. Also, I adopted a more adversarial role during the preliminary discussions: it seemed essential to sometimes play the devil's advocate in order to head off some of the objections likely to be posed by a western readership.

As well as further deepening our acquaintance, working on *Ethics* gave me a much better appreciation of the Dalai Lama's intellect. I have to admit that it soon became clear that his is superior to mine by a rather comfortable margin. There were many occasions when I found myself stammering to explain a point of view while challenging something he had said. He, on the other hand, hardly ever comes out with an utterance that is less than fully formed. I often felt as if I was wearing lead boots next to his plimsolls.

One particular observation from this time concerns the way in which His Holiness can be quite splendidly disconcerting. Too often I found myself jumping to conclusions, only to find them confounded a moment later. I had, for example, always assumed that Tibetans were, of necessity, highly conscious of the natural world, thanks both to their nomadic culture and to Buddhism's reverence for all forms of life. Not at all, he said. Tibetans were entirely ignorant in these matters. It had simply never occurred to anyone that there could be such a thing as pollution. But that does not mean they did not themselves pollute the environment. It was just that the conditions prevailing in Tibet (wide open spaces and very dry air) meant it had little impact.

Similarly, I gathered that at a science·conference His Holiness attended, he had caused consternation by telling the panel that he could imagine instances where it might be justifiable to use animals in experiments designed to further (human) medical science. (I noticed that in the transcript he used the plural 'instances' but in the book published subsequently, this was changed to the singular: 'an instance'. Was this censorship?)

One of His Holiness's most attractive characteristics is his disinclination to offer value judgements unless specifically asked for them and even then to be supremely careful in doing so. There are doubtless many good reasons for this. One is surely connected to his understanding of his role as Dalai Lama. He is, he insists, 'just an ordinary human being', though it is doubtful whether many people take this at face value. Few would travel thousands of miles, or queue for hours, or even listen to a stranger they thought merely to be an ordinary human being. Similarly, he maintains that he is not a religious leader but 'just a simple Buddhist monk'. Again, this is not the general perception. Yet it would help explain his reluctance to offer opinions.

Another reason for His Holiness's reluctance to speak out on certain issues is very likely connected to the Buddhist view of mission. A Buddhist teacher does not teach unless requested to do so. Nor does he (or to a much lesser extent, she) teach unless convinced of the motives of the supplicant. The bully-boy tactics of certain evangelical Christian missionaries in Mongolia are viewed with horror by many Tibetans, the Dalai Lama included.

Yet another factor is no doubt the western tendency to resolve everything into clear-cut, either–or dilemmas. This seems rather unsubtle to the Tibetan mind. And where this seems likely to lead to intractable argument, His Holiness prefers to remain detached, knowing that often the aim is to push him into a corner.

This does not mean he has no strong views. Moreover, he can be quick to state these unequivocally. I recall on one occasion telling him about some deep-green extremist who advocated that the world's population be reduced to a billion. His immediate response was to say that this person should set a good example and lead the way.

Similarly, I have observed many occasions when he was so distressed at something he had seen or heard that the very thought of it robbed him of speech. Then he will sit quietly for a moment or two, sometimes longer (offering a prayer?), sometimes taking off his glasses to wipe his eyes before continuing. A discussion about human embryo experimentation and the possibility of growing human body parts in sub-human creatures created for the purpose was one such.

I wonder though whether this reluctance to pontificate is not in large part the reason for the recent, rather disturbing, emergence of a sort of ersatz Dalai Lama living in the public eye. This is the Dalai Lama of cool, the Dalai Lama as friend to everyone—though most notably to a clutch of entertainment-world royalty—a spiritual hero who offers comfort to the victim in us all. This is the Dalai Lama of the Dalai Lama industry (an industry I must have helped create)—of countless books, articles, videos, television appearances and even two major feature films; the Dalai Lama as New Age icon, a religious leader who is popularly understood to reassure without requiring repentance, to console without demanding contrition.

At first sight, this looks like innocuous sentimentalization. But is such sentimentalization ever really innocuous? The problem with turning the Dalai Lama into the uniquely spiritual being of popular imagination is that it enables us to ignore anything he says that troubles us (such as his insistence that the economic disparity between North and South is immoral). It becomes the utterance of someone we cannot identify with other than superficially.

Yet one does not need to know him well to guess that the Dalai Lama is someone who would sooner bless than curse his enemies; someone who gives the same consideration to all; someone who pays no regard to social standing. Just by listening carefully, one can tell that here is someone who, to the utmost of his ability, seeks to be at peace with everyone; someone who is patient, who is kind, who is neither boastful nor conceited, who is never rude nor seeks his own advantage; that here is someone who neither takes offence, nor stores up grievances. On the contrary, he is evidently ready always to make allowances, to trust, to hope and, in adversity, to endure whatever trials come. (In saying this I am of course plagiarizing St. Paul: no one has better described what it means to be spiritual than he.)

If, then, we merely adore the Dalai Lama, the danger is we will overlook the fact that spirituality consists precisely in the exercise of virtue. Worse, there is every likelihood we will miss the most remarkable thing of all—which is that, just as he says, he is an ordinary human being. But therein lies our hope.

Making Kindness Stand to Reason

Pico Iyer

Though the Dalai Lama is famous as a speaker, his real gift, you quickly notice, is for listening. And though he is most celebrated in the west these days for his ability to talk to halls large enough to stage a Bon Jovi concert, his special strength is to address 20,000 people—Buddhists and grandmothers and kids alike—as if he were talking to each one alone, in the language he or she can best understand. The Dalai Lama's maxims are collected and packaged now as books to carry in your handbag, as calendar items and as advertising slogans, but the heart of the man exists, I think, in silence. In his deepest self he is that being who sits alone each day at dawn, eyes closed, reciting prayers, with all his heart, for his Chinese oppressors, his Tibetan people and all sentient beings.

Yet the curiosity of the Fourteenth Dalai Lama's life— one of the things that have made it seem at once a parable and a kind of koan—is that he has had to pursue his spiritual destiny, for more than half a century, almost entirely in the world—and, in fact, in a political world whose god is Machiavelli. His story is an all but timeless riddle about the relation of means to ends: in order to protect six million people, and to preserve a rare and long-protected culture that is years away from extinction, he has had to pose for endless photos with models and let his speeches be broadcast on the floors of London dance clubs.

To some extent, he has had to enter right into the madness and vanity of the Celebrity Age in order to fulfil his monastic duties. The question that he carries with him everywhere he goes is the simple one of whether the world-will cannot be avoided, whether it will scar him before he elevates it: in three centuries, no Ocean of Wisdom, Holder of the White Lotus and Protector of the Land of Snows has ever also served as guest editor of French Vogue.

I went to visit the Dalai Lama in Dharamsala as I have done at regular intervals since my teens. I took the rickety Indian Airlines flight from Delhi to Amritsar, which was often a restricted war zone (because it houses the Sikh stronghold of the Golden Temple), and from there took a five-hour taxi ride up into the foothills of the Himalayas. As I approached the distant settlement on a ridge above a little town—the roads so jam-packed with scooters and bicycles and cows that often we could hardly move (the Dalai Lama has, for security reasons, to drive for ten hours along such roads every time he wishes to take a flight)—Dharamsala came into view now and then, and then disappeared, like a promise of liberation, or some place that didn't really exist. Most of the time—the car collapsing on a mountain road, a group of villagers assembling to push it hopefully forwards, night falling and each turn seeming to be taking us farther and farther away from the string of lights far off—I felt sure we'd never get there.

As soon as you arrive at the dusty, bedraggled place, however, you realize you are very far from fairy tale, in the realm of suffering and old age and death. Windows are broken and paths half-paved in the rainy little village where the Dalai Lama has made his home for more than half his life now; even the happy cries and songs of the orphans at the Tibetan children's village on one side of town have a slightly wistful air, as the sun sets behind the nearby mountains. When you call the Dalai Lama's office, you will hear that 'All circuits are busy', or that the five-digit number changed yesterday. Sometimes my calls got cut off in mid-sentence, amidst a blur of static; sometimes I got put on hold—for all eternity, it seemed—to the tune of 'When London Bridge is Falling Down'.

It is, therefore, perhaps the perfect paradoxical setting for a humble monk who lives alone when he is not being sought out by Goldie Hawn or Harrison Ford. In the ante-chamber to his living-room, after you've been checked by a Tibetan guard and then an Indian one, you sit under a certificate of Honorary Citizenship from Orange County, an award from the Rotary Club of Dharamsala and a plaque commemorating an honorary professorship from Kalmyk State University. Ceremonial masks, Hindu deities and pietas shine down on you. On one wall is a huge, blown-up photo of the Tibetan capital of Lhasa, showing that the palace where the Dalai Lama once lived is now ringed by discos, brothels and a new Chinese prison, with armed soldiers stationed upon the city's rooftops.

The Dalai Lama has a singular gift for seeing the blessing in everything, and seeming unfazed by all the madness that swirls around him; he is always thoroughly human and always thoroughly himself. Sometimes, as you wait to see him, his exuberant new friend, a very puppyish German shepherd, runs into the room and starts jumping over a group of startled Tibetan monks here for a serious discussion, licking the faces of the Buddhist teachers before romping off into the garden again. Sometimes a pair of English hippies sits there, since the Dalai Lama is ready to take advice and instruction from anyone (and knows—such is the poignancy of his life—that even the most disorganized traveller may know more about contemporary Tibet, and the state of his people, than he does). As a photographer asks him to take off his glasses, pose with this hat, sit this way or sit that, he seizes the chance to ask him about what he saw when he photographed uprisings in Lhasa many years before.

As I sit across from him in his room with its large windows, looking out on pine-covered slopes and the valley below—*thangkas* all around us on the walls—the Dalai Lama makes himself comfortable, cross-legged in his armchair, and serves me tea. He always notices when my cup is empty before I do. He rocks back and forth as he speaks, the habit acquired, one realizes, over decades of long and gruelling meditation sessions, often in the cold. And part of his disarming power (the result, no doubt, of all that meditation and the dialectics of which he is a master) is that he launches stronger criticisms against himself than even his fiercest enemies might.

When first he met Shoko Asahara, he tells me one day (referring to the man who later planned the planting of deadly sarin gas in the Tokyo subway system), he was genuinely moved by the man's seeming devotion to the Buddha: tears would come into the Japanese teacher's eyes when he spoke of the Buddha. But to endorse Asahara, as he did, was, the Dalai Lama quickly says, 'A mistake. Due to ignorance! So, this proves [and he breaks into his full-throated laugh], I'm not a Living Buddha!' Another day, talking about the problems of present-day Tibet, he refers to the fact that there are 'too many prostrations there', and then, erupting into gales of infectious laughter again, he realizes that he should have said, 'too much prostitution' (though, in fact, as he knows, 'too many prostrations' may actually constitute a deeper problem). He'd love to delegate some responsibility to his deputies, he says frankly, 'but, even if some of my Cabinet ministers wanted to give public talks, nobody would come.'

The result is that it all comes down to him. The Dalai Lama is rightly famous for his unstoppable warmth, his optimism and his forbearance—'the happiest man in the world', as one journalist-friend calls him—and yet his life has seen more difficulty and sadness than that of anyone I know. He's representing the interests of six million largely unworldly and disenfranchised people against a nation of 1.2 billion whom nearly all the world is trying to court. He's the guest of a huge nation with problems of its own, which would be very grateful if he just kept quiet. He travels the world constantly on a yellow refugee's 'identity certificate' and, though regarded by most as a leader equivalent to Mother Teresa or the Pope, is formally as ostracized as Muammar Gaddafi or Kim Jong II. He is excited when meeting Britain's Queen Mother—because he remembers, from when he was young, seeing news clips of her tending to the poor of London during the Blitz—but the world is more excited when he meets Sharon Stone.

And so a serious spiritual leader is treated as a celebrity, and a doctor of metaphysics is sought out by everyone, from every culture, who has a problem in his life. As a monk, he seems more than happy to offer what he can, as much as he can, but none of it helps him towards the liberation of his people. I ask him one day about how Tibet is likely to be compromised or distorted by its complicity with the mass media, and he looks back at me shrewdly, with a penetrating gaze. 'If there are people who use Tibetans or the Tibetan situation for their own purposes,' he says, 'or if they associate with some publicity for their own benefit, there's very little we can do. But the important thing is for us not to be involved in this publicity, or associate with these people for our own interests.'

The razor-sharp reasoning is typical, even if it doesn't quite address the conundrum in which he finds himself. For precisely in order to satisfy his inner and outer mandate, the Dalai Lama is obliged to traffic in the world incessantly. He has to listen to a reporter asking him how he'd like to be remembered, which is, in the Buddhist context, akin to asking the Pope what he thinks of Jenifer Lopez. ('I really lost my temper,' he tells me, of the question, 'though I didn't show it.') He has to answer for every scandal that touches any of the many often highly suspect Tibetans and Tibetan groups around the world. And he has to endure and address every controversy that arises when his image is used by Apple Computers, or younger Tibetans deride him as an out-of-it peacenik who's done nothing to help Tibet for forty years.

As we spoke day after day in the radiant fall afternoons, young monks practising ritual debates outside his front door, the snowcaps shining in the distance, and the hopes of Tibet poignantly, palpably in the air around the ragged town of exiles, the time the Dalai Lama most lit up, in some respects, was when he spoke of some Catholic monks he'd run into in France who live in complete isolation for years on end, and 'remain almost like prisoners' as they meditate. 'Wonderful!' he pronounced, leaving it to his visitor to deduce that, left to his own devices, that's how he'd like to be.

To someone who reads the world in terms of temporal glory, it's a stirring story of a four-year-old peasant boy ascending the Lion Throne to rule one of the most exotic treasures on earth. To someone who really lives the philosophy for which the Dalai Lama stands, it could play out in a different key. At two, he lost the peace of his quiet life in a wood-and-stone house where he slept in the kitchen. At four he lost his home, and his freedom to be a real person, when he was pronounced king. Soon thereafter, he lost something of his family, too, and most of his ties with the world at large, as he embarked on a formidable sixteen-year course of monastic studies and was forced, at the age of six, to choose a regent.

The Dalai Lama has written with typical warmth about his otherworldly boyhood in the cold, thousand-roomed Potala Palace, where he played games with the palace sweepers, rigged up a hand-cranked projector on which he could watch Tarzan movies and Henry V, and clobbered his only real playmate—his immediate elder brother Lobsang Samten—in the knowledge that no one would be quick to punish a boy regarded as an incarnation of the god of compassion (and a king to boot). Yet the overwhelming feature of his childhood was its loneliness. Often, he recalls, he would go out onto the rooftop of the palace and watch the other little boys of Lhasa playing in the street. Every time his brother left, he recalls 'standing at the window, watching, my heart full of sorrow as he disappeared into the distance.'

The Dalai Lama has never pretended that he does not have a human side, and though it is that side that exults in everything that comes his way, it is also the side that cannot fail to grieve at times.

At the age of twenty-four, a few days after he finally completed his doctoral studies, and shone in an oral in front of thousands of appraising monks, he lost his home for good: the Wish-Fulfilling Gem, as he is known to Tibetans, had to dress up as a soldier and flee across the highest mountains on earth, dodging Chinese planes, and seated on a hybrid yak. The drama of that loss lives inside him still. I asked him one sunny afternoon about the saddest moment in his life, and he told me that he was moved to tears usually only when he talked of the Buddha, or thought of compassion—or heard, as he sometimes does every day, the stories and appeals of the terrified refugees who've stolen out of Tibet to come and see him.

Generally, he said, in his firm, prudent way, 'Sadness, I think, is comparatively manageable'. But before he said any of that, he looked into the distance and recalled how 'I left the Norbulingka Palace that late night, and some of my close friends, and one dog I left behind. Then, just when I was crossing the border into India, I remember my final farewell, mainly to my bodyguards. They were deliberately facing the Chinese, and when they made farewell with me, they were determined to return. So that means'—his eyes are close to misting over now—'they were facing death, or something like that.' In the four decades since then, he's never seen the land he was born to rule.

I, too, remember that drama: the fairy-tale flight of the boy-king from the Forbidden Kingdom was the first world event that made an impression on me when I was growing up. And, a little later, when my father went to India to greet the newly arrived Tibetan, he came back with a picture of the monk as a little boy, which the Dalai Lama gave him when he talked of his own three-year-old in Oxford. Since then, like many of us, I've run into him everywhere I go, it seems—at Harvard, in New York, in the hills of Malibu, in Japan—and have had the even stranger experience of seeing him somehow infiltrate the most unlikely worlds: my graduate-school professor of Virginia Wolf suddenly came into my life again as editor of a book of the Dalai Lama's talks about the gospel; at the Olympics, a long-time friend and sportswriter for the *New York Times* started reminiscing about how he covered the Dalai Lama on his first US tour, in 1979, and found him great because he was so humble. 'It sounds like he considers you part of the family,' a friend once said, when I told her that the Dalai Lama and his equally mischievous younger brother call me 'Pinocchio'. But really, this gift is for regarding all of the world as part of his family.

At the same time, the world itself has not always been very interested in the details of his faraway country, and a tradition that seems to belong to another world. When Tibet appealed for help against China to the newly-formed United Nations, it was Britain and India, its two ostensible sponsors, who argued against even hearing the motion. And as recently as the 1980s, I remember his press conferences in New York being almost deserted; when once I organized a lunch for him with a group of editors, one of them called up a couple of days before to call it off, because no one really wanted to come into the office on a Monday just to chat with a Tibetan monk. When first I visited him in Dharamsala, in 1974, I really did feel as if I was looking in on one of the deposed emperors of China or Vietnam, sitting in a far-off exile. As we sat drinking tea in his modest, colourful cottage, clouds passed through the room from the rains outside—all we could see through the large windows was mist and grey—and it felt as if we were truly sitting in the heavens, at least a mile above anything that felt real.

Yet one of the paradoxes of the Dalai Lama's life—a

paradox to answer the koan that has been his fulfilment of a spiritual duty in the world—is that it was, it seems, his monastic training that has allowed him to be so focussed and charismatic a presence in the world. In his early years in India, the Dalai Lama used the world's neglect of him to organize his exiled community and to write his country's constitution (in part to allow for his own impeachment). Even exile could be a hidden blessing, he was saying (and showing his compatriots): it freed him from the age-old protocol that so shackled him in Tibet and it brought the forever feuding groups of Tibet together in a common cause. Most of all, though, he used his free time to go on long meditation retreats, enjoying a solitude that could never have been his in Tibet (or, now, in Dharamsala).

Robert Thurman, professor of Tibetan studies at Columbia, and father of actor Uma Thurman, remembers first meeting the Dalai Lama in 1964, when he, full of spiritual ambitions, cross-questioned the young Tibetan about Shunyata, or voidness, while the Dalai Lama questioned him, no less eagerly, about Freud and the American bicameral system. 'It was fun,' Thurman says, using the word people often use of the Dalai Lama. 'We were young together.' At the same time, the answers that the monk, only in his twenties then, gave to complex theological questions were less good, Thurman feels, than those offered by more senior monks.

When the Tibetan leader emerged from his retreats, though, and came out into the world—Thurman saw him on his first US tour in 1979—'I almost keeled over. His personal warmth and magnetism were so strong. In the past, of course, he had the ritual charisma of being the Dalai Lama, and he's always been charming and interesting and very witty. But now he opened up some inner well spring of energy and attention and intelligence. He was glorious.'

And yet that air of responsibility—the word he always stresses in the same breath as compassion—has never left him. I remember going to see him the day after he won the Nobel Prize, when he happened to be staying (as is so typical of his life) in a suburban ranch house in Newport Beach. What struck me at the time was that, as soon as he saw me, he whisked me (as he would no doubt have whisked any visitor) into a little room, and spent his first few minutes looking for a chair in which I would be comfortable—as if I were the new Nobel Laureate and he the intrusive journalist.

But what I also remember from that moment was that, even as the world was feting him—congratulatory telegrams and faxes pouring into the rec room downstairs—he couldn't let himself off the hook. 'Sometimes,' he confessed, 'I wonder whether my efforts really have an effect. I sometimes feel that unless there is a bigger movement, the bigger issues will not change. But how to start this bigger movement? Originally, it must come from individual initiative.'

The only way, he concluded, was through 'constant effort, tireless effort, pursuing clear goals with sincere effort'. Every time he left a room, he said, he tried to switch off the light. 'In a way, it's silly. But if another person follows my example, then a hundred persons, there is an effect. It is the only way. The bigger nations and more powerful leaders are not taking care. So we poor human beings must make the effort.'

Meeting him now, I find him a lot more business-like than he was in those days (and, of course, much more fluent in English); when TV crews come to interview him, he knows how to advise them on where to set up their cameras (and when we begin talking, he is quick to point out that my tape recorder is moving suspiciously fast). He's not less jolly than before, perhaps, but he does seem more determined to speak from the serious side of himself, as the years go on, and as Tibet draws ever closer to oblivion. Where he used to greet me with an Indian namaste, now he does so with a handshake, though the Dalai Lama does not so much shake your hand as rub it within his own, as if to impart to it some of his warmth.

As we talk, though—every afternoon at 2 p.m., day after day—he takes off his glasses sometimes and rubs his eyes; his aides say that in recent years, for the first time ever, they've seen him exhausted, his head slumped back in his chair (this from the man usually seen leaning into the conversation, as if to bring to it all his attention and beady-eyed vigour). He doesn't have much time for spiritual practice now—only four hours a day (his duties increasing as he becomes a more senior monk). He still likes to do 'some repair work, of watches and small instruments', and he still loves tending to his flowers; one of the longest and most animated answers he gives me comes when I ask after his 'four small cats'. But these days the only real break he can take is in listening to the BBC World Service, to which he cheerfully confesses himself addicted.

This is the tendency of an engaging, still boyish character alight with curiosity; but it's also the confession of a man whose duties are almost entirely tied up with the dealings of the world, at a minute-to-minute level. One thing the Dalai Lama is not is otherworldly. He can explain in precise detail why the Tibetan cause is weaker than that of the Palestinians, or how globalism is, at best, advancing a kind of Buddhism in mufti. His references nearly always come from the day's most recent news, and he watches everything—from the fall of the Berlin Wall to the tragedy in Rwanda—both to see how it illuminates some metaphysical theory and to see what other kind of teaching it can impart. Exile, indeed, has allowed him, he will tell you, to become a student of the world in a way that no earlier Dalai Lama could, and to see a planet that previously he, and the Dalai Lamas before him, could glimpse only through the parted curtains of a palanquin. The best aspect of his travelling is that he can schedule meetings with scientists and psychologists and Hopi leaders, all of whom, he believes, can help him refine his understanding of his own tradition. Buddhists can and should learn from Catholics, from physicists, even from communists, he is quick to tell his startled followers—and if the words of the Buddha (let alone of the Dalai Lama) are not borne out by the evidence, they must be discarded instantly.

This is one reason why he seems much more interested in asking questions than in giving answers, and much more comfortable as a student (which he's been, in the context of Tibetan Buddhism, most of his life) than a teacher. It is also why I would say his sovereign quality is alertness: watch the Dalai Lama enter a crowded auditorium, or sit through a long monastic ceremony that has many others nodding off, and you will notice him looking around keenly, for what he can pick up—a friend to whom he can unselfconsciously wave, some little detail that will bring a smile to his face. Alertness is the place where the slightly impish boy and the rigorously trained monk converge, and though the world at large most responds to his heart—the pleasure afforded by his beam and air of kindness and good nature—the specific core of him comes no less from his mind and the analytical faculties honed in one of the world's most sophisticated metaphysical technologies. It's not unusual, I've come to see by now, for the Dalai Lama to remember a sentence he's delivered to you some years before, or to complete an answer he began ninety minutes ago, while lacing up his sturdy mountain boots. Sometimes, in large gatherings, he will pick out a face he last saw in Lhasa forty years before; once, as we were talking, he suddenly remembered something an Englishman had said to him twenty years before—about the value of sometimes saying, 'I don't know'—and asked me, searchingly, what I thought of it.

Again, the irony here is that the mindfulness he's cultivated in meditation—on retreats, and at the hands of pitilessly strict teachers—is what has helped him in his travels; spiritual training—this is one of the lessons of his life and his example—has constant practical application in the world. Much of the time he's speaking to people who know nothing about Buddhism—who may even be hostile to it—and he's mastered the art of speaking simply and ecumenically, from the heart, stressing, as he does, 'spirituality without faith—simply being a good human being, a warm-hearted person, a person with a sense of responsibility'. Talking to his monks, he delivers philosophical lectures which few of the rest of us can begin to follow; speaking to the world, he realizes that the most important thing is not to run before you can walk. The title of a typical book of his mentions not 'enlightening' the heart but, simply, 'lightening' it.

In a sense, he's turned his predicament to advantage in part by learning about western religions and meditation practices in other traditions, as earlier Dalai Lamas could seldom do. And he's also had to deal with a worldwide stampede towards a Buddhism for which it may not be ready (to such a point that, more and more as the years go on, he tells westerners not to become Buddhists, but just to stick to their own tradition, where there's less danger of mixed motives, and certainly less likelihood of confusion). Listening to him speak everywhere from Sao Paulo to Chicago, Philip Glass says, 'The word "Buddha" never came up. He talks about compassion, he talks about right living. And it's very powerful and persuasive to people because it's clear he's not there to convert them.'

Pragmatism, in short, trumps dogmatism. And logic defers to nothing. 'Out of 5.7 billion people,' he tells me one day, his eyes glittering with the delight of a student immersed in one of Tibet's ritual debates, 'the majority of them are certainly not believers. We can't argue with them, tell them they should be believers. No! Impossible! And, realistically speaking, if the majority of humanity remains non-believers, it doesn't matter. No problem! The problem is that the majority have lost, or ignore, the deeper human values—compassion, a sense of responsibility. That is our big concern, for whenever there is a society or community without deeper human values, then even one single human family cannot be a happy family.'

Then—and it isn't hard to see the still eager student

playing his winning card—he goes on, 'Even animals, from a Buddhist viewpoint, also have the potential of showing affection towards their own children, or their own babies—and also towards us. Dogs, cats, if we treat them nicely, openly, trustingly, they also respond. But without religion; they have no faith!' Therefore, he says triumphantly, kindness is more fundamental than belief.

Yet the deepest loss of all in the Dalai Lama's often bright and blessing-filled life is that all the friends he's made worldwide, all the presidents and prime ministers he's won over, all the analytical reasoning with which he argues for compassion and responsibility have not really helped him at all in what is the main endeavour of his life: helping the people of Tibet and sustaining a Tibetan identity among a scattered population, six million of whom have not seen their leader for two generations and the other 140,000 of whom have not, in many cases, seen their homeland. Many of those who see him flying across five continents in a year (in business class) and delivering lectures to sold-out halls don't know that he's working with a staff drawn from a population smaller than that of Warren, Michigan, and with a circle of advisors who'd never seen the world, or known much about it, before they were propelled into a premature exile.

A Simple Monk

Sulak Sivaraksa

A few years ago, leaflets were circulated by Christians outside a large public meeting at Diamond Head, Honolulu, stressing the fact that the Dalai Lama refers to himself as only a simple monk. They asked the following questions: What is he capable of? Why should people be attracted to—or even respect—him? Instead, the people should turn to Jesus, who was not only the Son of God but also the Saviour of the World.

On the other hand, both in public as well as in private, His Holiness has often praised Jesus, Mohammed and all religious leaders. He encourages Christians and Jews to practice their own religions wisely and mindfully. If they want to add Buddhist meditation to their spiritual traditions, it is all right, provided they do not belittle their own religions.

This reminds me of another simple monk, my own late teacher, Bhikkhu Buddhadasa, whom His Holiness also greatly admired. He asked all his followers to uphold three crucial tenets: (1) try to understand the essential teachings of the Buddha and put them into practice as selflessly as ·possible; (2) respect and honour others' religions, not regarding them as inferior to your own; and (3) unite with those of other faiths and non-believers so that together you can overcome greed, hatred and delusion, traits that are increasingly being manifested in consumerism, centralization of power and modern education, which concentrates only on intellectualism and is devoid of wisdom and compassion.

Bhikkhu Buddhadasa dedicated himself to working as the servant (*dasa*) of the Buddha. Indeed, the Buddha himself was a simple monk. When the Buddha was a prince, he revelled in all worldly pleasures, shielding himself from suffering in the world. Eventually, he encountered an old man, a sick man, a dead man and a monk. Suddenly it dawned upon him that sickness and death are a part of life. He wanted to overcome the suffering of life. He felt that abandoning sensual pleasures and family life and becoming a simple mendicant might be a way. In fact, the Buddha-to-be was a wandering monk for six years before he became truly awakened from greed, hatred and delusion. His understanding was so thorough that no selfishness remained. As a result, his wisdom was automatically transformed into compassion. That is the reason we call him the All Enlightened and the Compassionate One.

For us, being a simple monk (or a simple nun) is really essential for any human being to achieve the highest goal in life—overcoming suffering and being in the state of real happiness without depending on sensual or external conditions.

If we do not lead a simple life and depend so heavily on other factors, we have no time and energy left for deep concentration in order to be mindful, and to understand the reality of physical phenomena as well as the mystery of the universe. Scientific knowledge only helps us to understand some aspects of the universe, often compartmentally. On the other hand, deep meditation without selfishness will help one realize the truth holistically.

A simple monk finds it easier to overcome selfishness than a layperson attached to family life, because he/she is not tied down to sensual pleasure which is like a double-edged dagger. It is a fact that every gain, honour, sensual happiness or praise has its negative attribute: loss, dishonour, suffering and denunciation. According to the Buddha, these are the eight worldly conditions. Whoever is attached to any of these will not be free from the cycles of birth and death.

Unfortunately, some monks who have left the mundane world to pursue the truth are still caught in one or more of the eight worldly conditions. Losing their simplicity and sometimes even obsessed with fame and wealth, they are monks in name only. They no longer lead a celibate or a noble life and have become hypocrites, fooling themselves and others.

Morality or ethics is said to be the foundation of the successful development of human potential. According to the teachings of the Buddha, living within the discipline of the vows of morality—commitment not to harm any living being with one's body or speech by not lying, killing, stealing—is the most effective way of accumulating positive karmic energy or morality, literally a build-up of positive habits of mind, body and speech.

Vows or commitments are viewed not as moralistic restrictions but as practical guidelines for life. There are sets of vows for laypeople, but the vows for monks and nuns are said to serve as the most potent way to live within the commitments of morality. Fully ordained monks, for example, have 227 vows.

Logically then, the more vows one has and keeps—that is, one uses them as the tools they are meant to be—the easier it is to develop our innate potential for love, kindness, patience and wisdom. And it is commonsense that one is more likely to succeed at something by devoting more time to it than less and by living in an environment—internal and external—that totally supports the endeavour.

Put another way, the life of a monk (or a nun) is characterized by integrity, restraint and chastity in matters related to the sexual instincts of the body. In this day of consumerism and materialism, most people do not see the virtue of leading completely celibate lives.

An English monk, Bhikkhu Jayasro, expresses this issue beautifully:

It's only through taking this impeccable standard that we can begin to understand the whole nature of sexuality. We begin to see its conditioned nature, how it arises and passes away. We begin to see the suffering inherent in any attachment to it, how impersonal it is, what feeds it, what gives power to it, whether it be physical conditions, food, lack of sense restraint or indulgence in imagination. We begin to see it as a conditioned phenomenon. But we can only have a distance from it, be able to reflect on it and see it for what it is by refraining from its physical and verbal expressions.

There is an important point about defilements here: that we have to pin them down on the mental level before we can let go of them. And the way we pin something down on the mental plane is that we refrain consciously or endure through the intention to express it physically or verbally. This is where the relationship between *sila*, *samadhi* and *panna* becomes very clear. As long as we're still expressing sexual feelings physically, or indulging in lascivious or careless speech about sexual matters, then we can never isolate it. It's moving, it's still receiving energy. We're still keeping it in motion, we're still feeding the flames. So we seek to counter the stream of craving. And to do that successfully we must aspire to transcend sexuality altogether. It is that aspiration, as much as the actual restraint, that distinguishes the *samana* from the lay person.

So as celibate monks we take a whole new stance toward our sexual feelings, towards women—half of the human race. We practice looking on women who are older than us as mothers, if they're just a few years older than us as older sisters, if a few years younger than us as younger sisters. We substitute wholesome perceptions of women for the sensual. This is a beautiful gift that we can give women. An attractive woman comes into the monastery, and we refrain from indulging in sexual perceptions, sexual thoughts about that woman and substitute it with wholesome reflections, whether it is consciously trying to perceive the woman as a sister, or wishing that person freedom from suffering. Practising *metta* we reflect, 'may they be well'.

We offer women the gift of a wholesome response to them as human beings rather than following the instinctive attraction or obsession with their body or some aspect of their physical appearance. Through that intention we experience an immediate elevation from the blind instinctual level of our being to the uniquely human. It is a movement from the coarse to the refined. Indeed, the Pali word *brahmacariya*, which we translate into English as celibacy, literally means 'the way of the gods'. In other words, within the human realm, a chaste life led voluntarily and with contentment is the most refined, sublime and happy form of existence.

A simple monk endeavours to attain and uphold *upekkha*, which is tragically lacking in our richly violent world. Upekkha is the fourth stage of *brahmavihara*, the divine sentiments or sublime states of mind, and is generally defined as equanimity, neutrality, or poise. Venerable P.A. Payutto, a leading Thai monk, explains upekkha as follows: 'Seeing things as they are with a mind that is even, steady, firm and fair like a pair of scales; understanding that all beings experience good and evil in accordance with the causes they have created; [and the readiness] to judge, position oneself, and act in accordance with principle, reason, and equity.'

Raising a good example, the Venerable Bhikku argued that upekkha is detachment—without bossing around or interfering. It is compared to a carriage driver who, when the horses are running smoothly and on course, sits quietly and alertly in his or her seat. In this sense, a more comprehensive definition of upekkha, drawn from *Visuddhimagga*, may be 'passively watching when others are able to take responsibility for themselves, or when they deserve the results of the actions for which they are responsible'.

A point that needs to be emphasized is that upekkha does not mean hermetic isolation, apathy, insensitivity, or criminal negligence—sitting on a fence and doing nothing. Upekkha calls for mindful (temporary) detachment in order to cultivate wisdom; the latter is a prerequisite for helping others with compassion and understanding.

In the Theravada tradition there are ten stages of perfection, and it is recommended that the individual practice them. Upekkha is the final stage. The first nine stages are:

1. *Dana*: giving, charity, generosity and liberality
2. *Sila*: morality, good conduct, that is, respecting oneself and all sentient beings
3. *Nekkhama*: renunciation or trying to overcome sensual pleasures
4. *Panna*: wisdom, insight, and understanding
5. *Viriya*: energy, effort and endeavour
6. *Khanti*: forbearance, tolerance and endurance
7. *Sacca*: truthfulness
8. *Adhitthana*: resolution, determination
9. *Metta*: loving-kindness, friendliness.

In this tradition, the ten stages of perfection are divided into three levels. The first is ordinary perfection or *parami*. In the case of upekkha one becomes indifferent to praise and blame in the performance of one's duty. (Again, indifference to blame is not the same as being irresponsible for the negative consequences of one's action or inaction.) The second is superior perfection or *upaparami*. Here one is indifferent even when one is being harmed physically. Lastly is supreme perfection or *paramathaparami*. At this level one is indifferent even when one is being tortured to death. In other words, through the supreme perfection, one would achieve the stage of awakening from selfishness to selflessness—the 'I' is completely decentralized.

As pointed out, upekkha is always the last, because one needs to cultivate loving-kindness first and foremost. The *Mettakaraniyasutta* makes this clear.

He or she who wants to attain peace should [first] practice being upright, humble and capable of good speech. He or she should know how to live simply and happily, with the senses calmed, without being covetous and carried away by the emotions of the majority. Let him or her decline from doing anything that will be disapproved of by the wise ones.

[This is what he or she must contemplate.] May all people be happy and safe and may their hearts be filled with joy. May all living beings live in security and in peace—whether weak or strong, tall or short, big or small, visible or invisible, near or far away, already born or yet to be born. May all of them dwell in perfect tranquillity. Let no one do harm to anyone. Let no one put the life of anyone in danger. Let no one, out of anger or malice, wish anyone any harm.

Just as a mother loves and protects her child at the risk of her own life, we should cultivate Boundless Love and offer it to all living beings in the entire cosmos. We should let our boundless love pervade the whole universe, above, below and across. Our love will know no obstacles; our hearts will be absolutely free from hatred and enmity. Whether standing or walking, sitting or lying down, as long as we are awake, we should maintain this mindfulness of love in our own hearts. This is the noblest way of living.

Free from the wrong views, greed and sensual desires,
living beautifully, and achieving Perfect
Understanding, those who practice Boundless Love
will certainly transcend Birth and Death.

In sum, a simple monk is someone who is ever humble,
chaste, mindful and practises Boundless Love. He leads a
noble and celibate life. He wants so little for himself that all
his time and energy are sacrificed for the happiness and
welfare of other sentient beings. His happiness depends on
his thoughts, speech and actions being first and foremost for
the well-being of others.

His life is harmonious within himself, physically, mentally
and spiritually. And this harmony leads to harmonious
relationships with other monks and nuns, as well as with
laypersons. His lifestyle should influence the lifestyle of the
laity who will then try to imitate the simple and mindful
way of the monks. His lifestyle would also influence natural
phenomena, making them more harmonious and wholesome.
Even birds and bees would learn to be less harmful and
more compassionate.

The simple life of a monk can contribute much to social
welfare and environmental balance. Besides, a simple monk
would have the time for learning various sciences which
would be useful in helping humans and other beings
overcome suffering. As these sciences are interrelated and
necessary to prevent as well as to cure (not compartmentally
or commercially) contemporary personal or social ills, they
are advantageous indeed. His Holiness has successfully held
dialogues with leading scientists over the last few years. As
a result, some of them have become more humble and have
seen the value of the spiritual dimension in helping scientific
knowledge to transcend logic and materialism. Publications
on these series of dialogues are most meaningful. Publications
by His Holiness himself or by those who have been inspired
by him are likewise worthy.

Some ills are vastly damaging and horrendous such as

the Chinese invasion of Tibet and the dreadful events in that country. Yet, it is profoundly illuminating when a simple monk like His Holiness and his followers insist that we all learn to love and empathize with the Chinese people and forgive the Chinese government which has committed acts of aggression out of ignorance or delusion, not to mention out of greed and hatred.

Even when a simple monk is tortured physically or mentally he practices his mindfulness of loving kindness and compassion. Although His Holiness has not been tortured physically he is mutilated mentally every time he learns the hard fact that his subjects, monks and nuns are being tortured mercilessly. Yet he bears this pain magnanimously. And he reminds us all that the only way to overcome suffering is to cultivate seeds of peace within and to work nonviolently and patiently.

Being a simple monk in exile for over four decades, His Holiness has shown to the world that truth, beauty and goodness are not only possible but also practical. One only has to witness the deeds of His Holiness and his followers. Even lay persons who follow his footsteps lead a simple lifestyle based on compassion and nonviolence.

Although His Holiness is obliged to travel all over the world to meet people from all walks of life, as a simple monk he still manages to find the time to hold spiritual retreat, perform meaningful religious ceremonies, and teach young monks to walk the noble eight-fold path of the Buddha.

I believe that the influence of His Holiness in the world is not because he is a bodhisattva, a head of state in exile or a spiritual leader of a large Buddhist community. Neither is it because he possesses supernatural powers. Rather, it is because he is a simple monk who wants so little for himself and is devoting most of his time and energy in helping the people of the world who are being trammelled by greed, hatred and delusion. Yet, with good humour and humility, His Holiness, in bearing the tribulations of his people and his country, is showing the world that truth, forgiveness, love and compassion are the ultimate power.

Even religious leaders of other faiths, not to mention other heads of state and leading people in almost all walks of life, admire him because he steers clear of conversion. He only desires happiness and well being for all and he shows them that the best happiness depends on simplicity, truthfulness and compassion. With peace within himself, a simple monk like His Holiness is in an excellent position to guide others aspiring for world peace, social justice and environmental sustainability.

A Very Human Human Being

Mary Craig

It was September 1989. The monsoon rains were pelting down and Dharamsala's roads had turned to mud as I made my way up to Thekchen Choeling for my first audience with the Dalai Lama. A few months earlier, when I was searching for a subject for my next book, a friend had suggested Tibet. A crazy idea, I thought—a country in the back of beyond, a people with a language, religion and culture I knew nothing of whatsoever. Though I had, of course, heard of the Dalai Lama, I must admit my mental image was confused—owing more to dim memories of *Lost Horizon* than to reality. I had not heard of Dharamsala, nor of the large numbers of refugees there. Nor that it was where the Dalai Lama actually lived.

The idea took root and—especially after I was promised an audience with His Holiness—I began to explore the possibility of going to Dharamsala to see for myself. I boned up on recent Tibetan history and was overwhelmed by the horrors of what I discovered about the Chinese occupation. Arriving in Dharamsala and given access to the refugees, I found myself weeping with rage and pity and disgust as their stories unfolded. When the time approached for my audience with the Dalai Lama, somehow it began to seem unnecessary and self-indulgent, a distraction from the terrible reality in which I had become immersed. It was sure to be a brief formal encounter, more an exercise in protocol than a meeting of minds.

How wrong I was! The Dalai Lama was welcoming, warm and deeply impressive. Within moments I found myself thinking that here was the most radiantly human being I had ever met. There was a no-nonsense earthiness about him, but also a deep serenity and inner peace. Far from being a stiff and formal occasion, it was a person-to-person encounter in which I felt both challenged and healed. This man, I told myself wonderingly, could read me like an open book, yet was completely accepting of what he found.

He expressed interest in my half-formed plan to write about the refugees, and soon the questions came tumbling out—mainly about the current situation in Tibet and about the danger of young Tibetans in Tibet turning to violence (that very morning he had attended the stormy opening session of a Tibetan Youth Congress sympathetic to the idea). Time sped by, my allotted twenty minutes becoming half-an-hour, then an hour, an hour-and-a half, and still we were in full spate. When it was over, we had our photos taken, there were gifts of signed books, scarves, old coins, and it was like the parting of two old friends, with much pumping of hands and an invitation to come and visit next time I was in Dharamsala. Next time? With this meeting any remaining doubts about the book had vanished. I was well and truly hooked.

The following May I was back for a new crop of ever more harrowing interviews with the refugees. Once again I was to meet the Dalai Lama, and looked forward to a repeat performance of the first time. I had yet to learn that no two meetings with him are ever the same; every encounter is a new learning experience.

In the ante-room, waiting his turn, was a four-year-old lama, the recently discovered reincarnation of Ling Rinpoche, His Holiness's former junior tutor. An elderly monk was gently fussing over the child, making sure he knew what to do. As they left, the little boy gingerly put his hand in that of the older man.

A short time later, the child reappeared, wreathed in

smiles, hand in hand this time with the Dalai Lama. The latter gave him an affectionate hug, bent down to adjust the boy's shoe-strap, then stayed crouching down, waving, smiling and blowing kisses like a loving father till the boy was out of sight. It was a scene of immense tenderness—and I shall never forget it. Then His Holiness stood up and greeted my friend and myself with such warmth that it nearly took our breath away. I felt again that here was a person who could make you want to laugh aloud for the sheer job of being alive.

My companion was an American artist, Brigid Marlin, who had asked to paint a portrait of the Dalai Lama. As the Private Office had allocated her a mere forty minutes for a portrait that would normally take several days, Brigid was understandably nervous. I was supposed to talk to His Holiness and keep his face animated while she painted. I began by asking him about the Nobel Peace Prize he'd just received. 'Well,' he smiled deprecatingly, 'when I heard the rumour in the early evening, I was a little bit excited. But when I listened to the 8.30 news there was no mention. So I thought, oh well, it was just a rumour, and went to bed. Next morning I got up at 4 a.m. as usual, and heard that it was true after all. But by then, no more excited.' End of story.

He went on to talk about the new constitutional changes he was introducing, about Tibet's relationship with China, and of how much he had admired Mao Zedong until disillusion had set in. It was riveting stuff and I was swept up in it. Suddenly I realized that time was up and that Brigid was on the verge of tears. His Holiness noticed too. Walking over to inspect the sketchy beginnings of an oil painting, he teased her that his left eye looked too big. 'I've had no time,' Brigid wailed, bursting into tears. His Holiness gave her a sympathetic hug, went and sat down again, then held up a hand to tell her to wait. 'I'm—just—wondering,' he said slowly, before sending an official to ask the next visitor if she would mind an artist sitting in on her audience.

When the visitor agreed, Brigid's emotions got the better of her. 'Oh, I do love you,' she burst out. His Holiness hooted with mirth and prepared to greet the next arrival.

We both saw how he abstracted himself for a few moments, seeming to disappear somewhere deep inside himself, wiping the slate clean, as it were, so as to offer his undivided attention to the next arrival. As Brigid painted, I was a fly on the wall for the next couple of hours, observing how he could be different things to different people, paying each one the courtesy of total absorption in their concerns. With an American girl who planned to start an electronic newsletter for the Tibetans in Tibet, he was the practical, well-informed man of the world, discussing costs, logistics, sponsorships, exploring the merits and demerits of the scheme. Then—after he had dispatched the official a second time and once again collected himself—came a Swiss girl with a smart new exercise bike, a present from her father, a sports-shop owner who had been horrified to see a magazine picture of the Dalai Lama on a dilapidated old machine. Instantly, he dashed out to the corridor to see the bike, hitched up his robes and began pedalling with the enthusiasm of a small boy. Our unexpectedly extended visit had opened a window for us: that afternoon we saw several Dalai Lamas—loving father, compassionate friend, Nobel Prize winner unfazed by world renown, widely experienced politician, savvy businessman and enthusiastic child.

Tears of Blood was almost finished when I returned the following year. The Dalai Lama had been overseas, but as he was expected back any day the flags and banners were fluttering expectantly. Dharamsala is only a shadow of itself when he is not there. Somehow his absence is palpable. I was disappointed, however, having heard that he was due to leave again almost immediately and the audience list had been closed.

When I received news next day that I would be allowed to see His Holiness after all, I was so excited that I slipped and fell in the mud—it was monsoon time again—and arrived at the residence with my arm in a sling. It didn't matter, we joked about it momentarily, but my thoughts were full of a young Tibetan woman I'd just met who'd been used as a prostitute by the People's Liberation Army and had later witnessed fellow Tibetans being experimented on in hospital. I told His Holiness straight away. He knew the girl and shared my horror and disgust, proceeding to tell me about an Amdo woman who had been told by a Chinese doctor that to fulfil his quota of abortions he had often killed healthy babies, telling the mothers they had been stillborn.

The ghastliness of it reduced us to silence—it was the first time I had seen him like this, visibly overcome by the appalling fate of his people. When I left, he held my hand for several minutes, thanking me for the work I was doing for Tibet. He draped the *khata* round my neck. 'Here, you'd better have this,' he said, finally breaking into the familiar chuckle.

Tears of Blood came out in 1993, and the Dalai Lama gave me the green light for a second book on Tibet, a sort of family biography. When I returned in 1994 I was privileged to see him four times. Arriving at Thekchen Choeling for the last of these long audiences, I was introduced to a young woman in the ante-room. It was her first meeting with His Holiness and she looked apprehensive. 'Don't be nervous,' I said, 'He's the most human person you could ever hope to meet.'

She gave me a shocked glance. 'He's a living Buddha!' she protested.

'Well, isn't that the same thing?' I asked her.

To me, Living Buddha means a spiritually enlightened being who shows in his own person what it means to be human, and makes us want to follow his example.

Emerging from her audience, she looked transformed. We exchanged a few words in the corridor, arranging to meet later that day. Suddenly I looked up—there was His Holiness waiting at the far end of the corridor, doubled up with laughter. Embarrassed by my seeming discourtesy, I positively hurtled towards him, my white *khata* unfolding as I ran. 'Oh, Your Holiness, I'm so sorry,' I stammered, proffering the rumpled scarf. He went on laughing, tucked my arm in his, and we went into the audience room together.

I realized then how he relishes and thrives on informality. That afternoon, as we talked about his infancy in Amdo, he reminisced about how his mother would carry him on her back everywhere she went, and if he wanted her to change direction he would tug at her long earring. 'Sometimes very hard indeed,' he added cheerfully, leaning forward and yanking on my own earring for all he was worth. 'Just like that!' We both dissolved into laughter, and later when I was leaving he gave me a big friendly bear hug. I hugged him back.

In all my visits to the Dalai Lama—and he continued to delight and surprise me for a couple of years more—I came to realize that what I most valued in him was his genuine humility and his refusal, in spite of everything, to hate the Chinese. He sees himself as a simple monk and dreams of ending his days in a remote monastery in Tibet. He once talked to me about a monk he'd met, who after more than twenty years in a Chinese prison insisted that the worst danger he had faced was the fear of losing compassion for his torturers. 'Isn't that wonderful?' asked His Holiness with an admiration I both understood and shared. 'I feel sure that in his place I'd have let rage engulf me. Or I'd have given in and told them what they wanted to hear.' He showed the same humility in speaking of the tenth Panchen Lama, describing him as 'a true freedom fighter' whose courage he could not ever have matched. Perhaps it is because he is so accepting of his own perceived frailties that one feels so secure with him.

Both books (and a third one too) are long since published. I have not returned to Dharamsala, and I may never see him again except at the end of a long reception line in London.

You don't just drop in on His Holiness the Dalai Lama. His time is parcelled out carefully, and there is an endless list of those whose need to see him is greater than mine. Why should I complain? I had my hour in the sun—many hours, in fact. For almost a decade I had the unbelievable privilege of encountering a multi-faceted, very special human being, in whose presence I felt more of a human being myself. For that I shall always be grateful.

Compassion in Practice*

Matthieu Ricard

A t the foothills of the dark and imposing Himalayan peaks, Dharamsala is sleeping peacefully. A few lights shine at the top of a wooded hill. The Fourteenth Dalai Lama gets up. It is 3.30 a.m. This is how the day of one of the most remarkable persons of our century starts, with prayer and meditation. Wherever he might be, in whatever circumstances, every day, in the morning, the spiritual and temporal head of the Tibetan people meditates for four hours. It is a meditation which is above all a profound prayer for the good of all beings.

The room is a simple one, with varnished wood panelling, devoid of the usual rich decorations of the Tibetan temples. A statue of the Buddha, photographs of his spiritual masters and some sacred books are kept on a small altar. At around 6 a.m., the Dalai Lama has a hearty breakfast while listening to the news on the BBC, since, like all Buddhist monks, he does not eat in the evening. Then he continues to meditate till 8 or 9 a.m.

Come what may, the Dalai Lama maintains this discipline which gives him the strength he so deeply needs to untiringly pursue his activity for the Tibetan cause. When, in 1989, he

*This article is a revised version of the one earlier published in Buddhist Himalaya by Matthieu Ricard, Olivier Follmi and Danielle Follmi, Editions La Martiniere, Paris, 2002.

received the Nobel Prize, journalists rushed early in the morning to be the first to obtain the reactions of the Tibetan leader. The only response they could get from the courteous and discreet monk who, for the past thirty years, has been faithfully tending to the needs of the Dalai Lama, was: 'He has not yet got the news. We never disturb him when he is praying.'

To conclude his meditation the Dalai Lama goes to a room where some precious relics brought from Tibet are kept. Amongst those is a life-size statue of the Buddha, sculpted out of sandalwood, given to him by his followers who succeeded in saving it from destruction during the Chinese invasion. The Dalai Lama bows down a hundred times in front of this sacred image, which for him is the Buddha in person; this is the humble homage he offers not to a God but to Awakening, the Supreme Knowledge.

'At around 9 a.m. I go to my office if I have to meet people,' says the Dalai Lama. 'Otherwise, I work on some texts. I refresh my memory about writings which I studied in the past and I reflect more deeply upon the commentaries of the great masters of various schools of Tibetan Buddhism. I reflect upon the teachings and I do some meditation. At around 2 in the afternoon I eat my lunch. Then, till 5 p.m. I look after current affairs. I meet the elected ones of the Tibetan people, the ministers of the Government in Exile and other functionaries, and I meet visitors. At around 6 p.m., I have tea. If I am hungry, I take the permission of Buddha to eat some biscuits. [laughter . . .] Finally I do my evening prayers and I sleep at around 9 p.m. It is the best part of the day! I sleep soundly till 3.30 the next morning.'

At the end of the day, the Dalai Lama will conclude with a prayer, which he says inspires every moment of his life:

As long as space endures,
As long as beings exist,
May I too remain
To dispel the misery of the world.

Meeting the numerous visitors who have arrived from
Tibet is a particularly poignant moment. To see the Dalai
Lama at least once in their life, Tendzin, his wife and two
children have crossed snowy passes at a height of over 5000
metres, eluding the Chinese army which controls the borders
and denies Tibetans permission to go to India. Some of
Tendzin's companions have had to amputate their frozen
toes. But they are finally here, abundant tears flowing down
their cheeks, trying their best to contain their emotions so
as to reply to the Dalai Lama who, in his beautifully
resonant voice, is enquiring about their personal odyssey
and the situation in Tibet. He asks Guedun, a monk who,
during his twenty years in prison, has been tortured several
times, 'Did you ever experience fear?' Bowing his head, the
monk answers; 'My greatest fear was to feel hatred towards
my torturers.'

The residence of the Dalai Lama overlooks the vast
Indian plains which unfold to infinity under his windows.
To the north, some majestic peaks remind us that Tibet is
just a few hundred kilometres away as the crow flies,
beyond the imposing mountain range which circles the Roof
of the World. The country of snow, so near yet so far, is out
of access for the Dalai Lama so long as its inhabitants are
denied basic liberties.

A subdued atmosphere and a beneficial peace surround
this residence. Everyone talks softly, conscious of the vanity
of superfluous words and of the inexorable march of time,
this precious gift which ebbs away at every moment of our
life. Not a single superfluous gesture or word. This golden
silence is illumined only with the rippling sound of the
benevolent laughter of Kundun, the 'Presence', as the Tibetans
lovingly and respectfully call the Dalai Lama: He who is
never absent when you are in front of him and always
present when you are far away from him. Sometimes this
joyful laughter is replaced by a silent smile when the Dalai
Lama goes into retreat for a month or a few weeks each
year. His only words then are prayers which he communicates

through gestures or in writing. The retreat is a fertile alliance of an inward-looking contemplation and compassion which shines forth effortlessly to the outside world.

A typical day for the Dalai Lama at his residence seems to be simple and tranquil. However, for several months of the year this orderly schedule is disrupted because of his wide travels and the teachings he gives in India or abroad to crowds which sometimes run into several hundreds of thousands. The necessity to respond to everyone's aspirations and to support the cause of Tibet creates for this untiring peace pilgrim a busy schedule allowing little respite. In spite of this, Kundun maintains an unchanging serenity. For everyone, whether a visitor or a passerby met at the airport, he is totally and immediately present, with a look of overflowing goodness which penetrates your heart to leave a smile there before discreetly disappearing.

Goodness should not, however, be mistaken for weakness and so, when the opportunity appears, the power of the orator suddenly wakes up. To the Parisian bar which welcomed him very warmly, he made the following statement: 'My struggle for the Tibetan people is not one of those battles at the end of which there is a victor and a vanquished or, more often than not, two vanquished. What I endeavour to obtain with all my might is the victory of truth.'

He often explains how the main objectives of all his travels are to promote human values and contribute to better inter-religious understanding. For him it is obvious that an education which aims at developing the intelligence of the youth and at giving them a heavy load of information is not adequate. 'Those who prepared the 11 September 2001 disaster went about it with a lot of intelligence. But they used this intelligence to prepare an act as unthinkable as that of using an aircraft full of people as a bomb to kill other human beings.' He underscores that it is therefore imperative to help the youth to develop human qualities which will enable them to use their intelligence in a wise and altruistic way.

According to the Dalai Lama, it is equally essential to realize that it is our mind which experiences happiness and sufferings; in hoping to find happiness outside ourselves we are going on the wrong track. In November 2001, during a visit to Portugal, where he noticed that the building sector was very active, he used a striking image to illustrate this point. 'If someone who has just shifted to the hundredth floor of a luxurious apartment is unhappy within himself, the only thing he will be looking for is a window from where he can fling himself.' It is, therefore, essential to find happiness within ourselves and to realize that our happiness is intimately linked to that of others.

All this does not exclude humour or simplicity. How often have I seen him, just after having bid goodbye to a president or a minister, go and shake hands with the doorman in his box, or with the telephone operator behind her glass window, or mischievously give a tap on the back of the rigid republican guard with his sword and superb uniform, who in turn is surprised but happy that someone is treating him like a person. When Danielle Mitterand, wife of the erstwhile French president, came to visit the Dalai Lama, he took her round Dharamsala. In front of a big statue of the Buddha which is in a temple of the monastery the Dalai Lama respectfully pointed to it and said: 'My boss.'

His message is always the same and he does not tire of repeating it to those who want to hear it: 'Every person, even a hostile one, is, like me, a living being who faces suffering and aspires to happiness; he has every right to be spared suffering and attain happiness. This reflection makes us feel deeply concerned by others' happiness, be he a friend or an enemy. This is the basis of authentic compassion.'

The inexplicable power of compassion becomes most clear during surprise visits. I remember one night, at the end of a meeting with young students at the Bordeaux University, while the Dalai Lama was cutting through a compact crowd of those who did not find place in the amphitheatre, there was an old couple on the side, not daring to join the jostling crowd. The husband was standing behind his frail wife, who was sitting in a wheelchair. The ever alert gaze of the Dalai Lama fell on them; he cut through the crowd to go and hold the hands of the old lady in his and looked at her from up close, smilingly, without any words except the inexpressible ones of limitless love. After these few moments, which seemed to be an eternity, the old man said to his wife, 'You see, he is a saint.'

On another occasion, at the Amnesty International concert at Bercy in December 1999, when the Dalai Lama, who was a surprise guest, stepped onto the brightly lit stage between two rock songs, 15,000 young people got up as one person and offered a formidable ovation to the apostle of nonviolence. They then listened in silence, which is unusual at such places, to the warm words he spoke to them. After he spoke, once again a resounding ovation came from the hall. How does one explain such unanimity, such a heartfelt response coming from an unprepared crowd? It reminds one of Gandhi, Martin Luther King . . . this crowd had fathomed the depth of his heart.

When you ask the Dalai Lama why he evokes such reactions of warmth he answers: 'I do not have any special quality. Maybe it is because all my life I have meditated with all the strength of my mind upon love and compassion.'

One of the most powerful interactions of the Dalai Lama with others is during his teaching. There is no fiery rhetoric but a calm and profound philosophy (combined with down-to-earth advice and a solid sense of humour) on how to become a better human being. The Dalai Lama's way of teaching is extremely sensible and practical. Yet, because the simple things he says are the distillation of his life-long authentic spiritual practice and direct experience, they are never banal. When he tells you that a good heart is the most precious quality you can develop, it never sounds a cliché, because he himself has such an immense heart.

Sometimes he may read out a verse.

May I be a guard for those who are protector-less,
A guide for those who journey on the road.
For those who wish to go across the water,
May I be a boat, a raft, a bridge.
May I be an isle for those who yearn for landfall,
And a lamp for those who long for light;
For those who need a resting-place, a bed;
For all who need a servant, may I be their slave.
Like the earth and the pervading elements,
Enduring as the sky itself endures,
For boundless multitudes of living beings,
May I be their ground and sustenance.
Thus for everything that lives,
As far as are the limits of the sky,
May I provide their livelihood and nourishment
Until they pass beyond the bonds of suffering.

The reading of such a verse can bring tears to the Dalai
Lama's eyes. He stops and waits silently, unassumingly,
until he can speak again. There is no hint of showmanship
in this quiet display of feeling.

At other times, when he is illustrating his commentary
with anecdotes or remarking on something unusual in the
crowd, he may break into sonorous and spontaneous laughter
with the uninhibited freedom of someone who is detached
from worldly preoccupations. This reminds one of a verse
of the 19th century Tibetan yogi Shabkar:

Look at my delighted laughter!
The delight of a vast, free mind!
The experience of lightness of being
As when emerging from a narrow gorge
Onto a high, wide mountain pass!
Look how, free from mistaking things as real,
I am blissful, and yet more blissful,
Enjoying the realm of primordial wakefulness!

When His Holiness gives expanded teachings, such as the initiation of the Tantra of the Wheel of Time or Kalachakra, immense crowds gather to listen to him silently. In 1985 and in 2002, when he gave the Kalachakra in Bodhgaya, the place where the Buddha became enlightened, over 200,000 devotees gathered to attend the teachings, including the main spiritual masters of the different Tibetan Buddhist traditions. Several thousand people managed to come down from Tibet. They braved the border guards to escape for a while the relentless repression of the communist regime, crossing the high snowy passes in hazardous journeys that cost a few their lives.

It was an amazing sight to watch them, seated in the first rows, their dreams fulfilled beyond imagination—not only being able to get a furtive glance at their beloved leader and spiritual master, but also being able to sit all day long for a week right in front of him! In the warm climate they were still wearing their felt boots, sheepskin coats and torn down Chinese jackets that had hardly protected them from the biting cold during their journey. Their eyes looked at things in a different way than those of the Tibetans who had been refugees in India for more than thirty years. Everything was new to them, especially freedom. Amidst this attentive audience, theirs were faces of astonishing character and beauty, their gaze as clear as the sky as they looked at the Dalai Lama with a fervour that welled up from their very bones.

The Ocean of Wisdom

Brother Wayne Teasdale

It is not easy to write about the Dalai Lama, and specifically Tenzin Gyatso. He is such a rare and totally unique spiritual teacher, there is always the tendency to slip into hyperbole in praising his extraordinary, divine-like position and the whole aura surrounding this 'simple monk', or the opposite extreme of hiding behind a dry, scholarly objectivity that is often sceptical. Here, like the Buddha, I will try to walk a middle path. Personally, I am convinced there are certain figures, saints and bodhisattvas about whom it's not really possible to exaggerate. Such are Mahatma Gandhi, Thomas Merton (the Trappist sage) and Mother Teresa. Tenzin Gyatso is also one of them.

When we encounter great holiness in anyone, there is evident a superhuman degree of virtue and sensitivity, a transcendence of self-concern, an availability and responsiveness to others. As an example from the Dalai Lama's life—an example so characteristic of who he is beyond his position—let me offer an incident from one of his many visits to America. Some years ago at Harvard University there was a special conversation between His Holiness and three or four professors before a huge audience that included a film crew. The first professor who spoke was hogging the limelight, and he went on and on, way past his allotted time. As his talking became excessive, and there was no sign that he would stop, the other professors, fearing their own time would be used up, became impatient, then indignant and angry.

Through it all, His Holiness patiently, calmly, attentively, and with a smile, listened to this man. His Holiness's sensitivity was such that he knew this person needed to feel that he was being heard. He needed attention and affirmation. His Holiness's compassion was in responding to the professor's deeper agenda, instead of descending into resentment, frustration and anger as the other participants were doing. He chose quite spontaneously to respond compassionately, even if it meant a slight inconvenience to others. This little story is typical of His Holiness and illustrates the nature of his sensitivity.

In what follows I would like to explore His Holiness's commitment to inter-religious dialogue, which is really a dialogue of life itself, not a stiff, formal activity as it often is in academic forums. The first part of this article will consider the Dalai Lama's encounters with Thomas Merton and Bede Griffiths. Then I will share my own meetings with His Holiness, meetings that essentially continued the line of experience and development initiated with Merton. I will then present some impressions of His Holiness that have occurred to me over time. The next section of the essay will examine His Holiness's interest in the integration of science, wisdom and all the other areas of knowledge, and this will be done primarily within the context of the synthesis dialogues.

I will then move on to the Buddhist/Christian monastic dialogue, and reflect on the prophetic dimension of this very valuable relationship. This reflection will then crystallize into what I call the 'matrix' as a way to integrate the essential metaphysical, existential principle of Buddhism and Christianity. A brief section will look at the Tibetan issue and the Catholic church. Finally, in the last section, I will reflect on the significance of the Fourteenth Dalai Lama in this millennium.

Thomas Merton and Bede Griffiths

Tibet's first experience of Christians involved a mission of the Jesuits in the latter part of the 17th century led by Father Desiderio. He had learned Tibetan and written a work in that difficult and little-known language. Of course, the Jesuits were missionaries, and their methods were innovative and even visionary. They tended to be way ahead of their time because they respected the cultures they worked and lived in, and eventually came to modify their evangelical objectives with the realization that in China, India, Japan and Tibet they were dealing with very advanced systems of wisdom.

This realization certainly also characterizes the outlook of Thomas Merton, a Trappist monk from Kentucky, especially in the last years of his life. Merton had been absorbing eastern wisdom on a deep level long before his fateful trip to Asia in the autumn of 1968. Thomas Merton had only three audiences with His Holiness in Dharamsala in November 1968. This was the whole extent of their relationship in terms of time. His Holiness said later that he never realized Christians were spiritual until he met Merton. Here was a Christian monk completely unlike any Christian the Dalai Lama had ever met before; he was nothing like the missionaries of the time, most of whom were bent on conversion.

His Holiness discerned in this Christian geshe a profoundly learned man in matters of spirituality, comparative religion and culture. He found an openness in Merton rarely seen in other Christians. Thomas Merton discovered in His Holiness a brother and fellow monk, equally open, and very curious about Catholic monastic life and practice. The two men liked each other immensely and looked forward to a wonderful friendship, a friendship that now awaits its unfolding in eternity.

Father Louis, Merton's monastic name, and His Holiness talked about everything. They shared their experience of monastic life in their respective traditions, looking at various practices, education, the formation of monks and nuns, their ways of prayer and meditation, their sacred texts. They reflected deeply on the differences and similarities of the Buddhist and Christian faiths. They discussed the horrific tragedy of the Tibetan people, the Tibetan diaspora and their focus on securing and preserving their culture and tradition in India. They also talked about the Vietnam war, the superpower rivalry, the civil rights movement in the United States, and the peace movement in Europe and America.

His Holiness and Thomas Merton made a deep impression on each other. The impact of Merton on the Dalai Lama was considerable. He often speaks of this American monk, a literary genius, with affection and wistfulness. In a wonderful documentary on Merton's life released in the early 1980s, His Holiness was interviewed by the film-makers. His Holiness spoke affectionately of Merton on that occasion and, with profound emotion and a higher pitch to his voice, he remarked, 'If Thomas Merton had lived, we would have done something for peace together.'

The Dalai Lama met with Bede Griffiths on three occasions, as in Merton's case, but these encounters were spaced by years. They were together twice in India at conferences in which both were participating. But their most telling conversation occurred in Australia in the early 1990s. It was an eventful exchange. Both were completely relaxed and open. They discussed many theological and mystical teachings of each tradition. Although I never knew Merton, I did know Bede, and had a twenty-year friendship with him.

At the time of their third encounter, Father Bede was greatly interested in Dzogchen. He told me of this wonderful meeting with His Holiness. The Dalai Lama, on his part, said to me, 'Bede Griffiths is a great teacher!' Father Bede and the Dalai Lama both had a lot of respect for each other, and had Bede lived longer, they might have achieved something of importance together. Bede's knowledge of Hinduism and Buddhism was far greater than that of Thomas Merton, but both were Christian prophets drinking from the well of eastern wisdom and reinvigorating western contemplation. Both had a similar mission, but with different circumstances.

First Encounters and Impressions

Passing through Britain for a month's rest after a long period in India, I had my first fascinating experience with His Holiness. This happened in April 1988 at the residence of Basil Cardinal Hume, O.S.B., the archbishop of Westminster and Catholic patriarch of England. Although I had seen His Holiness at St. Patrick's Cathedral in New York City in 1979 when I was a graduate student at Fordham University, it was not until this encounter that we actually met for the first time. Cardinal Hume was a Benedictine monk who had also been an abbot before being named patriarch of England. He had an interest in a dialogue, and welcomed a Catholic/Tibetan monastic exchange.

I was invited to this historic dialogue. There were twenty of us—Christian and Buddhist monks, with a few nuns—seated around an oval table. His Holiness entered and was introduced by the abbot of Prinknash Abbey, Bede Griffiths' monastery before he had gone to India. This gathering was an intimate situation, and from the very beginning there was a strong rapport between His Holiness and me. After the seventy-minute conversation, His Holiness came over to me with an extended hand. It was a warm and meaningful introduction.

Afterwards, I followed up with a letter to Tenzin Geyche, his long-time secretary and good friend, and not much later found myself in Dharamsala in early January 1989. My second encounter with His Holiness was a two-hour conversation. It proved to be eventful, because it resulted in our jointly producing a document entitled *The Universal Declaration on Nonviolence*. This declaration is a brief, one-page statement. It was later ratified by His Holiness and Monastic Interreligious Dialogue (MID) (formerly known as the North American Board for East/West Dialogue), the organization I represented. MID took responsibility for the document after I had written the first draft. Other members of MID and I refined the final form of the document.

I have often felt, or had a sense, that the unique position I have been placed in helps to continue the relationship with His Holiness, Tibetan Buddhism and the Tibetan people that Thomas Merton initiated with his historic visit to Dharamsala in 1968. I have always remained conscious of His Holiness's words about doing something substantial for peace, and have hoped that maybe I could contribute to that important aspiration. Though I'm certainly no Merton, I share with him an openness to the east, a keen interest in the Dharma and in Hinduism, Taoism and Sufism, as well as the powerful hope for a lasting, just and comprehensive peace—a peace that is more than simply the absence of conflict, a peace that reflects, as St. Augustine called it in his time, 'the tranquillity of order', a spiritual harmony animating an enlightened humankind, and a human civilization based on love and compassion. Such a peace is based on our ultimate potential, and that requires the engagement of our spiritual resources for self-transformation leading to social change grounded in awareness.

Over the years, His Holiness and I have seen each other a couple of times a year, and I am also a friend of his younger brother, the Ngari Rinpoche, and his family, as well as many other Tibetans. These encounters have become progressively more profound in depth and friendship. I have formed many impressions as to who the Dalai Lama is as a person. I remember so well a visit I made after the 1993 Parliament of the World's Religions in Chicago. We sat together for two hours as he talked with others, participated in an interview and shared stories with me. On that occasion

I saw very clearly how Christ-like he actually is, and I said to him: 'I see Christ in you more than I have perceived Christ in most Christians!' I suppose I could have used different language to express this spiritual perception. Perhaps what I had really discerned was the sanctity, love and compassion of this man.

Another impression that has taken root is his gift for intuition, or we can say, for clairvoyance, even telepathy. This gift is not a light matter, and I view it as a by-product of spiritual realization. So many times in his presence I have become conscious of how completely he knows me and knows where I'm coming from, or what I'm preoccupied with. He seems to draw me into a larger state of awareness, including me in his own. There is no need to say anything, since in these moments our communication is perfect and words would only detract from what we experience and know and possibly only confuse the issue.

A further impression that has struck me in his intellectual profundity, his ability to understand virtually anything. His intellectual gifts, however, are not abstract abilities, but are always in the service of his quintessential humanity, his good-heartedness. His knowledge is always grounded in compassion and wisdom, and these are practical qualities, qualities found in the saints of all traditions. But there is so much more. In addition to these attributes, there is his sense of humour and playfulness, indomitable strengths that not even tragedy and suffering have eclipsed. Basically, what I discern in him is a highly developed humanism rooted in spiritual practice and extended to all sentient beings.

Interest in the Integration of Knowledge

His Holiness has been interested in science and other areas of knowledge for many years. He has attended many conferences round the world attempting to discover the common ground between science and spirituality. He has found most of these meetings disappointing for one reason or another. Usually they have fallen short of his expectations either because—as he puts it—the scientists were too 'hard' or too 'soft'. By 'hard' he means that they were closed to the spiritual dimension of life, and adhered to a purely uncritical reductionist view of science, a view that really isn't very scientific at all! The problem with the 'soft' scientist is that he/she is too quick to jump to a common ground or a spiritual view of science and the cosmos. The science in this case is suspect even though the 'soft' scientist may actually be wiser than the 'hard' scientist.

His Holiness has been and is intrigued with the notion of synthesis, the conscious attempt to find common ground among all areas of knowledge, and a grand unifying paradigm that harmonizes science, religion, spirituality, social justice, peace and the environment. The work towards finding such a paradigm took form for the first time in Synthesis I, or the Dharamsala Dialogues, held in Dharamsala from 11 to 16 September 1999. His Holiness participated in this significant gathering in which 110 people were present, thirty-five of whom were active synthesizers, while the remaining were observers and the media. The synthesizers represented all the major disciplines and areas of activity. There were physicists, mathematicians, biologists, astronomers, spiritual teachers and theologians, people in government and diplomacy, as also activists working for the promotion of the cause of peace, justice and the environment.

This event was in many ways historic, not in what it achieved, since it was only a beginning and so there were no dramatic results, but in the recognition of spirituality as the basis to integrate all knowledge. In this recognition, there is an insight that all knowledge has to have a practical relationship with the improvement of human nature and that of other sentient beings. Spirituality, the mystical life, provides such a unifying vision for knowledge, and allows science and religion to have a more positive, indeed friendly, collaboration.

Synthesis II was convened in Trent, Italy from 26 June

to 1 July 2001. Around thirty synthesizers participated in this event in the beautiful surroundings of the Dolomite mountains. This meeting was far more focussed than the Dharamsala Dialogues. The important aim of this conference, and these dialogues, is simply to have a number of relevant conversations free from egos and hidden agendas, in a spirit of friendship and community in such a way that a tangible sense of communion surfaces and a new vision emerges.

The Buddhist/Christian Monastic Dialogue

Another important interest of His Holiness is inter-monastic dialogue. This interest has been ongoing since Thomas Merton's visit to Dharamsala, though there has been contact between Christian monastics and members of the Zen and Theravadan traditions prior to Merton's journey to India. The connection with Catholic monastics is very dear to His Holiness's heart, and he has said as much to many people over the years. With the Parliament of the World's Religions in Chicago in 1993 and the Gethsemani Encounter at Merton's monastery in Kentucky in July 1996 inter-monastic dialogue has advanced much. April 2002 witnessed another round when Gethsemani II was convened. The Dalai Lama participated again as he had in the previous two sessions. The focus of the Parliament dialogue was highly specific: *Sunyata and Kenosis: The Rising of Universal Compassion in the Spiritual Journey.* Gethsemani I was more general and explored numerous topics of mutual interest like monastic life in each tradition, the role of the teacher, monastic education, mystical experience and meditation. It was profoundly historic and useful, a watershed in Catholic/Buddhist relations. Gethsemani II was equally momentous.

The increasing importance of inter-monastic relationships and inter-religious dialogue can be seen with the publication of the first *Encyclopedia of Monasticism*.[1] This two-volume work encompasses Hindu, Buddhist, Christian and Jain monasticism, and represents a much needed contribution to a hitherto neglected area. The intense conversations that are taking place, coupled with the inter-monastic hospitality exchange initiated by MID and His Holiness, have no doubt heightened interest in what is unfolding.

The inter-monastic hospitality exchange between Catholic and Tibetan monastics has been going on since 1980. From its very inception, the Dalai Lama has enthusiastically supported it and continues to do so. The exchange works in this manner. Four or five Tibetan monks and nuns come over to the United States and spend six months visiting a number of monasteries and convents of the Cistercian, Trappist and Benedictine communities. The longest they stay in one place might be three weeks to a month, with a minimum of a week. The Christian monks and nuns, again four or five of them, spend a similar amount of time in the great Tibetan monasteries in India. The Catholic groups always visit His Holiness. In each case—whether Tibetans coming to America, or American monastics going to India to visit Tibetan monasteries—they enter deeply into the monastic observance of each community. The quality and richness of dialogue both at the Parliament of the World's Religions and at Gethsemani I owes much to these extraordinary exchanges over the years.

His Holiness always emphasizes the necessity of friendship as a basis for genuine dialogue, one that reaches a profound level of mutual recognition of each other's tradition. In his numerous relationships with Christians, as well as Hindus, Jains and Jews, the Dalai Lama has followed his own teaching: he has made friends with persons of other traditions, and from the openness and affection emanating and surrounding these friendships he converses with those close to him from other traditions.

Such is my experience with him since the beginning of our friendship and collaboration. Because we are well-disposed to each other, that is, because we are friends, spiritual friends with a strong bond, we are able to talk about any subject, even those regarded as sensitive in each of our traditions. It is this kind of friendship that makes possible a very vital kind of work that will one hopes lead to humankind's ultimate destiny: liberation and salvation.

The Prophetic Vision of the Buddhist/Christian Relationship

This vital work is a prophetic collaboration that, through the process of deep dialogue, propels consciousness forward in each tradition and in a global, universal sense. From the open-ended character of the dialogue, something new will emerge for humankind and, eventually, for all sentient beings. The working towards common ground and greater understanding will generate a new awareness, a more enhanced view that unites what is truest in each tradition. This work may take centuries, even millennia, but there will come a day when Christianity and Buddhism will together offer a new vision to the world.[2]

During Synthesis I at Dharamsala, an insight occurred to me near the close of the conference, an insight I call a seed of synthesis, and it is related to the Buddhist/Christian dialogue and collaborative relationship. This 'seed' of synthesis can be formulated in this way: the Divine as a matrix of dependent arising. His Holiness was present for this and other 'seeds' from other participants in the Dharamsala Dialogues. Let me briefly elaborate here. I believe this integration of the two principal insights represents an embodiment of Divine Incarnate Wisdom.

The Divine as a matrix of dependent arising relates and unites the essential insight of each of these traditions. Dependent arising is the interconnection of all sentient beings; their intrinsic interdependence exists within the boundaries of the matrix of boundless consciousness, and this consciousness is the Divine itself. A matrix both defines and contains, and in the case of the Divine matrix, it defines and contains the interconnection of all sentient beings. The Divine, in Christian mystical experience, is the very connection, or connectivity, of all the sentient beings that co-arises together. It is infinite consciousness animated by divine compassion and love. Consciousness as loving, compassionate, merciful, kind, intelligence and knowing connects all beings in a cosmic, ontological community. This is an insight that must be considered with great care.

There are many other points of common ground between the Buddhist and Christian traditions and a number of these are being discussed in the inter-monastic dialogues, in the forums of the Society for Buddhist/Christian Studies, and in hundreds of academic fora around the world. They are being thought about by individual practitioners and writers, pioneers of the spirit, opening up new vistas of realization and universal culture. Again, His Holiness often leads the way by his openness and his own insights into where the common ground might be, as, for instance, when he met with Christians and reflected on the inner meaning of the Gospel.[3] Buddhists and Christians who are friends and engaged in ultimate levels of dialogue are servants of a purpose larger than either's tradition, and they are responsible for this work because they have the consciousness which makes it possible. With their consciousness comes a burden of responsibility that they cannot shun or escape. His Holiness has a sense of this when he speaks of our universal responsibility.

Tibet, Monasticism and the Catholic Church

For many years now, many of us from the monastic world have stood in solidarity with His Holiness and the Tibetan people, have tried and continue to try to awaken the Catholic church to the moral responsibility it has to similarly support the Tibetan struggle. In Catholic theology and culture we like the term *conscientization* to refer to the moral awakening to issues of justice. We are engaged in such a labour of conscientization, and not simply in the church, but extending to all the other religions and the world at large.

His Holiness has been following this development with keen interest and realism. To date we have not been successful in raising the level of concern in Rome on Tibet to a high-priority status. At the 1993 Parliament of the World's Religions, in the midst of the Buddhist/Christian Monastic Dialogue session, MID introduced the document *Resolution on Tibet*. It was read and presented to His Holiness.[4] He was very pleased with this action.

I believe there will come a day when the church will come out vigorously, standing with the Tibetan people, but this will still take some time. I feel the time is much nearer than many think. We need to keep pushing, that is, raising the issue whenever opportunities present themselves, and be willing to converse with anyone willing to listen. Relentless pursuit of justice will eventually yield a rich harvest. I am convinced that the voice of the Catholic church will provide the kind of support that will result in the concretization of humankind on the Tibetan tragedy.

The Significance of the Dalai Lama

There are many reasons why I feel unqualified to evaluate His Holiness's contribution to our planet and to suggest his historical significance. He is such a rare figure, so unique and so precious, made further so by the circumstances of his people and the fascinating role he is playing as a global spiritual teacher. A number of attributes enhance his contribution and are extremely valuable in this new age.

The first is what I call his spiritual humanism, his ability to relate to all kinds of people, with and without any particular commitment to a tradition. He has seen clearly what is really important: primarily how we treat one another, including other sentient beings. In his book *Ethics for a New Millennium*,[5] His Holiness offers a vision of ethics that can be said to be a form of natural spirituality, a moral understanding that reveals those qualities in our human nature that are universal and are the basis not simply of ethics but of the best of religion and spirituality. He is committed to presenting a practical guide to ethical life founded on the commonality of the human traits of compassion, love, kindness and mercy to people who do or do not belong to any of the world's religions. In this teaching he offers solid advice to the whole of humanity.

His significance is as an icon of spiritual and human depth, a powerful presence gently but firmly advocating change, transformation of the heart and justice for his people. His human and spiritual presence in history is reinforced by a humble, accessible style of leadership, often conveyed with humour and laughter. The nature of his presence and his teaching are also revealed in who he is as a person, rather than his position. His generosity as a teacher benefits us all, and has played an essential role in the lives of thousands of westerners and millions of Tibetans. His Holiness's subtle teaching on universal responsibility represents something new and refreshing; it manages to steer clear of a provincial view, or the pitfalls of nationalism, and evokes what is deepest, most authentic in all of us. It appeals to our basic and common humanity. The Dalai Lama, like other world spiritual leaders, is an eloquent voice of advocacy for the planet and no other spiritual leader has equalled his contribution to ecological awareness.

All in all, His Holiness is a person with far-sighted vision. In this respect, like a circle, I'd like to return to that moment when we first met so many years ago in Britain. When he spoke on that occasion, he said something that has always stayed with me, making an indelible impression. He remarked, 'We must keep our attention and determination fixed on the far horizon, and not be distracted by what is unimportant.' He is a master of that destiny towards which we are all moving. His ultimate significance concerns this destiny.

A Buddha of Compassion

Nicholas Ribush

I first encountered Tibetan Buddhism at Kopan Monastery, Kathmandu, Nepal, towards the end of 1972. My first teachers were Lama Thubten Zopa Rinpoche and Lama Thubten Yeshe, who were just starting to introduce the Dharma to westerners, an activity that continues apace to this day. I was immediately attracted to this path and have been trying to understand and practice it since.

From the start, Lama Yeshe and Lama Zopa Rinpoche manifested extraordinary respect for and devotion to His Holiness the Dalai Lama, and as a cynical westerner from a predominantly materialistic and atheistic upbringing I was struck by their attitude towards what I imagined was simply another human being.

I was able to meet His Holiness for the first time about fifteen months later when, in January 1974, I went to Bodhgaya, India, to attend the Kalachakra initiation he was to confer. I also planned to take novice ordination, along with nine other prospective western monks and nuns. There were well over 100,000 people there and we were lost in a vast and wonderful sea of Tibetans.

Out of his customary kindness, Lama Yeshe had requested His Holiness to perform the very first part of our ordination ceremony, where the last tuft of hair is snipped off the crown of one's otherwise freshly-shaved head. Accordingly, on the last day of the initiation, we lined up with everybody else to receive a blessing from His Holiness and view the mandala.

As we approached His Holiness, Lama Zopa Rinpoche pulled out a pair of scissors and explained who we were and what we wanted. His Holiness smiled, laughed out loud, and exclaimed, 'I hope it lasts!' (In my case it did, but not for life, as intended, but for only about twelve years.) That brief but warm encounter, that individual attention despite a million other things going on, was my first taste of His Holiness's astonishing kindness, compassion, focus and love.

I met His Holiness a few more times in the next couple of years, mainly in the company of Lama Yeshe and Lama Zopa Rinpoche, when they would seek His Holiness's advice on their work in the west and report to him what had happened on their travels. In 1977, my mother visited me in India and I took her to Dharamsala to meet His Holiness and his two tutors, Kyabje Ling Rinpoche and Kyabje Trijang Rinpoche. They were all amazingly kind, especially His Holiness, who gave my mother a forty-five-minute private interview (they let me in, too), patiently answering all her questions about past and future lives and the six realms of cyclic existence.

I have heard His Holiness described in many ways over the years. He always describes himself as a simple Buddhist monk, but to various writers he has been the god–king of Tibet; to the Chinese, a 'splittist'; to most politicians, the true head of Tibet; to Dharma students everywhere, a great teacher and a perfect living example of what he teaches; and to the world at large, a Nobel Laureate, a great statesman, the leading advocate of nonviolence and peace, the voice of Buddhism and, in general, our best hope for the future. To the Tibetan people, His Holiness has always been the living manifestation of Chenrezig—Avalokiteshwara, the Buddha of Compassion. I've often wondered what this means.

While never for a moment agreeing that he is indeed a manifestation of Avalokiteshwara, in his teachings at the Kalachakra initiation in Los Angeles, 1989, His Holiness described Avalokiteshwara as a deity, a bodhisattva or a Buddha. As a deity, Avalokiteshwara is not a separate being but a manifestation of the compassion of all Buddhas, a quality of all enlightened beings. When a person striving for enlightenment attains his or her goal through practising the yoga method of Avalokiteshwara, we can call that person an Avalokiteshwara. Also, the compassion of a particular Buddha, for example Shakyamuni Buddha, can manifest as Avalokiteshwara.

As His Holiness Dudjom Rinpoche has explained, historically Tibetans claim to be descended from Avalokiteshwara, who in ancient times is said to have come to Tibet from his reputed abode in south India, Mount Potalaka, manifested as a monkey and mated with an 'ogress of the rocks'. The first religious king, Songtsen Gampo (AD 617–650) is said to have been a manifestation of Avalokiteshwara. So, too, are Nyatri Tsenpo, the first human king to rule the whole of Tibet; Drom Tönpa, translator for the great Atisha, who restored pure Buddhism to Tibet about a thousand years ago and founded the Kadam tradition; and all fourteen Dalai Lamas, including, of course, the present one.

Also, the mantra of Avalokiteshwara, *Om mani padme hum*, is the 'official' mantra of Tibet. Many Tibetans, both lay and ordained, recite it constantly, and it may be found painted and carved into rocks and stone tablets all over the Himalayas.

Thus, the practice of Avalokiteshwara is central to Tibetan Buddhism and as a part of that Tibetans regard their spiritual and temporal leader, the Dalai Lama, as the living embodiment of Avalokiteshwara and everything he represents.

The Buddha's intent was that all sentient beings attain enlightenment. In order to do so, sentient beings have to follow the path that leads to enlightenment; we have to make the effort ourselves—the infinite Buddhas cannot do it for us. In other words, we have to practise Mahayana

Buddhism and, if we want to attain enlightenment as quickly as possible, we have to practice Vajrayana, the form of Mahayana Buddhism that was practised and preserved in Tibet.

His Holiness has also said that of all the Buddha's teachings, the most important is that of compassion, and of all the qualities of a Buddha, the best is again compassion. Even a Buddha's omniscience depends on compassion; it is only through the power of compassion that it is possible to attain the ultimate wisdom of a Buddha.

What are the activities of a Buddha? The main activity is to reveal the teachings that lead to enlightenment to those who are open to them, that is, according to the karma of potential disciples. First, however, how does one become a Buddha? How does one become enlightened?

As I understand from the teachings of my own precious teacher, Lama Zopa Rinpoche, the principal cause of enlightenment is *bodhicitta*, the determination to reach enlightenment for the sake of all sentient beings. Bodhicitta arises from great compassion, which is generated in dependence upon each and every sentient being. With great compassion, one not only feels the suffering of all sentient beings as one's own but is also compelled to do something about it. This feeling only grows as one approaches enlightenment and remains with one forever, even after enlightenment. Therefore, a Buddha has no choice but to help sentient beings in whatever way possible.

Since sentient beings have to make the effort themselves, they need to be shown the path. Showing the path and inspiring others to follow it is a Buddha's main job. But, if one were a Buddha, how would one go about it?

One couldn't remain in the enlightened sphere of the Dharmakaya, because there one could communicate only with other Buddhas. One could manifest in the Sambhogakaya, but only advanced bodhisattvas can be taught at that level. Instead, one would have to manifest in a form with which lower beings could communicate.

However, very few sentient beings have the capacity, let alone the interest, to practise Dharma, so one would have to manifest among those who do—in other words, as a human.

Manifesting among humans, one could appear in some kind of miraculous form, but while that would attract attention, it wouldn't really be of that much benefit. People need to be inspired to follow the path to enlightenment by being able to see that they, too, can become enlightened. To inspire people in this way, one would have to manifest in a form they can relate to—as a person. Then people can think, 'I'm a person; she's a person. I can become like her'. In that way, they open themselves to the teaching. Thus, if the people on earth at this time were open to benefit, one would manifest as a human teacher.

Watching His Holiness, even from afar, as I've had to do, it's easy to see how he could indeed be the living embodiment of an enlightened consciousness. He radiates love and compassion; everybody wants to be near him all the time. His wisdom is also clearly apparent—he can teach a range of students from rank beginners to highly learned geshes and advise the most sophisticated hermits in retreat. He takes responsibility not only for his land and his people, but also for the whole world, striving constantly to bring peace, reason and understanding to as many people as he possibly can.

Day after day, His Holiness extends himself as much as any man on earth, but all for the benefit of others. He is constantly travelling the world, teaching Dharma and giving initiations, holding audiences for all manner of visitors, meeting politicians, giving speeches and press conferences, appearing at this function or that, participating in conferences and so forth. From morning to night, in Dharamsala and abroad, His Holiness runs from one appointment to the next, taking great responsibility every time—responsibility for the spiritual welfare of not only the sentient beings on this planet but also countless others throughout all of space; for peace on earth; for the welfare of Tibetan refugees and the oppressed people in Tibet; and for the freedom of Tibet itself.

I don't see His Holiness all that often, perhaps a few days each year, but each time I feel exhausted just watching how busy he is, how constant are the demands on his time and how amazing is the energy he puts into each and every person he meets.

His Holiness never forgets unimportant people either. Once I was at an event in Indiana where His Holiness was consecrating a stupa built by his elder brother, Taktser Rinpoche. Everybody was lined up, three-deep, along the path; I was at the back somewhere. I'd disrobed a year previously and hadn't seen His Holiness since that time. As His Holiness moved down the path, looking back and forth at the people on either side, he noticed me, slightly bent over, hands folded at my heart. In Tibetan, he called out, 'What happened to being a monk?' or words to that effect, and swept on. I was amazed—that he would see me, remember who I was and that the last time we met, more than a year before, I was a monk. He also knew that I wasn't just wearing lay clothes but had actually disrobed.

Ten years later, His Holiness was visiting Brandeis University in Boston. Moving rapidly from one meeting to the next, His Holiness, surrounded by security, was walking through a crowd of people, smiling at everybody he could, when again he saw me, bent over, about twenty yards away. 'Old friend,' he called out, motioning me to come over. 'Old friend!' I was so touched that in all this busyness he could be so kind. And of course, it's not just me. His Holiness is like this with most people he knows, and he knows so many.

Surely His Holiness the Dalai Lama is the Buddha of Compassion. Who else would have the wisdom, power and compassion to accomplish all that he does? Of course, I wouldn't even pretend to see or know but a fraction of what His Holiness does for others, but anybody who observes him with clear sight and an open mind will see more than an extraordinary person among us.

Universal Responsibility in the Dalai Lama's World View

*Bharati Puri**

Among the debates on rights and responsibilities that are both fascinating as well as interminable, is the argument offered by the Dalai Lama. Considered as one of the foremost arbiters of human and environmental rights, the Dalai Lama determines to put forth the rights of the human being as inherent in the Buddhist notions of human dignity and compassion and conceptualizes them by postulating reciprocity of human rights and responsibilities of all human beings. Although lacking a formal character, his thesis springs from his Buddhist concerns, offering a normative understanding of the issue.

The idea of reciprocity as found in Buddhist theory encapsulates, as also conceptualizes, its theory of rights. Scholars who accept the concept of human rights as implicit in classical Buddhism contend that

> under Dharma, husbands and wives, kings and subjects, teachers and students, all have *reciprocal*

*Bharati Puri's doctoral thesis is entitled 'Engaged Buddhism in the Modern World: A Study of the Dalai Lama's Worldview', in which she has deconstructed the various writings of the Dalai Lama for the first time and which is to be published. This chapter is a part of her doctoral thesis.

obligations [italics added] which can be analyzed
into rights and duties. We must qualify this belief,
however, by noting that the requirements of Dharma
are almost always expressed in the form of duties
rather than rights . . . Until rights as personal
entitlements are recognized, as discrete and integral,
part of what is due under Dharma, the modern
concept of rights cannot be said to be present.[1]

Even though Buddhist etymology does not categorically
refer to rights—a concept, incidentally, with a long
intellectual history in the western philosophical tradition[2]—
this does not simply mean that Buddhists cannot agree with
the substance of the human rights discourse. Peter Harvey
explains that

Buddhists are sometimes unhappy using the language
of rights as they may associate it with people
demanding their rights in an aggressive, self-centred
way, and may question whether talk of inalienable
rights implies some unchanging, essential self that
has these, which is out of accord with Buddhism's
teaching on the nature of selfhood.

Nevertheless, as duties imply duties, Buddhists
are happier talking directly about duties themselves:
about 'universal duties', or to use a phrase much
used by the Dalai Lama, 'universal responsibilities'
rather than 'universal rights'.[3]

Etymologically, the word 'responsibility' comes from
the verb 'respond', which means to answer or reply;
responsibility must therefore involve answerability. A
reference to the term responsibility is expressive of and
concerned with every individual in the society, as also the
society itself,[4] and is therefore in accordance with the
Dharmapada which points out that the 'concept of one
world' is theoretically realized when we accept the sense of
relatedness between one individual and another. The
Dharmapada says:

So although the world may become large or small, ultimately it is the relation between two individuals only. As soon as the second man is visualized, the concept of the world also arises. The second man, therefore, includes in him all the rest of individuals in the world.[5]

This ontological assumption essentially describes the existence of all beings in one, that is, in the other. Even if one does not come into contact with every individual in society, yet, it is this relation which is its formative principle.[6] Reflected in contemporary writings too, this assumption emphasizes the necessity of considering the effects of personal and social actions on others, in the realms of speech and symbolic manipulation in the present information age, and in the policies, programmes and products of large and small institutions. '"The others" affected by [these] actions must be understood not only as a unit, but as significant collectivities: families, neighbours and workplace teams; social, ethnic and economic groups; national and international populations; and, not least just as biological species and ecosystems.'[7]

The concept of *vasudhaiva kutumbakam*, which in Sanskrit literally means, 'to regard the whole world as one's family', the Kantian insistence on the universalization of the maxims of moral will, as well as the concern of Utilitarian philosophers with the ideal of the 'common good', all go to reveal that as a concept, universal responsibility has, in the history of thought, been accorded a wide range of ethical reflection. A genuine sense of universal responsibility advocated by the Dalai Lama cannot arise from an individualism bred by an economic world view.[8] Through universal responsibility he attempts to articulate a 'moral vision'[9] in which 'universal connectedness' is emphasized. He sees in this unity a universal feeling of being linked with, as also a responsibility towards, all people.[10] First used by the Dalai Lama, the term 'universal responsibility' has been put to more than just linguistic use and has become a rallying point for movements, as also the foundational principle for institutions.[11] Defining this concept, he says: 'True compassion is universal in scope. It is accompanied by a sense of universal responsibility. To act altruistically, concerned only for the welfare of others, with no selfish or ulterior motive, is to affirm a sense of universal responsibility.'[12] In the Tibetan language, the term closest to universal responsibility is *chisem*, which literally means universal consciousness (*chi* means universal and *sem* means consciousness).[13] In a speech the Dalai Lama made at the Parliamentary Earth Summit, held under the auspices of the United Nations Conference on Environment and Development at Rio de Janeiro, Brazil on 7 June 1992, he said that universal responsibility is the real key to human survival.[14] '[It] is the best foundation for world peace, the equitable use of natural resources and, through concern for future generations, the proper care of the environment.'[15] From the point of view of awareness, universal responsibility is not even a principle; it is an inherent aspect of everyone's deepest sense of being: 'The principle of universal responsibility is what every person fundamentally is; we, by birth, embody it.'[16]

Human dignity in Buddhism lies in the infinite potential or capacity of human nature to participate in goodness. Emerging from Buddhist philosophy, the Dalai Lama's Weltanschauung is representative of the fundamental sameness of all human beings.[17] It is with such an understanding that he sees Buddhahood as 'within the reach of all human beings'. Carrying the argument further by seeking similarity between Buddhist thought and the Universal Declaration of Human Rights, he suggests that it [the Universal Declaration of Human Rights] facilitates the advancement of human beings towards the 'Buddhist goal'. Other comparative studies of the Buddhist conceptualization of rights and the Universal Declaration of Human Rights discuss similar paradigms.[18]

The argument put forth by those who are opposed to the Universal Declaration of Human Rights is that this concept, produced from a western imagination of individualism, attempts to impose international human rights standards on all cultures as a form of imperialism. This has been criticized for various reasons.[19] Samuel Huntington explores through his controversial analyses of how clashes between civilizations are the greatest threat to world peace, how an international order based on civilizations appears to be the best safeguard against war. His understanding of the western ideas of individualism, liberalism, constitutionalism, human rights, equality, liberty, the rule of law, democracy, free markets, the separation of church and state is that often these have little resonance in Islamic, Confucian, Japanese, Hindu, Buddhist or Orthodox cultures. And, that the western efforts to propagate such ideas produce instead a reaction against 'human rights imperialism' and 'a reaffirmation of indigenous values . . .'[20] This, however, has been strongly criticized on the grounds that such a relativist thesis is not entirely convincing. 'It assumes that there is a single set of Western, Islamic or Asian cultural values respectively. This is patently untrue . . . Huntington's list—Confucian, Japanese, Hindu, Buddhist—refutes the popular catchall of "Asian" values. There are many traditions and beliefs, some of them hostile to each other, even within each of these.'[21] Those subscribing to the 'Asian' view of human rights suggest that the standards laid down in the Universal Declaration of Human Rights are basically advocated by the west, and that these 'universal' human rights cannot be applied to Asia and other parts of the Third World, not simply because of differences in culture but also owing to differences in economic development,[22] and that the Universal Declaration of Human Rights does not take into due consideration the equitable, economic development of the Third World.

Opposing such a view, the Dalai Lama insists that fundamental human rights are as important to the people of Asia as they are to those in Europe or the United States of

America.[23] This is because all human beings, whatever their race, religion, sex or political status, are basically the same, by virtue of the fact that they share common human needs and concerns.[24] For this reason, he stresses not only the logical need to respect human rights worldwide, but more importantly, the definition of these rights.[25] The Dalai Lama emphasizes that all human beings yearn for freedom, equality and dignity. Since the Universal Declaration of Human Rights upholds all these three beliefs, the Dalai Lama too agrees with this declaration. This in a way also spells out the Dalai Lama's departure from his predominantly Buddhist position on the issue; although this stance can also be interpreted as strengthening the arguments in which he unifies all human beings.

The Dalai Lama's position can be assessed on the basis of the understanding of political economy amongst Tibetan scholars of the trend that has gained currency the world over which lays stress on economic gains rather than on national glory.[26] The Dalai Lama has completely understood the implications of this trend. Contrary to the apprehension of the advocates of Asian human rights, as to whether economic development can suffer due to human rights protection, the Dalai Lama turns the argument around and suggests instead that it is with economic coercion, sometimes, that human rights may be protected.[27] He concludes: 'The universal principles of equality of all human beings must take precedence.'[28]

He reasons that individuals and nations can no longer resolve many of their problems by themselves and are forced to be *interdependent*. The principle of interdependence basically emphasizes and encourages a growing awareness in people about the responsibility they share as individuals, vis-à-vis one another, and the responsibility they owe to the planet they live in.[29] Such a thought process in the Dalai Lama's thinking is especially influenced by the Buddhist doctrine of *pratityasamutpada*, or interdependence, which is considered the foundation of all teachings of the Buddha,[30] and which Buddhism identifies as the doctrine that leads to the cessation of all plurality. It is in this sense that the Dalai Lama says: 'It is a major error, a "root-error", to isolate human life, to attribute to it an essence, in itself.'[31] This ensures that the dignity, growth and evolution of the individual is not of great regard. In Buddhism, human dignity flows from the capacity of human nature to reach perfection, as demonstrated by the historical figure of the Buddha. Therefore it is suggested that the Buddha is the living embodiment of human perfection. It is the profound qualities of wisdom and compassion, which the Buddha exemplifies, which can cultivate human dignity.[32]

In his attempt to fuse the metaphysics of Buddhism with consciously lived reality, the Dalai Lama has entirely reinterpreted the doctrine of karma in which the active role of the human agency is emphasized. In this respect, perhaps, the Dalai Lama's formula fundamentally differs from Gandhi's, especially when seen in the context of karma and human rights. Where Gandhi considers an individual human condition as designated by the karmic law, the Dalai Lama goes a step further by making the individual larger than karma.

As a concept, karma is seminal to Buddhism. In Buddhism, the various manifestations of suffering, natural as well as unnatural, are taken to be the consequence of karma.[33] Yet, in the Dalai Lama's view, an individual cannot shirk the responsibility of finding himself/herself in a particular situation. The Dalai Lama says, 'To say that every misfortune is the result of karma is tantamount to saying that we are totally powerless in life.'[34] Going to the root of the word karma, the Dalai Lama sees it as denoting an active force, the inference being that the outcome of future events can be influenced by our actions. To suppose that karma is some sort of independent energy which determines the course of our whole life, he suggests, is incorrect. He questions, 'Who creates karma?' and answers his own question in the following words:

We ourselves. What we think, say, do, desire and
omit creates karma . . . In everything we do, there is
cause and effect. In our daily lives the food we eat,
the work we undertake, and when we relax, these
are all functions of action: our action. This is karma.
We cannot, therefore, throw up our hands whenever
we find ourselves confronted by unavoidable
suffering. If this was so, there would be no cause for
hope.[35]

This stance exemplies the difficult task that the Dalai Lama
has chosen, of treading a middle way between the
preservation of tradition and the necessity of progress.[36]

Envisioning the human condition on the principle that
all human beings are essentially equal and each has an equal
right to life, liberty and happiness, regardless of economic
condition, education or religion, as the Dalai Lama does
(and that karma ought not to predetermine these), is a
logical corollary to the Buddhist understanding that each
human being is equal to every other human being by virtue
of being a human being.[37] However, a rational authentic
appeal of any discourse on rights lies in its 'correct'
application. Mrinal Miri's succinct analysis brings this out
in his theory of rights, where he strives to balance the
freedom of the human agency, besides rescuing human
rights discourse from absurd nominalism: 'Human rights
are rights, which belong to human beings, qua human
beings, as beings who can exercise freedom through reason.
Such rights, therefore, are unique to human beings and
apply universally to all human beings.'[38]

It is in this sense that the Dalai Lama argues that each
human being can seek to live in a society where everyone is
allowed free expression and each person can strive to be the
best he/she can be.[39] However, he emphasizes, 'To pursue
one's own fulfillment at the expense of others would lead to
chaos and anarchy. So what is required is a system whereby
the pursuits of the individual are balanced with the wider

well-being of the community at large.'[40] Without the motivation for striking a balance, violence could find a perfect situation in which to breed; he reasons that universal responsibility is this balancing principle.

Nonviolence is the bedrock of the Dalai Lama's commitment to universal responsibility.[41] Buddhism is deeply associated with nonviolence and peace, both strongly represented in its value system.[42] It is important in Buddhism to see humans as a part of the community of 'sentient beings' in a conditioned world where suffering is endemic, and thus to kill or harm another being deliberately is to ignore the fragility and aspiration for happiness that one has in common with it.[43] Buddhism also suggests that it is in understanding the impermanent nature of phenomena that one can eschew violence.[44] 'Impermanence', as referred to in Buddhism, is radically different from violence. Even though impermanence stresses the phenomenon of 'transitoriness', which means that nothing is permanent and therefore could, by the very logic of its definition, suggest rectitude in resorting to violence, the difference between the two can be drawn by understanding that whereas impermanence is essentially based on the nature of phenomenon, violence calls for a change brought about by a human agency and thereby becomes a violation of the natural law of change. In Buddhist thought, it is said: 'Let the law of impermanence, not lawlessness of violence, determine the life-span of all that lives: individuals, species, cultures, the earth as a whole.'[45] The Buddhist law of impermanence supports nonviolence. 'Nonviolence,' the Dalai Lama says, is 'compassion in action.'[46] Hence, responsibility when it refers to a compassionate concern for mankind is called universal responsibility in the Dalai Lama's thought. It can be defined as developing of the 'sense', to work not merely for one's individual self, family or nation but for the benefit of all mankind.[47] This Buddhist approach, which concentrates on the individual, does not lose sight of a necessary corollary, which is a meaningful individual life interrelated with a lived social condition.[48] In an argument 'tautological' to this, he states that it is important to reassess the rights and responsibilities of individuals, peoples and nations in the context of globalization and interdependence.[49]

It is his faith in interdependence which not only ensures a sense of respect for the rights of others, but also ensures that the rights of others are recognized above one's own. He suggests that a keen awareness of the interdependence phenomenon is only possible with the help of compassion. For the Dalai Lama, 'the practice of compassion is not idealistic, but the most effective way to pursue the best interests of others as well as our own.'[50] To experience genuine compassion is to develop a feeling of closeness to others, combined with a sense of responsibility for their welfare.[51] Enumerating the Buddhist belief in freedom, equality and compassion for all as being fundamental to any discourse on rights,[52] he has consistently argued that the most important 'moral quality' that individuals need to cultivate is compassion.[53]

While some philosophers restrict duties to the public sphere and establish the sanctity of the private, the most important thing about a discourse on rights grounded in compassion is that it has the capacity to address moral life in what the liberal regards as the private domain.[54] The Dalai Lama's discourse on rights, grounded in compassion,[55] does not see true happiness emerging from limited concerns, but from developing love and compassion 'for all sentient beings'. His earnest wish is that all sentient beings can find happiness and compassion. This means that they can all be free of suffering. This spirit finds a true echo in Tsong Khapa's words 'The character of the great ones is limited to the benefit and happiness of others',[56] and in Schopenhauer's explanation of this as a situation in which 'distinction[s] between individuals ceases'.[57] For the Dalai Lama, to begin with, compassion is to have the good of others in one's heart, or as one's motive for action. He ventures to give a

social face to compassion and extends it from the individual
to the society at large and, much in consonance with
Schopenhauer, holds that differences between individuals
are not real. Schopenhauer describes the apparent difference
between persons by saying that 'according to experience,
the difference between my own person and another's appears
to be absolute. The difference and time that separates me
from him separates me also from his weal and woe.'[58] Again
he says, 'My true inner being exists in every living thing as
distinctly as it makes itself known in my self-consciousness
only to me . . . It is this that bursts through as compassion
on which all genuine . . . virtue therefore depends',[59] a vision
that echoes the non-dualistic philosophy of the Advaita.
According to the Dalai Lama:

> Different philosophies and traditions have different
> interpretations of the meaning of love and
> compassion . . . The Buddhist interpretation is that
> genuine compassion is based on a clear acceptance
> or recognition that others, like oneself, want
> happiness and have the right to overcome suffering.
> On that basis one develops some kind of concern
> about the welfare of others, irrespective of one's
> attitude to oneself. That is compassion.[60]

The Dalai Lama postulates that it is possible to have
compassion without any physical proximity to the situation
or person one is feeling compassionate towards.[61] A similar
insight is encountered in Tibetan Buddhist philosophy, where
visualizing each sentient being as one's mother becomes a
'means' to extend natural sympathy into universal
compassion.

Arguments which concur with the Dalai Lama's position,
that rights are not merely rights but are also duties and that
both rights as well as duties are interdependent,[62] would
also suggest that at present there is no endogenous theory
capable of unifying contemporary societies and no imposed
or imported ideology which can be *simply* substituted for it.

Therefore, some scholars have suggested the need for 'a mutual fecundation of cultures'.[63] For a concept to become universally valid, it is imperative for it to fulfil at least the condition that it should be the universal point of reference for any problem regarding human dignity. In what emerges as their criticism, they assert that 'the culture which has given birth to the concept of "Human Rights" should also be called upon to become a universal culture.'[64] Even where scholars discount the concept of rights as a peculiarly western notion, they explicitly affirm that the world should not renounce declaring or enforcing human rights. Rights are imperative and a 'technological' civilization without an assertion of rights amounts to the most inhuman situation imaginable. They insist, however, that room should be made for other traditions to develop and formulate their own 'culture specific' views corresponding to or opposing western rights, for it would otherwise be impossible for non-western cultures to survive let alone to offer viable alternatives. It is here that the role of a cross-cultural philosophical approach becomes important. 'Human pluralism' must be recognized in principle as also practised, and an intermediary space must be found for mutual criticism that strives for 'mutual fecundation' and enrichment. Pannikar observes, 'Perhaps such an interchange may help bring forth a new myth and eventually a more humane civilization. The dialogical dialogue appears as an unavoidable method.'[65] It may be said here that the Dalai Lama has constantly emphasized the need for dialogue as paramount in establishing mutual understanding and harmony. A cross-cultural critique, on the whole, considers new perspectives for an internal criticism and sets the limits of validity of human rights. It offers, at the same time, two possibilities: of 'enlarging its realm and of a mutual choice with other conceptions of man and reality'.[66]

Arguments however counsel, and at the same time inform, that claiming universal validity for human rights in the formulated sense, as of the Declaration of Human Rights, implies the belief that most peoples of the world today are engaged in much the same way as the Western nations in a process of transition and thereby transformation from more or less mythical Gemeinschaften[67] [feudal principalities, self governing cities, guilds, local communities, tribal institutions] to a 'rationally' and 'contractually' organized 'modernity', as known to the Western industrialized world.

Such arguments also indicate that 'no one can predict the evolution (or eventual disintegration) of those traditional societies, which have started from different material and cultural bases and whose reactions to modern Western civilization may therefore follow hitherto unknown lives.'[68]

As a vision and a response to these various debates, the Dalai Lama's interpretation of rights and responsibility can be seen as a plea for upholding and preserving the dignity of humankind, an ideal which he foresees to be the necessary foundation for every society.[69] The connection he articulates between rights and responsibility is representative of his 'engaged Buddhist ethic', wherein the individual does not debunk her/his social responsibility and neither does the society undermine the humanity of an individual.

Universal Responsibility and the Roots of Empathy and Compassion

Daniel Goleman

L ittle is known about the Dalai Lama's intense personal interest in the sciences; he has said that if he were not a monk, he would have liked to have been an engineer. As a youth in Lhasa it was he who was called on to fix broken machinery in the Potala Palace, be it a clock or a car. That early interest in science burns as brightly today. In part, I believe, this interest is motivated by his instinct that scientific truths lend yet another base of support to his most basic beliefs, such as the principle of universal responsibility.

Over the last decade or so I have had the privilege of convening or participating in a series of dialogues with His Holiness and scientists and scholars. These dialogues have been a rich source for finding the agreements between science and the spiritual views that support a philosophy of universal responsibility. The topics have been wide-ranging: the philosophical bases of physical reality; the nature of time, emotions and health; neurophysiology and states of consciousness; and the nature of suffering. But an underlying, unifying theme has been the interconnectedness of phenomena, and particularly the web that ties together all life.

Throughout these discussions I have been struck by the attitude of His Holiness: one of openness, deep curiosity, keen insight and a high level of scientific sophistication. Often, for example, a scientist would describe an experiment and its results—whether in neuroscience or quantum physics—and His Holiness would ask a question about whether such and such a proposition or some other possibility had been tested, only to have the scientist say, 'Your Holiness, that is exactly the next experiment we want to do.' He is, as it were, a natural scientist.

His attitude towards finding the truth is that of the true scientist: ideas and beliefs are hypotheses, to be investigated, explored and tested. Where the weight of evidence lies, there is truth to be found. His openness extends even to his own faith, Buddhism. He has said that if some belief of Buddhism were to be tested scientifically and irrefutably shown to be false, then it would have to change. Indeed, he sees investigation of the truth as vital to the spirit of Buddhism. As he told one scientist, 'From the Buddhist perspective, the more explanation and insight there is, the better.'

His view that science and the life of the spirit are complementary was aptly summed up in His Holiness's introductory remarks to a dialogue with neuroscientists at Harvard Medical School:

Science has made tremendous progress in understanding and harnessing matter. Buddhism, on the other hand, has a profound philosophy and over the centuries has developed a systematic method of shaping and developing the mind. Whether we are scientists or spiritual practitioners, our basic needs and aspirations are the same. Scientists may study mainly matter but they cannot ignore the human mind, or consciousness; spiritual practitioners may be engaging mainly in developing the mind but they cannot completely ignore their physical needs. It is for this reason that I have always stressed the importance of combining both the mental and the material approach to achieving happiness for humankind.

The Roots of Empathy

In this spirit of seeing the complementarity of science and spirit, I would like to explore one of the taproots of universal responsibility as seen in my own field, psychology, in the development of a child's sense of connectedness with others, of empathy and of compassion. For the newborn infant, this feeling revolves around the sense of touch, the intimate contact of mother and baby. When infants are deprived of human touch, they fail to thrive. A therapy for premature infants is to pick them up and gently stroke them regularly several times each day. Its effect in increased body weight and brain size is measurable—a finding His Holiness has cited many times in talking of the basic human need for connection.

From this base of intimate contact comes the older infant's sense of rapport and attunement with its caretakers. When an infant smiles or laughs or utters sounds, the caretaker's response in turn begins to build a rudimentary feeling of being emotionally connected with others—the feeling that someone will respond appropriately, rather than the communication falling into a void.

From this sense of emotional connectedness springs the earliest signs of altruism in year-old toddlers. At this age there emerges a capacity psychologists call 'sympathetic distress'. A toddler sees another fall down and starts crying, and tears well up in her own eyes as she watches, as though she herself was hurt rather than the other child. In one study of sympathetic distress, for example, a typical incident occurred when a fifteen-month-old child got hurt and was crying, and his playmate tried to comfort him by offering him a favourite teddy bear. These small acts of caring are the beginnings of compassion, the early precursors of empathy.

Developmental psychologists have found that infants feel sympathetic distress even before they fully realize that they exist apart from other people. Even a few months after birth, infants react to disturbances in those around them as if they were their own. By one year or so, they start to realize that the misery is not their own, but someone else's, though they still seem confused over what to do about it. In research conducted by Martin L. Hoffman of New York University, for example, a one-year-old brought his mother over to comfort a crying friend, ignoring the friend's own mother who was also in the room. This confusion is seen, too, when one-year-olds imitate the distress felt by someone else, possibly to better comprehend what they are feeling. For example, if another baby hurts her finger, a one-year-old might put her own finger in her mouth to see if she too hurts. On seeing his mother cry, one baby wiped his own eyes, though he had no tears.

Such 'motor mimicry', as it is called, is the original technical sense of the word 'empathy', as it was first used in the 1920s by E.B. Titchener, an American psychologist. This sense is slightly different from its original introduction into English from the Greek *empatheia*, 'feeling into', a term used initially by theoreticians of aesthetics for the ability to perceive the subjective experience of another person. Titchener's theory was that empathy stemmed from a sort of physical imitation of the distress of another, which then evokes the same feelings in oneself. He sought a word that would be distinct from 'sympathy', which can be felt for the general plight of another with no sharing whatever of what that other person is feeling.

Motor mimicry fades from toddlers' repertoire at around two and a half years, at which point they realize that someone else's pain is different from their own, and they are now better able to comfort them. A typical incident from a mother's diary is as follows:

A neighbour's baby cries . . . and Jenny approaches and tries to give him some cookies. She follows him around and begins to whimper to herself. She then tries to stroke his hair, but he pulls away . . . He calms down, but Jenny still looks worried. She continues to bring him toys and to pat his head and shoulders.

At this point in their development toddlers begin to diverge from one another in their overall sensitivity to other people's emotional upsets, with some, like Jenny, keenly aware and others tuning off. A series of studies by Marian Radke-Yarrow and Carolyn Zahn-Waxler at the National Institute of Mental Health showed that a large part of this difference in emphathic concern had to do with how parents disciplined their children. Children, they found, were more empathic when the discipline included calling strong attention to the distress their misbehaviour caused someone else: 'Look how sad you've made her feel', instead of 'That was naughty'. They found, too, that children's empathy is also shaped by seeing how others react when someone else is distressed; by imitating what they see, children develop a repertoire of empathic responses, especially in helping other people who are distressed.

The Well-attuned Child

Sarah was twenty-five when she gave birth to twin boys, Mark and Fred. Mark, she felt, was more like herself; Fred was more like his father. That perception may have had the seed of a telling, but subtle, difference in how she treated each boy. When the boys were just three months old, Sarah would often try to catch Fred's gaze, and when he would avert his face, she would try to catch his eye again. Fred would respond by turning away more emphatically. Once she looked away, Fred would look back at her, and the cycle of pursuit and aversion would begin again, often leaving Fred in tears. But with Mark, Sarah virtually never tried to impose eye contact as she did with Fred. Instead

Mark could break off eye contact whenever he wanted and she would not pursue it.

A small act, but telling. A year later, Fred was notably more fearful and dependent than Mark; one way in which he showed his fearfulness was in breaking off eye contact with other people as he had done with his mother at three months, turning his face down and away. Mark, on the other hand, looked people straight in the eye; when he wanted to break off contact, he'd turn his head slightly upward and to the side, with a winning smile.

The twins and their mother were observed minutely when they took part in research by Daniel Stern, a psychiatrist then at Cornell Medical School. Stern was fascinated by the small, repeated exchanges that took place between parent and child; he believes that the most basic lessons of emotional life are laid down in these intimate moments. Of all such moments, the most critical are those that let the child know her emotions are met with empathy, accepted and reciprocated, in a process Stern calls 'attunement'. The twins' mother was attuned with Mark, but out of emotional synch with Fred. Stern contends that the countless repeated moments of attunement or misattunement between parent and child shape the emotional expectations adults bring to their close relationships, perhaps far more than the more dramatic events of childhood.

Attunement occurs tacitly, as part of the rhythm of relationships. Stern has studied it with microscopic precision through videotaping hours of mothers' interactions with their infants. He found that through attunement mothers let their infants know they have a sense of what the infant is feeling. A baby squeals with delight, for example, and the mother affirms that delight by giving the baby a gentle shake, or coos, or matches the pitch of her voice to the baby's squeal. Or, if a baby shakes his rattle and she gives him a quick shimmy in response. In such an interaction the affirming message is in the mother more or less matching her baby's level of excitement. Such small attunements give an infant the reassuring feeling of being emotionally connected, a message that Stern finds mothers send about once every minute when they interact with their babies.

Attunement is very different from simple imitation. 'If you just imitate a baby,' Stern told me, 'that only shows you know what he did, not how he felt. To let him know you sense how he feels, you have to play back his inner feelings in another way. Then the baby knows he is understood.'

The Costs of Misattunement

Stern holds that from repeated attunements an infant begins to develop a sense that other people can and will share in its feelings. This sense seems to emerge at around eight months, when infants begin to realize they are separate from others, and continues to be shaped by intimate relationships throughout life. When parents are misattuned to a child it is deeply upsetting. In experiment, Stern had mothers deliberately over- or under-respond to their infants, rather than matching them in an attuned way; the infants responded with immediate dismay and distress.

Prolonged absence of attunement between parent and child takes a tremendous emotional toll on the child. When a parent consistently fails to show any empathy with a particular range of emotions in the child—joys or tears, the need to cuddle—the child begins to avoid expressing, and perhaps even feeling, those same emotions. In this way, presumably, entire ranges of emotion can begin to be obliterated from the repertoire for intimate relations, especially if through childhood those feelings continue to be covertly or overtly discouraged.

By the same token, children can come to favour an unfortunate range of emotions, depending on what moods are reciprocated. Even infants 'catch' moods. Three-month-old babies of depressed mothers, for example, mirrored their mothers' moods while playing with them, displaying more feelings of anger and sadness, and much less spontaneous curiosity and interest, compared to infants whose mothers were not depressed.

One mother in Stern's study consistently under-reacted to her baby's level of activity; eventually her baby learned to be passive. 'An infant treated that way learns, when I get excited I can't get my mother to be equally excited, so I may as well not try at all,' Stern contends. But there is hope in 'reparative' relationships: 'Relationships throughout life—with friends or relatives, for example, or in psychotherapy—continually reshape your working model of relationships. An imbalance at one point can be corrected later; it's an ongoing, lifelong process.'

Indeed, several theories of psychoanalysis see the therapeutic relationship as providing just such an emotional corrective, a reparative experience of attunement. 'Mirroring' is the term used by some psychoanalytic thinkers for the therapist's reflecting back to the client an understanding of his inner state, just as an attuned mother does with her infant. The emotional synchrony is unstated and outside conscious awareness, though a patient may bask in the sense of being deeply acknowledged and understood.

The lifetime emotional costs of lack of attunement in childhood can be great, and not just for the child. A study of criminals who committed the most cruel and violent crimes found that the one characteristic of their early lives that set them apart from other criminals was that they had been shuttled from foster home to foster home—life histories that suggest emotional neglect and little opportunity for attunement.

Such neglect can lead to psychopathy in adulthood, the incapacity to feel empathy or compassion of any sort, nor the least twinge of conscience. Robert Hare, a University of British Columbia psychologist, believes that the callousness of criminal psychopaths is based in part on a physiological pattern he discovered: psychopaths about to receive an electric shock show no sign of the fear response that is normal in people about to experience pain. Because the prospect of pain does not trigger a surge of anxiety, Hare contends that psychopaths lack any concern about future punishment for what they do. And because they themselves do not feel fear, they have no empathy—nor compassion—for the fear and pain of their victims.

Empathy is typically, and tragically, lacking in those who commit the most mean-spirited of crimes. The blotting out of empathy as these people inflict suffering on their victims is part of an emotional cycle that precipitates their cruel acts. This absence of empathy for their victims is one important focus of the new treatments being devised for violent offenders. In one of the most promising treatment programmes, the offenders read heart-wrenching accounts of crimes like their own, told from the victim's perspective. They also watch videotapes of victims tearfully relating what it was like to be molested. The offenders then write about their own offences from the victim's point of view, imagining what the victim felt. They read this account to a therapy group, and try to answer questions about the assault from the victim's perspective.

Finally, the offender goes through a simulated re-enactment of the crime, this time playing the role of the victim. The empathy they gain from this perspective-taking is an impetus for them to take responsibility for their own crimes, and to try to reform themselves. From empathy arises compassion, even in the most hardened heart.

The Neurology of Empathy

As is so often the case in neurology, quirky and bizarre case reports were among the early clues to the brain basis of empathy. A 1975 report, for instance, reviewed several cases in which patients with lesions in the right area of the frontal lobes had a curious deficit: they were unable to understand the emotional message in people's tone of voice, though they were perfectly able to understand their words. A sarcastic 'Thanks', a grateful 'Thanks' and an angry

'Thanks' all had the same neutral meaning for them. By contrast, a 1979 report spoke of patients with injuries in other parts of the right hemisphere who had a very different gap in their emotional perception. These patients were unable to express their own emotions through their tone of voice or by gesture. They knew what they felt, but they simply could not convey it. All these cortical brain regions, the various authors noted, had strong connections to the limbic system, the brain's emotional centre.

These studies were reviewed as background to a seminal paper by Leslie Brothers, a psychiatrist at the California Institute of Technology, on the biology of empathy. Reviewing both neurological findings and comparative studies with animals, Brothers points to the amygdala—a structure in the limbic system that stores emotional memories—and its connections to the visual cortex as part of the key brain circuitry underlying empathy.

Much of the relevant neurological research is from work with animals, especially primates. That primates display empathy—or 'emotional communication', as Brothers prefers to say—is clear not just from anecdotal accounts, but also from studies such as the following. Rhesus monkeys were trained first to fear a certain tone by hearing it while they received a mild electric shock. Then they learned to avoid the electrical shock by pushing a lever whenever they heard a certain tone. Next, pairs of these monkeys were put in separate cages, their only communication through a closed-circuit TV which allowed them to see pictures of the face of the other monkey. The first monkey, but not the second, then heard the dreaded tone, which brought a look of fear to its face. At that moment, the second monkey, seeing fear on the face of the first, pushed the lever that prevented the shock—an act of empathy, if not of altruism.

Having established that primates do, indeed, read emotions from the faces of their peers, researchers used long, fine-tipped electrodes gently inserted into the brains of monkeys. These electrodes allowed the recording of activity in a single neuron. Electrodes tapping neurons in the visual cortext and in the amygdala showed that when one monkey saw the face of another, that information led to neuron-firing, first in the visual cortex, then in the amygdala. This pathway is a standard route for information that is emotionally arousing. But what is surprising about results from such studies is that they have also identified neurons in the visual cortex which seem to fire only in response to specific facial expressions or gestures, such as a threatening opening of the mouth, a fearful grimace or a docile crouch. These neurons are distinct from others in the same region which recognize familiar faces. This would seem to mean that the brain is designed from the beginning to respond to specific emotional expressions—that is, empathy is a given of biology.

A similar physiological basis to empathy in us humans is suggested in research by Robert Levenson, a University of California psychologist who has studied married couples trying to guess what their partner is feeling during a heated discussion. His method is simple: the couple is videotaped and their physiological responses measured while talking about some troubling issues in their marriage—how to discipline the kids, spending habits and the like. Each partner reviews the tape and narrates what he or she was feeling from moment to moment. Then the partner reviews the tape a second time, now trying to read the other's feelings.

The most empathic accuracy occurred in those husbands and wives whose own physiology tracked that of the spouse they were watching. That is, when their partner had an elevated sweat response, so did they; when their partner had a drop in heart rate, their heart slowed. In short, their body mimicked the subtle, moment-to-moment physical reactions of their spouse. If the viewer's physiological patterns simply repeated their own during the original interaction, they were very poor at surmising what their partner was feeling. Only when their bodies were in synch was there empathy.

This suggests that when the emotional brain is driving the body with a strong reaction—the heat of anger, say—there can be little or no empathy. Empathy requires enough calm and receptivity so that the subtle signals of feeling from another person can be received and mimicked by one's own emotional brain. In other words, when we are less caught up in our own worries and ruminations, less trapped by the small concerns of the everyday self, we are more receptive to the needs and feelings of others. And from that receptiveness flows the impulse that undergirds a personal sense of universal responsibility.

Empathy and Ethics: The Roots of Altruism

One of the most famous lines in English poetry is an expression of the principle of universal responsibility: 'And therefore never send to know for whom the bell tolls; it tolls for thee.'

John Donne's sentiment speaks to the heart of the link between empathy and caring: another's pain is one's own. To feel with another is to care; in this sense the opposite of 'empathy' is 'antipathy'. The empathic attitude is engaged again and again in moral judgements, for moral dilemmas involve potential victims: should you lie to keep from hurting a friend's feelings? Keep a promise to visit a sick friend or accept a last-minute invitation to a dinner party instead? When should a life-support system be kept going for someone who would otherwise die?

These moral questions are posed by the empathy researcher Martin Hoffman, who argues that the roots of morality are to be found in empathy, since it is empathizing with the potential victims—someone in pain, danger or deprivation—and so sharing their distress that moves people to act to help them. Beyond this immediate link between empathy and altruism in personal encounters, Hoffman proposes that the same capacity for empathic effect, for putting oneself in another's place, leads people to follow certain moral principles.

Hoffman sees a natural progression in empathy from infancy onward. As we have seen, at one year of age, a child feels distress herself when she sees another fall and starts to cry. Her rapport is so strong and immediate that she puts her thumb in her mouth, buries her head in her mother's lap, as if she herself is hurt. After the first year, when infants become more aware that they are distinct from others, they actively try to soothe another crying infant, offering them their teddy bears, for example. As early as two years of age children begin to realize that someone else's feelings differ from their own, and so they become more sensitive to cues revealing what another actually feels. At this point they might, for example, recognize that another child's pride might be hurt if undue attention is called to them, and that the best way to help them deal with their tears is to ignore them.

By late childhood the most advanced level of empathy emerges, as children are able to understand distress beyond the immediate situation, and to see that someone's condition or station in life may be a source of chronic distress. At this point they can feel for the plight of an entire group, like the poor, the oppressed and the outcast. That understanding, in adolescence, can buttress moral convictions centred on wanting to alleviate misfortune and injustice.

Empathy underlies many facets of moral judgement and action. One is 'empathic anger', described by John Stuart Mill as 'the natural feeling of retaliation . . . rendered by intellect and sympathy applicable to . . . those hurts which wound us through wounding others', which Mill dubbed the 'guardian of justice'. Another instance in which empathy leads to moral action is when a bystander is moved to intervene on behalf of a victim. The research shows that the more empathy a bystander feels for the victim, the more likely she will intervene.

There is some evidence that the level of empathy people feel shades their moral judgements as well. For example, studies in Germany and the US found that the more empathic people are, the more they favour the moral principle that resources should be allocated according to need; the less empathic, the more they favoured the principle that people should be rewarded according to the effort they expend, regardless of need. Empathy, then, is the natural root of the altruistic impulse to take responsibility for those in need.

A Final Word

The Dalai Lama represents Tibet, the one great culture centred on a wisdom tradition that has survived from classical times into the modern day world. But the perilousness of our times is symbolized by the fact that even that future survives intact only in exile. Tibet represents a time capsule of sorts for the modern world, a message from an age when life was centred on the spirit, when the inner sciences—the art of being—were developed to the highest levels. At a time when the modern world is adrift and in crisis, we need more than ever to bring this wisdom to bear on our collective challenges.

Science and technology have brought immense control over nature, but power without wisdom is dangerous. We need to balance our modern capabilities with an ancient wisdom. His Holiness often speaks of the interconnectedness of all beings and the universal responsibility that this brings. In a sense, that means we are all in this together. He has said, also, that because these times are so dire, it is a great honour to be alive now, at this moment, on this planet. It is we who bear the responsibility, who face the challenge, who must take care of the planet, not just for ourselves, but for the future of our children.

Universal Responsibility:
A Christian Consideration

Raimon Panikkar

The Dalai Lama has asked all people to meditate on the principle of universal responsibility. In fact, practically all saints of all traditions have preached and lived this principle. A saint, runs a Chinese saying, is a person who has the soul of the whole people; for the Indic tradition, such a person is a *mahatma*, and according to the western classics, *magnanimitas* is the feature of saintliness. A 'great soul' feels responsible for a wider field than a 'narrow-minded' individual.

The extremely important call of the Dalai Lama to explore the notion of universal responsibility does not consist in asking us to work on one concept so as to get some further clarity on a particular subject. The call of His Holiness existentially extends the field of our responsibility by inviting us to become aware of its universal area. Most studies of this notion tell us that we are not responsible for things we are not aware of. We are only responsible if we are aware that we have to respond to a certain situation and are free in our response. This is why the notion is generally restricted to ethics.

The call of the Dalai Lama widens the horizon and reminds us of the otherwise traditional doctrine that our awareness is not limited to what we see with our eyes, comprehend with our reason or, worse, 'see' by means of satellites and mass media information. Our awareness, and thus our responsibility, extends also to what opens up to our third eye, our faith, our deepest intuition. By doing this he expands our responsibility into areas which until now were outside the concerns of modern man. Many people can go on with business as usual because they do not see beyond their private and individual fields.

'Responsibility only enters insofar as one can be called in question by another, and insofar as one can answer this summons,' says Molinski in Rahner's *Sacramentum mundi*. The Dalai Lama urges us to question. We have to add, of course, that he is not alone in this call. This is the call of practically all religions.

This spiritual head of one branch of the Buddhist tradition, in tune with the cosmology of ancient Buddhism, is not satisfied with just human history, and enlarges the field of human responsibility to all sentient beings. As a modern man, following our increasing ecological consciousness (which I prefer to call ecosophical), His Holiness suggests we should include in our responsibility the entire ecosystem of our planet and soon of our solar system. The shrinking of our human responsibility is the fruit of modern individualism, which limits man's concerns to himself and his immediate surroundings.

To be sure, these voices of concern, which the powers-that-be and the routine of the mind are still reluctant to hear, come today with increasing consensus from all the intellectual and spiritual corners of the world. Humanity as such is responsible for its own destiny. Human history is confronting us with the dilemma of a radical anthropological and thus civilizational change (*metanoia*) or a collective suicide. If some survive they will be not the 'fittest' but the most unscrupulous—those who will destroy each other soon afterwards. What we call human consciousness may 'transmigrate' onto another non-historical realm. Hope might not be lost, but humanity as we know it will collapse.

*

What follows is a Christian consideration on one single aspect of this formidable problem. It is a Christian commentary, however, which keeps in mind the reader of other traditions. I could as well have written a Hindu or a Buddhist reflection on the topic and it would be worth the effort to undertake a comparative study. We should be cautious, however, not to centre every reflection on the single concept of responsibility, ignoring the many homeomorphic equivalents in other cultures. The Buddhist notion of *pratityasamutpada* (co-dependent origination, universal concatenation or radical relativity), for instance, will stress more the awareness of a common belonging than the ability to respond. We need a plural perspective to the problems of the world. This is a requisite for a healthy approach.

I choose the Christian tradition because His Holiness moves quite often among people of Christian extraction who have almost forgotten the Christian archetypes of their religion—an oblivion to which modern Christianity has heavily contributed. For this reason I shall describe what I think belongs to the genuine Christian tradition, although expressed in simple language for contemporaries to whom the old parlance may offer some difficulties.

A consideration means the effort at bringing all the stars (*sidera*) together into one intelligible constellation. I could cite teachings from the Gospels to Teilhard de Chardin (to quote just one name) passing through the Greek, the Oriental and the Latin Fathers of the Church, the Middle Ages, Renaissance and modern Christian thinkers to substantiate the Christian notion of universal responsibility. But I will not use any telescope to gaze at those giant stars and shall use just my naked eye to present this consideration.

The very notion of universal responsibility entails at least three fundamental aspects: human freedom, the universal connection of all things, and the capacity of things or events to respond to the human being.

Anthropological Freedom:

We would not be responsible if we were robots or puppets in the hands of a higher instance of whatever type, be it a god, a society or a machine. I am responsible if I have in me the capacity to respond to the summons of what makes me precisely responsible. Human freedom is an essential ingredient of responsibility.

Universal Solidarity:

We are not responsible for what lies absolutely outside our field of action, or rather, outside the effluvia of our being. Responsibility implies certain solidarity, the *karma, sarvam sarvatmakam, Buddha-kaya* or the *pratityasamutpada* of other traditions.

Dialogical Cosmology:

We are not responsible either if the 'other', for which we are allegedly responsible, is a merely automatic or fixed thing under the law of necessity impervious to human interference. If in one way or another I cannot influence that 'other', I cannot have any responsibility. My response has to affect that for which I am supposed to be responsible. In a Newtonian universe, for instance, we are not responsible for an eclipse. In an astrological cosmology our co-responsibility with the course of the eclipse is altogether another matter. Responsibility is meaningless in an utterly mechanical universe.

*

I shall limit myself exclusively to the second point, as much as I would like to touch upon the third problem since it concerns a burning issue of our times: the modern scientific cosmology.

Most religious traditions have underscored the unity of the world, whether it be considered a creation or otherwise.

Many traditions, including the Christian, have stressed in a special way the unity of humanity, without disputing the oneness of creation. Another pitiful restriction has also occasionally occurred. Some religions have de facto limited 'humanity' to the people of their own tradition. Outsiders have been, if not totally forgotten, certainly neglected in the doctrinal elaborations of this unity of the human race.

The history of Christianity has from the very beginning been torn between an *inherited* idea of a chosen people and an *inherent* idea of universality. The Jewish idea of chosenness does not claim universality. The Greek idea of universality does not pretend any privilege. This tension is not yet quite resolved in the present time. But after two millennia of history I detect that the prevalent trend today is to qualify chosenness and to reinterpret universality. 'Catholicity', for instance, is not understood as a rather modern geographical universalism nor as being holder of an exclusive truth, but as something closer to the universality of a mirror which reflects the whole without pretending to be the sole image of the whole. This was incidentally the primitive understanding of the word 'catholic' up to times past St. Augustine's.

*

'Am I perchance my brother's keeper?' asked the first human being in the Bible (Adam and Eve certainly were not ordinary people). 'Yes, you are!' was the unambiguous answer. In order to escape this universal responsibility, the human race has ever attempted to reduce the extension of our 'brother'. Responsibility was restricted to our 'neighbours'. 'But who is my neighbour?' someone asked the rabbi from Nazareth, and he boldly replied that it was the foreigner, the stranger, the 'pagan', the *goi, kafir* or *mleccha*. Our responsibility includes all people. Jesus summed up 'salvation' as having an active responsibility for the welfare of the downtrodden and identifying oneself with the naked, hungry and suffering.

Let us reintroduce the problem from another more elementary perspective.

Why on earth should I be responsible for a murder committed in a distant island by an unknown fellow for reasons totally incomprehensible to me? Language is treacherous, for I should not have said 'fellow', since the very word denotes a certain partnership which is precisely what is at stake in the example. Is that distant person my fellow? Or have we fellowship only with our family, clan, caste, nation, religion, culture?

The only rational answer is to say that willingly or unwillingly, knowingly or not, we belong together and are not isolated individuals, unconnected monads, independent beings.

In a word, universal responsibility implies a certain type of universal solidarity. Individuals can only be linked by external ties, like a common interest. The moral responsibility which flows from a common goal is limited to the means used in the acquisition of that goal. It is a legal notion.

F.H. Bradley wrote, 'For practical purposes we need make no distinction between responsibility and liability to punishment.' This is the usual way of understanding responsibility in a predominantly economic world view. I cannot be accountable for what lies outside my accounts. If there is no ontological unity of the human race there is no universal responsibility. There is only accountability for the accounts into which we have put our investments. This individualism is what lies outside my accounts. This individualism is what leads modern citizens to express strongly: 'If power lies exclusively with the people and I am the people, and I have not voted [for] the constitution [of a country, for example], why am I obliged to obey that law as sacrosanct?' Individuals feel united only if there is a common purpose (nationalism and communalism of all sorts) or if there is a threat from the law, the police or the army. No wonder that our planet has more than 40 million in the armed forces. They 'enforce' law and order because there is no sense of responsibility.

Legal responsibility implies a prior contract, at least implicitly. Ethical responsibility demands at least a tacitly acknowledged moral code. We have responsibility towards others (legal), and towards ourselves (ethical). None of this alone can be the basis for universal responsibility. Here is the place and role of religion in general. It re-links man with something above the *merely* 'human' by the active acknowledgement of a vertical dimension. Here is the place and role of God in the Christian tradition. Our response to this one God oversteps the boundaries of a mere responsibility towards society or towards one's own Self. God is not a discriminator of persons, says Christian scripture. The Other in front of God, *in conspectus Domini* repeated the scholastics, has the same rights as I have.

We should not understand universal responsibility to mean a single universal moral code. The mores of people are very different and so are their ways of thinking. Each world view offers the possibility of deriving from it a sense of universal responsibility, but each culture may have different visions and interpret and justify this responsibility in diverse forms. To be sure, our contemporary situation calls for working towards a political consensus for dealing with the problems of human conviviality, but no culture should impose its views on another.

We urgently need a political dialogical dialogue for our world, but this is different from assuming, for instance, that we should proclaim a global ethic ignoring the function of the Divine (so central in many traditions) just because it seems irrelevant in today's politics. The needed pragmatic rule of political behaviour is something different from a global ethic and, furthermore, different from our problem.

In sum, there is only universal responsibility if there is a universal human link of an ontological nature. My example is the Christian dogma of the mystical Body—to which I now turn.

The Hebrew Bible from its first lines stresses the unity of creation. The entire universe is the creation of one God, and the whole world sings the glory of its Creator. The world is a unity.

The Christian scriptures, while fully accepting this oneness, emphasize the unity of the human race. The 'recapitulation' of all things is done by one Man who becomes the Head of this Cosmic Body. Christ is a cosmic Christ, but he is foremost the head of humankind, besides being also the head of the whole cosmos, called a *makranthropos* (not dissimilar to the Vedic *purusa*) by the Greek Fathers. The 'heresy' of the Ebionites was not to deny that Jesus was the son of Mary, but to deny that 'Christ was before Mary' (to defend *Christum ante Mariam non fuisse* in the words of St. Jerome).

The confusion between Jesus and Christ has had dire consequences in Christian history. 'Jesus is the Christ' is the Christian *mahavakya*, the Christian confession. Yet the Mystical Body of the Christian tradition is not just Jesus, the son of Mary, but the Mystical Body of Christ. This Christ, 'light which illumines all Men', 'splendour and image of the Godhead', 'upholding all things by his word', 'superior to all angels', 'alpha and omega', 'only begotten and firstborn of all creatures', who was 'before Abraham', 'in whom all things find their support', etc, this Christ, 'mystery hidden since the beginning in God', is discovered by Christians in and through Jesus of Nazareth.

Human solidarity in the Christian tradition has two pillars and one ground. The two pillars are the first Adam, created in the image and likeness of God, and the second Adam, Jesus the Christ, incarnated in time and history in order to re-establish the image and likeness of the Divine in Man. The ground is the eschatological expectation of a 'new heaven and a new earth' at the *apokatastasis panton* or time of the 'universal restoration' which St. Augustine sums up saying, 'And there will be one Christ loving himself' (*et erit unus Christus amans seipsum*).

The very word Adam means simply Man, the Man, and not just an individual. All have been under 'original sin' because of the universal human solidarity between the first Adam and the rest of mortals (otherwise why should we share the responsibility of Eve?). All have been restored to the undistorted divine image because of the human solidarity between the second Adam and all the rest of humanity—theological distinctions and philosophical problems notwithstanding.

This is the explicit teaching of the Apostle Paul, confirmed by most of the so-called ecumenical councils. And all will be integrated into the *regressus* or the return of all things to their origin from which they have emerged (*egressus*) so that at the end 'God will be all in all things'. This is the reason why St. Thomas, in the footsteps of Augustine's idea of evil as lack of being (*privatio*), dares to affirm that sinners are not (*peccatores in quantum peccatores non sunt*). The Christian solidarity is universal and complete.

It is obvious that both the language and the ideas are all couched within a particular cultural context against the background of the world view of the time. Just as Adam is a common name particularized in the story of creation, Christ is also a common name applied to the son of Mary. The action of the first Adam takes place at the birth of every person, and the action of the second Adam is witnessed in the rebirth of every human being. Both are historical and transhistorical events, even if a particular Christian theology has afterwards interpreted the rebirth in a very particular manner—although never so exclusive as to deny many forms of that initiation into eternal life, which Christians call baptism.

Similarly, traditional Christianity has believed in the final oneness of both human history and the cosmos, so as to understand the entire reality as a radical Trinity: Father, Christ and the Holy Spirit. This Christ encompasses the whole history of the universe, the complete temporality of reality integrated in the Divine Mystery. *In rebus tantis trina coniunctio mundi* sings the Christian liturgy in a slightly different but applicable way. This radical trinity is the truly *mysterium conjunctionis*, the 'threefold conjunction' of the real.

In this manner the Christian believes in the total solidarity of the human race—extended also to the entire universe as so many scriptural passages affirm and as has been elaborated by the later tradition. It is the entire creation that 'groans and waits for the total transformation of the cosmos' towards the 'new heaven and the new earth'. Little meaning it would have to believe in one creator if there was not one creation. This is religion: We are all 'linked' in the same adventure. It has been, in fact, a certain notion of universal responsibility which has triggered, in all its ambivalence, the missionary urge of the Christian churches. They felt, rightly or wrongly, responsible for the whole world.

We may now 'bring all the stars together' by citing exclusively one single luminous planet of the Christian solar system. Our choice should be significant for the modern west in as much as we choose not an oriental, a Greek or a modern witness, but a man who has decisively influenced (be it a blessing or not) the self-understanding of the most powerful branches of Christianity: St. Augustine.

St. Augustine's leading idea follows in the wake of St. Paul and, of course, the Gospels:

> Extend your love over the entire earth if you want to love Christ, since the members of Christ are to be found everywhere in the world. If you love only one part you are divided, if you are divided you are not in the Body, if you are not in the Body, you are not under the Head (*Epistula ad Parthos* 10 [PL 35, 2060]).

Or again,

> All Men are one Man in Christ, and the unity of Christians constitutes but one Man (Psalm 127 [PL 37,1686]).

And more:

> If he is the Head, and we are the members, then
> together he and we are the whole Man (Johanem 21
> [PL 35,1568]).

There are dozens of such sentences. For Augustine we can
understand Christ in three ways (*tribes modis intelligitur, et
nominator*): as God equal to the Father, as Man (*assumpta
carne*) and, thirdly, as the 'whole Christ in the fullness of
humanity' (*totus Christus in plenitudine ecclesiae*) (Sermo,
341,I).

For brevity's sake I shall not quote from the entire
Christian tradition regarding this central tenet of the Mystical
Body. The reader may refer to the outstanding multi-volume
work, *The Whole Christ*, by Emile Mersch, written just
before World War II for further knowledge.

*

Many writers discussing the problem of responsibility stress
the moral responsibility of the person concerning our human
actions. We are responsible for our actions, we are told, and
according to them we shall be 'judged'. One of the best
descriptions is that of Maurice Blondel stating that *la
responsiabilite est la solidarite de la personne avec ses actes.*
It is interesting to note that already a century ago Blondel
spoke of solidarity and not of congruence between our
being and our actions. Responsibility is not the logical
consequence of our ideas (as Kierkegaard would be inclined
to defend) but the very manifestation of our being. Our
responsibility is not the conclusion of a syllogism or the
application of a rule, but the free response of our being to
the very challenge that existence confronts us with.

In one word, we are not just responsible for our actions
but also for our thoughts (as the famous incident of Ananias
and Sapphira in the *Acts of the Apostles* shows: 'You have
lied not to Men but to God'). The responsibility is not only

towards ourselves, but towards the in-dwelling Divine Spirit in us. This is why Jesus also said that we shall be held responsible for every idle word coming out of our mouth, that is to say for every word which does not effect what it says.

To use the example cited earlier, I cannot know why that distant person in that distant island did what he/she did. I cannot know the results of my actions, and with the best of intentions I cannot foresee the good or bad effects of my words. The seat of our responsibility lies not in the good or bad example we set, not in the good or bad effect we have on others, but in our very being. The seat is inside us, it is ourselves. Responsibility is not mere prudence, and much less the fruit of an objective calculus foreseeing the effects of our words or actions. It is not cunning, nor a strategy for prestige, good name and better results.

Responsibility is an ontological virtue because our being is dialogical and we are neither a solipsistic monad nor a dialectical individual. Our responsibility is based on the response we give to ourselves, to our being, because our being is constitutively related to all other beings. And this relatedness is a human relation, that is, dialogical, sharing our *logos* with all beings (*homo loquens*). What links us with other beings, the traditional Christian answer will be, is not that we know about that distant person, but that we are all equally linked with the Ground of our Being or God. God is the warrant of our universal solidarity. If I am not as I have to be, if I betray myself, if I do not live up to the divine calling which constitutes me, the entire universe suffers from my infidelity, and that 'distant person' will commit that hideous act because, though in a minimal way, I have contributed to it.

It would be an undue extrapolation if we were to interpret this in a mechanicistic way and say, for instance, that my responsibility towards that distant fellow is simply one-sixth billionth part of the share. The greater my 'soul', the bigger is my responsibility. The being of a saint hallows an entire society: 'To whom less has been given, less will be demanded'. Every being is unique and we cannot judge others. Interconnectedness is not a quantitative dimension, nor is relationship a mechanical one.

Paradoxically enough, this awareness of our universal responsibility bestows on us calmness and peace which saves us from the messianistic syndrome of wanting to be the saviours of the world and falling into despair or indifference when we realize we cannot perform the task. It is not that we skip our duty or dilute our responsibility so thin that it does not matter what we do. On the contrary, aware of our intrinsic responsibility in our very being, we do not frantically run to influence other people or 'convert' them (to our ways) by extrinsic means. Instead it is the purity of heart that counts and the transparency of our lives. Not even the left hand should know the good acts that the right is doing.

Needless to say ideas similar to the traditional Christian idea of God as the foundation for universal responsibility are present in other religions with some variations. I mentioned the notion of karma and pratityasamutpada as other homeomorphic equivalents for the foundation of universal responsibility.

It is an interesting feature of our times that there is rooted in our human experience an increasing shared awareness of human problems common to all in any doctrinal approach to reality. Our contemporary awareness does not respond to deductive morality: There is a God, therefore I have to behave in a certain way; the Buddha said so therefore I should do it; the Veda prescribes it, therefore I should behave in a particular manner. It is rather the other way round. We perceive the deterioration of the earth, the increasing human exploitation by other human beings, man-made injustices, hunger, etc, and we then find both strength and remedies to address the issues, within our cultural context, later analysing which methods or beliefs were the most effective.

The description of this modern myth needs but one important proviso. It would be a degradation of religion and demeaning to humans to see religion as a mere means and man as force in the universe. All religions warn us that man is not the absolute boss, neither in heaven nor on earth, that our solidarity is not something we create, but that this *solidum* is something given, and that our responsibility is precisely this human capacity primarily not to ask but to respond. Our responsibility entails the intuition that as beings we respond to a question we have not ultimately formulated. Universal responsibility does not mean universal lordship over reality, but a distinctly human power to respond freely to the mystery of reality and, thus responding, steer also the very destiny of that reality. The Christian believes that he is not alone in this task.

Gentle Bridges and Golden Seeds:
The Dalai Lama's Dialogues with Science

*Swati Chopra**

I am on my way to Dharamsala to cover the tenth Mind and Life Conference: a series of dialogues between eminent scientists and the Dalai Lama. It is a jolting overnight bus journey from Delhi. I am excited to be in the presence of the Dalai Lama and keen to witness the interaction between what appears to me to be the sciences of life and a science for living.

My thoughts are a jumble. My editor has agreed to this assignment because of the celebrity stir caused by Hollywood stars Richard Gere and Goldie Hawn walking the narrow streets of this hill town. But that is not my motivation. As a journalist I have my, well okay, 'triple gems'—openness, awareness and sharing. And in the darkened night, I think of these as being the qualities that drive both science and Buddhism too—being open beyond beliefs and mindful of facts and experience.

I recall my conversation with my editor. 'Science and Buddhism? The Dalai Lama and scientists?' I told him what I knew. That Mind and Life conferences are part of an ongoing process of dialogue between modern science and

The writer attended the Tenth Mind and Life Conference at the official residence of His Holiness the Dalai Lama in Macleodganj in October 2002.

Buddhism initiated by a scientist (Francisco Varela) and a businessman (Adam Engle) in 1987 with active support from His Holiness.

'Why?'

Because Buddhism is among other things an ancient science of the mind. It has uncovered notions of reality that quantum physics is now slowly but surely arriving at. Because it also has a sophisticated science of ethics that can give geneticists and bio-engineers a perspective with which to resolve their dilemmas. Because for the sake of our planet and ourselves, we must understand more about the interconnectedness that Buddhism talks about. Because a vocabulary is emerging, through interactions such as Mind and Life, for the two to talk meaningfully to each other.

And because, as the Dalai Lama says, 'with the ever growing impact of science on our lives, religion and spirituality have a greater role to play reminding us of our humanity . . .'

As the rickety bus inches towards mist-cloaked Macleodganj, a tender dawn breaks out over the Dhauladhar range. The Tenth Mind and Life promises to be an engagement in openness and learning.

A cold morning. I race madly through the streets and bazaars to reach by '9 a.m. sharp', as the lama-in-charge had strictly warned me. Weaving through a crowd of little monks-in-training giggling at my haste, I arrive at the entrance to the 'temple', the Dalai Lama's official residence. After a perfunctory security check, a tag bearing the legend 'Mind and Life Institute, Dharamsala 2002' is placed round my neck with a smile. Multiple head-silhouettes merge into a single, circular whole on the tag—an appropriate logo for the institute that has brought wonderful minds, scientific and Tibetan, at one table for the past fifteen years.

A gong sounds. 9 a.m. All participants must gather.

Up the steep, double helix-like winding gravelled path to the Dalai Lama's residence, people walk in groups of twos and threes. I hear snatches of conversations peppered with terms like 'dharma of gene expression', 'cognition and consciousness', 'physical reality/ultimate reality' that convey a sense of a hybrid sciento-Buddhist idiom that the dialogue has bred. My guardian-angel lama materializes by my side and promptly introduces me to several participating scientists, and the French monk Matthieu Ricard, who breaks off an animated discussion to say hello. Others' reactions are less enthusiastic, somewhat bordering on the frosty.

The issue is, as I gather, one of secrecy, which was apparently promised to scientists from the first conference onwards. The Mind and Life conferences were to be semi-private meetings, away from the media spotlight and, I imagine, the rest of the scientific community that mightn't take too kindly to its members hobnobbing with religion. A journalist's presence, therefore, is somewhat unwelcome.

Later, I discover that the one-sided, celebrity gossip reports in Indian newspapers have also angered the scientists who see it as a trivializing of the conference. They would rather have nothing to do with any journalist at this point, least of all an Indian one. A request is made to His Holiness who, in his great compassion, lets me stay.

The meetings are being held in a large room overlooking the snow-covered Dhauladhars. Sunlight streams in from wide windows and warms the gleaming wooden floors. *Thangkas* depicting Buddha's past, present and future line the walls. The participating scientists—Nobel Laureate Steven Chu, physicists Michel Bitbol and Arthur Zajonc, biologist Ursula Goodenough, geneticist Eric Lander and chemist Pier Luigi Luisi—sit in a semi-circle in the middle of the room, with the Dalai Lama's seat in the centre. The 'observers' sit to his right, the monks to his left. The Dalai Lama himself would sit in the shadow of a gold Buddha, seated in *samadhi*, eyes half closed in deep contemplation.

A young monk wearing trendy dark glasses walks in and takes his seat among the scientists, somewhat self-consciously. I recognize the Seventeenth Gyalwa Karmapa, Ugyen Trinley Dorje. In fact, of all the Mind and Life conferences, this one has the largest contingent of monks in attendance who, I am told, are being taught western science in their monasteries upon the Dalai Lama's encouragement. Tsoknyi Rinpoche, a gentle lama who has come from Nepal, explains that His Holiness is of the view that if Buddhism is to survive into the future, it must continue to change and adapt. In the present context, this means studying science and dialoguing with it.

So, is this a sort of a survival tactic, a Heimlich manoeuvre to remain relevant by a community struggling under the pressures of exile?

A sudden hush descends upon the gathering. A silence, and then . . . a belly laugh! His Holiness walks in, shaking hands all-round. He takes his seat, with translators Geshe Thupten Jinpa and B. Allan Wallace by his side. Under the ever watchful gaze of the golden Buddha, the conference begins.

In approximately ten sessions—morning and afternoon, spread over five days—the Mind and Life conference discusses 'the nature of matter, the nature of life'. Mornings are reserved for presentations by scientists about their respective fields, while in the afternoons the Dalai Lama presents related topics in Buddhism. The starting point is physicist Erwin Schrödinger's question which he asked in 1943: 'Can that which takes place inside a living organism be accounted for by physics and chemistry?' In many ways, this has been the perennial quest of science, to understand the mysterious nature of life and its equally enigmatic equation with matter.

In their presentations, Luigi Luisi and Ursula Goodenough talk about the origin of life on earth and subsequent biological evolution. From very simple molecules increasingly complex phenomena emerge. Molecules become cells that form organisms, which have consciousness. So, a quality emerges that the original elements didn't have—consciousness. How does it arise? What is its nature?

His Holiness listens to the presentations with a great

aliveness, and his occasional questions seem to arise from a deep understanding. As Matthieu Ricard, a veteran of several Mind and Life conferences, tells me over a doughnut during the mid-morning coffee break: 'I have noticed in this and previous meetings that the best brains in the world of science come here not really knowing what to expect. They are almost always pleasantly surprised to see the depth of Buddhist philosophical thought and how vast and complex it is. So a meaningful dialogue is built quickly, more than many of them expected in the first place. And His Holiness is always very eager to know and learn. The scientists discover that they can talk to him not as a beginner but even about the deepest issues, of ethics, of the natural world.'

Quickly comprehending the essence of what is being said, I find that the Dalai Lama is able to look at it both from the scientist's point of view as well as that of his tradition and form the gentle bridges that enable one to reach out to the other. As the dialogue develops, there are several occasions to remember that one is in the presence of a fiercely modern mind which never quite lets go of his Buddhist perspective, often coming to rest in the middle ground between the two.

A delicate balance is in play. In the Dalai Lama's person, the Gelug lineage-holder seems to exist in tandem with the adventurer who looks with wonderment at every new thing and thought. As he has often said: 'I would have been an engineer if I had not been a monk!'

The group breaks up for the meals and coffee breaks that punctuate the conference day, but the discussions find a way of continuing. During car rides, at the guest house, while walking through the bustling lanes of Macleodganj at dusk, the Tenth Mind and Life Conference constantly evolves through informal exchange. Many scientists request private audience after the day's proceedings end at 5 p.m. to discuss issues further with the Dalai Lama.

Daniel Goleman, author and psychologist, who is

attending his sixth successive Mind and Life conference, tells me that these tête-à-têtes often help break the ice. 'Most scientists who come are not Buddhist practitioners, nor is it a requirement at all,' he says, as the setting sun leaves its ochre imprint on the Dhauladhars. We are sitting in the veranda of the guest house where the scientists and observers are staying. 'Some are quite sceptical, understandably so,' he continues. 'There are those who have not been as willing as we would like them to be to engage in dialogue. Some might think that they have to come here and teach the Dalai Lama their point of view, whereas actually this is a collaboration of different perspectives.'

On the conference grapevine, however, I hear a marvellous story of a powerful spiritual transformation. During a private audience with His Holiness during Mind and Life 2000, psychologist Paul Ekman suddenly felt as though he were consumed with heat. He said later that something happened in that moment that transformed him emotionally. Before that, he would have episodes of angry outbursts at least once a week. These completely stopped after the meeting. The tremendous insights he achieved during his conversation with His Holiness moved him enough to rewrite a considerable part of a book on emotions that he had been working on for thirty years.

How open can we really be? How much a dialogue depends on this alone, I think, as I trudge uphill in the swiftly gathering darkness.

The discussions in the conference turn to consciousness, as they often do in most Mind and Life dialogues. The Buddhist position on consciousness and its evolution is that there is no evolution. In fact, there is no evolution not only for the physical matter, but also for consciousness, which is seen as part of an endless continuum. His Holiness explains:

> Science talks of a Big Bang, formation of matter, appearance of life, and so on. But is this the full story? Is it all we have? In Buddhism, there is no

concept of a beginning. It is impossible to accept nothing becoming something. So the Buddhist perspective is of beginninglessness, of infinite Big Bangs, and not only of matter but of consciousness. 'No beginning' might be difficult to imagine but it is more logical, if you really think about it.

As this is hotly debated, I suddenly wonder how difficult it is for Buddhism and science to really converse at the same level since they have in common neither paradigms nor basic assumptions. There are times in the conference when the dialogue seems to be going nowhere. When this happens, both the Dalai Lama and the scientists maintain their viewpoints, without one putting the other down. There is no sense of competitiveness, perhaps because of the privacy of the meetings that frees the scientists from their constituencies, and perhaps because there is an unsaid agreement not to hurt, to be gentle with one another. The Dalai Lama plays facilitator in those awkward moments, his laughter easing things along.

In times when tradition would dictate otherwise, the Dalai Lama has the rare quality to listen and be open to contrary views, modifying his own when sufficiently convinced. His is a dynamic mind that refuses to be dogmatic about anything, least of all his own tradition: very much in the spirit of the Buddha Shakyamuni, who instructed his followers never to accept anything, not even his own teachings, without adequate questioning and reasoning. Only those that stood the test were to be applied, the others discarded, not unlike the research method of the contemporary scientist.

The bridges become visible again, spanning the turbulence of debate, riveted together by the search for truth, for reality that is as much the Buddhist's as it is the scientist's.

The breakfast buzz before one morning session revolves around Steven Chu. 'He is of Chinese origin,' I am told, the remark laden with obvious political undertones. The Dalai

Lama mentions this fact, but in passing, not as a political statement but to emphasize the need for greater participation of Asian scientists in Mind and Life conferences. That Dr Chu is a Nobel Laureate is also significant and his presence is seen as being responsible for ratcheting up the conference's acceptability as a serious dialogue within the scientific community.

Dr Chu presents the physicist's view of matter and life. He starts with outlining the quantum theory: that atoms are made up of electrons, protons and neutrons, of which the last two can further be broken down into quarks. 'Electrons and quarks are the most elementary particles,' he says. 'According to our current understanding of them, they have no size and are described as "fields".' He goes on to describe how the very act of observing the elementary particles changes their behaviour.

The Dalai Lama is able to see subatomic particles and their behaviour as an illustration of the Buddhist perception of reality. Says he:

> According to Madhyamika philosophy, there are two levels of reality—conventional and ultimate. At the ultimate level, nothing exists, it is Sunyata [emptiness], while at the conventional level what we perceive through our senses exists. But here too, things cannot stand the test of deconstructive analysis and are proven not to exist intrinsically. Clinging to things obstructs the individual's ability to relate to the world openly, just as observing the quarks changes their behaviour. So Buddhism deconstructs the solidity of things we grasp at. In the end, everything we undergo has to do with human experience. And this is why ethics have to be part of research.

Ethics and science are further examined with Eric Lander's presentation about modern genetics and the choices it faced in the light of the human genome project. The human control of genetic material, literally the matter of life, is forcing the making of certain choices. What should be the framework within which these are made? For instance, after unravelling the genome it is known that a particular disease, say Alzheimer's, is caused by one particular gene. Would it then be right to replace it? And if it was known that an embryo had genetic abnormalities, would it be right to abort it?

Motivation is the key, says the Dalai Lama, aligning the karma of choosing with intentionality. A variety of factors must come into play: extent of suffering involved, motivation, the short- and long-term effects, and so on. Not once does he talk in absolutes and say something like, 'I am a Buddhist, so all violence is bad', but insists on examining every question on an individual basis. 'It is the motivation at the core of every choice that makes it ethical or unethical,' he says. This gives scientists a point to ponder, since, as Arthur Zajonc points out, their research is often supported by companies whose 'motives might not be pure but mixed'.

Altruistic motivation must stem from compassion, the Dalai Lama's touchstone for any choice-making that needs to be done. No discussion in which he participates can be complete without a mention of compassion, the active loving-kindness for all sentient beings that arises from the Buddhist understanding of interdependence of life. This is a natural corollary to the theory of co-dependent origination according to which everything exists because of everything else. There is no independent existence—we are all part of the gigantic web of life. Apart from its obvious implications for ecology and environmental awareness movements, here, in the dialogue with science, compassion becomes the tool with which to make good choices. It recurs during Ursula Goodenough's presentation about intelligence and awareness.

'Is there a biological evolutionary basis for compassion? Where does it come from?' His Holiness asks her.

'Well, part of it is a question of survival. We are social beings because of that. There are examples in nature of empathy. For instance, when two chimps are fighting, an older chimp takes them by their hands and effects a reconciliation.'

'Working together for survival is not really compassion,' says His Holiness. 'Honey bees don't know the Dharma, yet they work together beautifully. But these supposed examples among animals can only be of limited altruism, as they arise from necessity of some kind. Only human beings can develop infinite altruism because of their highly developed intelligence.'

One is reminded of the bodhisattva's vow to defer nirvana, enlightenment, until he can help all sentient beings into it and its centrality to the Dalai Lama's Mahayana Buddhism. Looking back at previous Mind and Life conferences, I find that then too His Holiness often turned the conversation towards compassion and its place in human life—the practical never sacrificed for the theoretical and the abstract. For instance, in Mind and Life III, the Dalai Lama argued in favour of universal ethics based as much on compassion as on rationalism and individualism, overturning objections by participants who sought to link compassion with religion, or deemed it an 'unreliable' human trait. 'If we look at history over all the millions of years that human beings have existed, I think there has been more construction than destruction. Ordinarily, when something destructive happens, we are shocked, because by nature we are compassionate,' he said.

However, His Holiness is mindful enough of both the harsh reality of worldly suffering as well as the possibility of transcending it to point out that compassion is not necessarily a stand-alone, nor is it a sugar-coated medicine that will magically cure the world's ills. It needs to be coupled with wisdom and right action. Giving the simple example of making the choice between alleviating a person's hunger by feeding him once or finding him a livelihood, His Holiness says: 'If you applied wisdom, you would think further: How can I alter circumstances so that this person doesn't suffer in future? Unless people make an effort to improve themselves, nothing can be done. It takes wisdom, not just sympathy, for people to move forward.'

I coax my mind back to the interesting if somewhat dense presentations related with physical sciences that comprise most of this conference. I cannot help but feel that the dialogue is somewhat richer, more relevant with the behavioural sciences, where you deal with the human condition and with ethics. This might be because there is a closer relation and much more commonality between the two. In the fields of psychology and neurosciences, for instance, Buddhist techniques are directly applicable and so the dialogue is rendered more relevant.

It is the last day. Everyone gathers for the final session. There is much satisfaction about the levels of synergy that were achieved during the conference. Luigi Luisi says good humouredly, 'Earlier, there was occasional flirting, but now it is a real marriage [between science and Buddhism].' But he has spoken too soon.

During his closing comments, Allan Wallace illustrates the need for provability of emergent phenomena by citing the example of reincarnation. 'Of all religions, the Buddhist view is the only one that can be tested, since it involves a coming back into the world, unlike the Christian or Islamic views where the soul goes away into a hell or heaven never to come back.'

'Not so fast!' immediately interjects Eric Lander. 'Reincarnation' seems to be the magic word that opens the doors of dissent in the conference. Barbed wires appear where there were bridges and the room stands sharply divided. All scientists voice their denial strongly, while Wallace and Ricard try and argue the case for reincarnation, pleading for a lowering of 'cultural resistance' to reincarnation.

'I remember a neuroscientist who once told me that he would believe in reincarnation if a yogi would direct his consciousness to a particular place and leave a letter giving the details of where he will reappear,' says Alan. 'And I told him that this has already happened seventeen times, in the lineage of the Karmapas of Tibet, who leave detailed instructions about where and when they will be reborn!'

All this while, as the debate rages on, the Dalai Lama sits watchfully, listening quietly. He neither assents nor dissents. Reminds me of the Buddha's response of silence to the hair-splitting among scholars of his day over the issue of the existence or otherwise of God. Not wishing to get involved in any debate that was purely in the realm of conjecture and not directly connected with the practicalities of the human condition, the Buddha would simply become silent. As does His Holiness now.

Later, when the acrimony has settled and everyone is friends once again, he turns to the scientists and says: 'I am an old man. If you promise there is no reincarnation, then I can relax. Else I will have to start the customary preparations for my next birth!' A belly laugh and a gentle bridge once again. No judgement, only quiet awareness.

As the day draws to a close, everyone lines up to receive the customary white silk *katas* (scarves) as blessings from the Dalai Lama.

The bus curves along the serpentine hill roads taking me further and further away from the pine-scented mountain air of Dharamsala. My editor comes into focus again, and I think that I did get the scoop, only rather than being about the Hollywood glamour, it is about synergy of the ancient and the modern, about gentle bridges and golden seeds, about frank dialogue and open minds. I marvel at the sustained effort that has kept the dialogue going for the past fifteen years. And this despite the odds, the prejudices against all religion and spirituality that modern science harbours. I remember Daniel Goleman saying: 'When we started fifteen years ago, it was a rare scientist who would be open to a dialogue with the Dalai Lama, or anyone from any religion. It seemed not the thing a scientist should do. The level of scientists involved in the dialogue has gone up over the years. The scientific community has also started taking the dialogue much more seriously.'

Gaps, fissures exist, but so do the golden seeds of shared wisdom, carefully sown and nurtured by His Holiness over the years. And the dialogue continues, with sincerity and commitment, mindfulness and sharing, over bridges past and present.

The Dalai Lama as a Political Strategist

Senthil Ram

'[A] young man who is much more intelligent and is better informed regarding world affairs than his advisors . . . [and who] is deeply conscious of the need for social and other reforms in Tibet,' commented Loy Henderson, US ambassador to India in 1951, about the young Dalai Lama. From Lhasa to Dharamsala, throughout the troubled times following the Chinese occupation of Tibet in 1950, the Dalai Lama's politics reflect the Buddhist notion of realistic understanding, in other words, pragmatism. In this essay I analyse the political philosophy of the Dalai Lama, who is revered by millions of Tibetans. While still at the height of his authority as the political and temporal leader of Tibetans, the appointment of Kalon Tripa—the Tibetan equivalent of prime minister—has at least theoretically placed him on the back seat of the democratic vehicle of the Tibetan Government in Exile that is manoeuvreing towards a politically free Tibet. Therefore, at this juncture, taking stock of the Dalai Lama's political contribution is crucial to comprehend the essence of Tibetan polity apart from visualizing its future course. Given the problematic in separating religion and politics, this essay proceeds with a modest objective of highlighting the Dalai Lama's political role without undermining the influence of Tibetan Buddhism.

Background to the Tibetan Question

The 20th century has been a turning point in the Tibetan conflict, widely known as the 'Tibetan question', that is rooted in the unfathomable depths of centuries-old historical specifics as claimed and constructed by both the main parties: the People's Republic of China (hereafter PRC) and the Tibetan Government in Exile (hereafter TGE). The British invasion and conquest of Tibet under Younghusband in 1903 and 1904 marked the beginning of the end of isolation of the kingdom of Tibet. The Qing dynasty in China, which had a representative in Tibet and treated Tibet as 'politically subordinate', perceived this as an act of imperial aggression against its hegemony and attempted to increase its control over Tibet. Long before this, the sudden overthrow of the Qing in 1911 resulted in the proclamation of independence by the Thirteenth Dalai Lama. From 1911 to 1951, Tibet functioned as a de facto independent nation and conducted all its local and international relations without interference from China or any other country. On the contrary, the Chinese claims on Tibet as part of its territory, the recognition of Chinese suzerainty over Tibet by the United States and the United Kingdom, and the simultaneous refusal of these countries to recognize Tibetan independence resulted in the invasion and occupation of Tibet by the Chinese communists in October 1950.

Whether the Chinese intention was to liberate then occupy, or occupy then liberate, Mao's 'peaceful' strategy routed the poorly equipped Tibetan army of approximately 10,000 troops and forced the Tibetans to negotiate and relinquish their political sovereignty for the first time in Tibetan history. In return, the seventeen-point agreement promised to preserve the political and religious status of the Dalai Lama and not to introduce political and economic reforms until the Tibetans sought them. But the Chinese religious and economic reforms in eastern Tibet and the consequent protests slowly spread to central Tibet and created fear and mistrust among the Tibetans. As a result both the Chinese and the Fourteenth Dalai Lama could not honour the agreement. Finally, the Dalai Lama fled Tibet in March 1959 after a major revolt in Lhasa, followed by an exodus of nearly 80,000 Tibetans to India. He subsequently established the TGE and denounced the seventeen-point agreement and claimed Tibet's right to self-determination and independence. PRC gave up the agreement as well, and established a people's government in Tibet. Here lies the root of the disagreement over the issue of Tibet's political status vis-à-vis China. Over the years the conflict has become complex by encompassing various issues ranging from cultural survival, identity, governance, human rights, environment and development.

From exile the Dalai Lama pursued various landmark reforms, on the one hand to democratize the Tibetan polity and on the other to nonviolently handle the conflict with China. Though his democratization initiatives are constrained by practical reasons like 'economic insecurity, traditional normatic decorum and lack of education', it is principally accepted as a method of polity due to his impartiality in dealing with various sects and regions and also the loyalty and affection of the Tibetan people. Without struggle or loss of human life, the Tibetan democracy that originated from the ideas of the leader and came down to the masses is fittingly called the Dalai Lama's democracy or 'one man's democracy'. Importantly, his single democratic vision has united the three diverse Tibetan regions of U-Tsang, Kham and Amdo, and has successfully controlled the conflict so as not to reach an overt level over the last fifty-odd years.

Though nonviolence as a political tool of Tibetan policy sounds very natural, given the nonviolence potential of Tibetans and Buddhist tradition and culture, it should not be over-emphasized. First, it is important not to overlook the violent potential of the Tibetan people. Like any other culture, Tibetans too, though less prominently after Buddhism became the state religion in the 13th century, held on to weapons, waged wars and maimed people for land and wealth. There were several violent exceptions in the 'non-coercive regime' of Tibet, particularly against foreign incursions, including the British invasion of 1904. Tibetans bravely fought the advancing Chinese People's Liberation Army in 1950. Often monks too joined in the battles against the Chinese to regain territories, and also fought with other monks belonging to different sects. The 1959 Lhasa uprising witnessed many monks carrying guns alongside the Khampas. Later, the Khampas used the guerillas tactics of 'hit and run' with the clandestine support of the CIA, on and off until 1974. Secondly, the political transformations to democracy in Buddhist countries have not taken place in a nonviolent manner. For instance, in Thailand, Burma and Sri Lanka, Buddhism was (and is) used to justify the violence of the nationalistic political activists. Therefore, at the political level, Tibetan nonviolence is more a choice than inherent. What I want to stress is the deliberate choice of nonviolence becoming a political means with roots in Tibetan Buddhism during adversities, and the chief role of the Dalai Lama in contributing to a philosophical base called *middlepath* with pragmatic political elements. Particularly from the 1980s, the policy of the Dalai Lama has formed the backbone of the TGE's middlepath policies and has become the driving force of the Tibetan nonviolent movement aimed at stopping the Chinese population transfer policy that threatens the ethnic composition of Tibet.

The Middlepath Policy of the Dalai Lama

The middlepath is not an end or a goal of the Tibetan movement. It is not a peace proposal either. According to Thubten Samphel, middlepath as conceived by the Dalai Lama is a method of conducting the struggle for freedom and justice for Tibetans. Thus, middlepath does not represent or reflect the overall belief system of the Tibetans. Rather, it is a nonviolent technique advocated by the Dalai Lama which can be crudely compared to the Gandhian satyagraha. The essence of the middlepath is avoiding extremes. On the one side there is the necessity of not submitting to communist Chinese policies that are against the survival of Tibetan culture and religion. The other side is the extreme measure of achieving a free Tibet at the cost of a vicious cycle of violence that might work against Tibetan culture and religion. Thus, taking a middlepath is a moderate position that could guarantee the common minimum interests of all concerned parties. For the Tibetans, it is the protection and preservation of Tibetan culture and religion; for the Chinese it is the security and territorial integrity of the motherland; and for the neighbours and third parties, peace at their borders and peaceful international relations. In essence, middlepath becomes a pragmatic tool of policy to peacefully handle the conflict with China to achieve the Tibetans' goal. The goal of the Tibetan struggle, according to the Dalai Lama, is to achieve a spiritual, religious and cultural freedom conducive for Tibetans to perform their universal responsibility of preserving, maintaining and disseminating the sublime cultural traditions of the unique inner sciences for the sake of the whole world in an autonomous political arrangement within the PRC.

Though the Tibetan conflict is defined by various researchers as 'intractable nationalistic conflict', 'ethnonationalistic conflict', 'nonviolent conflict', and an issue of 'identity and autonomy', for the Dalai Lama it doesn't have any political motivation. The problem between Tibet and China, in the Dalai Lama's words, 'is not the difference in ideology, social system or issues resulting from clashes between tradition and modernity. Neither is it an issue of human rights violations nor about a struggle based on ethnic claims. The root of the Tibetan issue lies in Tibet's long, separate history, its distinct and ancient culture, and its unique identity.' Under his leadership, the Tibetan movement has a spiritual motivation to protect the religious tradition of Tibet that is rooted in compassion and nonviolence and to facilitate Tibetans to perform their broader responsibilities to humanity. Although the Tibetans have at times highlighted on political platforms the issue as a political problem, the current prime minister of the TGE has reiterated the Dalai Lama's words:

> The people of Tibet have inherited for centuries a responsibility' to preserve, promote and disseminate a unique culture and spiritual tradition for the benefit of all sentient beings. To enable people of Tibet to fulfil these duties, we require a conducive social, political, economic and environmental situation. Human intelligence cannot awaken to its fullest extent in an atmosphere of oppression and terror. An uprooted cultural heritage cannot be properly preserved and promoted through replantation elsewhere. Therefore, political freedom is a means for Tibetans to fulfil their bounden duties.

For the Dalai Lama, although religious and political freedom are inseparable and one can't exist without the other, in the Tibetan nonviolent movement religious freedom becomes central and political freedom becomes subsidiary. He firmly believes that adequate political freedom will be the solution for the present predicament of the Tibetans. Therefore, the Dalai Lama had proposed an autonomy arrangement within the PRC as a solution. He said:

> I do not seek independence for Tibet. I hope that negotiations can begin and that they will provide for genuine autonomy for the Tibetan people and the preservation and promotion of their cultural, religious and linguistic integrity, as well as their socio-economic development. I sincerely believe that my 'Middle Way Approach' will contribute to stability and unity of the People's Republic of China and secure the right for the Tibetan people to live in freedom, peace and dignity (statement made on 10 March 1999).

The Dalai Lama has been advocating the political demand for genuine autonomy informally from 1979 when Deng Xioping invited the Tibetans to discuss anything but independence, and formally from 1989, when he formulated the Strasbourg Proposals as a realistic proposition to settle the issue through negotiations. The Dalai Lama's 'greater autonomy' proposal has been appreciated as reasonable by various parties to the conflict. Further, his proposal falls within the conflict management processes recommended by conflict resolution experts. Particularly when it comes to protracted social conflicts similar to Tibet that are about protecting unique cultural identities and seeking a suitable form of governance, Edward Azar has suggested different forms of political structures within existing national set-ups. Tedd Gurr and Deepa Khosla have gone one step further in suggesting autonomy as a realistic solution to the Tibet issue.

The most important constituent of a nonviolent movement is the precise and agreed goals. Setting goals is not an easy task, as history has shown—from the Gandhian movement which was caught between moderates and extremists in deciding the route of the movement, to the democratic opposition in Serbia which could not reach a decision in conducting the 2000 elections against Milosevic till few months before the date. Decision-making over the goals often divided the house during difficult times. Similarly in the Tibetan case, the non-establishment line of thinking is in favour of a politically independent and democratic Tibet. Their central argument is that the TGE has failed miserably to convince the unwilling Chinese for negotiations even by giving up independence for nearly two decades. Therefore, groups like the Tibet Youth Congress (TYC) are against relinquishing Tibetan sovereignty and demand complete independence for the whole of ethnic Tibet, encompassing the three traditional provinces of U-Tsang, Kham and Amdo. The root of this divisive stand lies more in the process of decision-making than in positions.

Nonetheless, the TGE's stance, which is open for negotiation, on the demand for autonomy sounds, at least theoretically, practical as it satisfies the basic needs of both Tibetans and Chinese without separation. For the Tibetans it guarantees basic human rights and the right to protect their unique cultural traditions. For the Chinese it respects territorial integrity and contributes to a stable and strong motherland. Thus, by addressing the national concerns of Tibetans and Chinese, this goal seems politically achievable.

Essentials of Middlepath

For Gandhian satyagraha the basic precepts are: truth, nonviolence (ahimsa) and self-suffering. For the Dalai Lama, the basic precepts of middlepath are nonviolence and dialogue. He has said:

> . . . to live with less conflicts and bloodshed and in order to achieve this, it is important to follow nonviolence and to have dialogue . . . if our struggle through nonviolence with a compassionate feeling succeeds we will be creating a new way to solve problems and conflicts and thereby serve the interests of entire humanity.

As is evident from his words, the Dalai Lama believes that nonviolence and dialogue can be the only basis for peaceful conflict resolution. Over the years, nonviolence and dialogue have occupied a central place in his middlepath policy. Dialogue, without doubt, points to negotiations with the Chinese. Therefore he conceived peace initiatives like the Five-point Peace Plan and Strasbourg Proposals to be the flexible basis for negotiations with the Chinese. Though the Dalai Lama has not explicitly said what he means as nonviolence in the context of the middlepath, it essentially points to nonviolent action.

Dialogue is a central component of Tibetan Buddhism and, in turn, middlepath. In the context of politics, he strongly advocates · dialogue as a practical approach to solving the Tibet issue. He emphasizes dialogue at two levels: one, between the TGE and the PRC and two, between the Tibetans and the Chinese people. He has said:

> After a half a century of 'liberation' the Tibetan issue is still very much alive and remains yet to be resolved. Obviously this situation is of no benefit to anyone, either to Tibet or to China. To continue along this path does nothing to alleviate the suffering of the Tibetan people, nor does it bring stability and unity to China or help in enhancing China's international image and standing. The only sensible and responsible way to address this problem is dialogue. There is no realistic alternative to it (statement made on 10 March 1998).

He has often stressed the importance of dialogue in his speeches and statements. According to him, the distrust between the Chinese and Tibetans can be overcome 'only through face-to-face meetings and sincere dialogues'. For his part, he has said, 'I remain committed to the process of dialogue as the means to resolve the Tibetan problem. I do not seek independence for Tibet. I hope that negotiations can begin and that they will provide for genuine autonomy for the Tibetan people and the preservation and promotion of their cultural, religious and linguistic integrity, as well as their socio-economic development.' In his 10 March 1996 statement, the Dalai Lama also encouraged dialogue between Tibetans and Chinese so as to promote 'a better understanding of our mutual concerns and interests'. Thus, the Dalai Lama firmly believes that a lasting solution to the Tibet issue can be found through people-to-people contact between the Tibetans and Chinese.

The Dalai Lama, the chief architect of Tibetan nonviolent politics, is a staunch follower of Mahatma Gandhi. His endorsement of the Universal Declaration of Nonviolence which states that 'all forms of violence, especially war, are totally unacceptable as a means to settle disputes between and among nations, groups and persons' made him radical among other religious and political leaders. He strongly believes that nonviolent resistance is for the strong-willed and the principled who refuse to rely on the warped illogic of stopping the enemy's bad violence with one's good violence. The Dalai Lama states that it is shortsighted to believe that a lasting solution can be found through the use of force. He always expresses his firm conviction in following a nonviolent path. According to him, force and confrontation can only bring temporary gains. Therefore the Dalai Lama encourages nonviolent resistance inside Tibet. Though he has acknowledged that 'Tibetan people expressing their deep sorrow through nonviolence is the correct way', he does not put in plain words the dynamics or the workings of Tibetan nonviolent resistance. This has made the holistic understanding of the ongoing Tibetan nonviolent movement hard to grasp, unlike the Gandhian or Kingian movements. Therefore, I am focusing here on the less-known pragmatic elements of Tibetan nonviolence than on the well-known Buddhist and Gandhian influences.

First, for the Dalai Lama, nonviolence is the most effective and appropriate method to resolve conflicts. He firmly believes in nonviolence as a political technique. He points out that, 'events such as the end of dictatorial regimes of Marcos in the Philippines and Pinochet in Chile, as well as the changes in Moscow and other countries, show quite clearly that the upheavals in the heart of the population were . . . the result of nonviolent action.' Further, he understands the importance of nonviolence for a friendly neighbourhood. Since China and Tibet are neighbours—past, present and future—he argues that they must have a peaceful and harmonious relationship. Therefore it is essential that the problems dividing them should be resolved in a nonviolent way. Using violence in such situations leaves people with a feeling of contempt and enmity for generations and thereby results in further violence. He gives the examples of protracted conflicts like Israel and Palestine, and Bosnia where violence was used to curtail violence. He also gives the examples of the Philippines, Chile and the erstwhile Soviet Union where democracy has been established through nonviolent means.

Secondly, nonviolence is used in politics due to the understanding that the means of the struggle should not contradict its social goals or ends. Violence cannot be used to create a political system based on self-government and grassroots participation and bring about peace. Only through nonviolent methods can one attain nonviolent results. It is also important to note the connections between nonviolence and democracy as established by the Dalai Lama. Another crucial element of the pragmatic nonviolent approach is the recognition that both parties have needs that have to be resolved. Therefore, the Tibetans are dedicated to pursuing problem-solving negotiations as exemplified by such peace initiatives like the Five-point Peace Plan to achieve a solution equally beneficial to both the Tibetans and Chinese.

Thirdly, in the Tibetan situation violence is not considered a realistic option against the Chinese and is seen as counter-productive to the Tibetans' objective. Even though non-governmental organizations like the TYC advocate 'violent means of struggle', the Dalai Lama strongly believes that nonviolence is the most effective means to deal with the Chinese under the present circumstances. He also feels that a violent struggle against militarily powerful China is an impossible task. The Dalai Lama has said, 'I ask the hotheads, let them visualize this. If we follow violent methods, a few hundred guns will not be effective. At least we need several thousand, at least a few thousand . . . around 100,000. Now from where will we get these weapons? Is there some country willing to supply us with them?' Elsewhere, the Dalai Lama has reiterated that no one will give weapons to the Tibetans, and even if a country were to do so, transferring them to Tibet would not be easy. 'If half a million Tibetans took up arms against China, it would be suicidal.' He believes that an armed uprising would be the best excuse for China to obliterate the Tibetans. Further, the dwindling Tibetan population definitely discourages the violent option and promotes nonviolence, as the latter would save lives.

Lastly, the Tibetan nonviolent position mobilizes support from many quarters, including the Chinese people. The Dalai Lama has said, 'because of our nonviolent attitude, Chinese people both within China and abroad have already expressed sympathy and concern for our cause and as a result are openly demonstrating their support for Tibet's struggle for independence.' He firmly believes that through nonviolence they can arrive at a solution that is mutually beneficial to the Chinese and Tibetans. According to the Dalai Lama, the tremendous international support Tibetans now enjoy is due to the nonviolent character of the movement. The Dalai Lama has often acknowledged the media's sympathy towards the nonviolent movement and its importance to Tibet's cause. He has said that media interest on Tibet has attracted 'people the world over . . . [to] the Tibetan cause.' Therefore the Dalai Lama attaches 'great importance to this interest . . . [and] the fact that our cause will gain recognition in this way will, I believe, inspire the Chinese government to show greater restraint in its dealings with the Tibetan people, and to take their needs into account.' Thus, the Tibetan nonviolent struggle has indispensable pragmatic elements where nonviolence is realistically used as only one of several possible methods with which to respond to the conflict situation with China for a mutually beneficial settlement.

The Strategy of the Tibetan Nonviolent Struggle

When the Dalai Lama visited India in 1956, he met many Gandhians and discussed the Tibetan situation. They advised the Dalai Lama to return to Tibet and carry on the freedom struggle. The Dalai Lama did exactly that. But there were no results. So, finally in 1959, when there were no alternatives, he went into exile. From exile, he tried to solve the issue through negotiation by initiating direct contacts with Beijing. The lack of progress in direct initiatives and the serious threat to Tibetan culture in the form of Chinese population transfer policies compelled him to take the Tibetan nonviolent movement to a different level without wavering from his chosen path of nonviolence and dialogue: internationalizing the Tibetan issue in the hope that it would pressure China to come to the negotiating table. In his second Tibet Support Group conference address in Germany in June 1996, the Dalai Lama clearly explained that the deadlock in the Sino-Tibetan negotiations had compelled him to internationalize the Tibet issue. He said:

> Because of this lack of response from the Chinese side, I was compelled to publicly announce my Five-point Peace Plan for Tibet. This was the result of lack of response from the Chinese side and thus there was no other alternative except to seek support from the international community.

Here the Dalai Lama emphasized the lack of response from the Chinese side for negotiation and lack of alternatives to deal with China as important reasons for internationalizing the Tibet issue. Since his immediate objective then was a dialogue with China to preserve the Tibetan culture from Chinese policies, the Dalai Lama firmly believes that international moral, political and economic pressure is the only feasible option the Tibetans are left with to find a timely solution. Therefore, he has often publicly solicited for 'immediate international pressure [to] be exerted upon the Chinese government, with an aim to beginning significant negotiations as soon as possible.'

Thus, with nonviolent action and dialogue as central components, the middlepath policy attempts to mobilize international pressure so as to compel China to agree to a negotiated political settlement over Tibet. Pressure has been exerted on China through legislative effort, that is, taking

Tibet into governmental fora, particularly legislative branches, and effecting changes in government policies worldwide. This has become the core strategy of internationalization. This strategy has evolved since 1987 by encompassing four dimensions: nonviolent resistance inside Tibet, dialogue with PRC, Constructive Programme in Exile to protect Tibetan culture and religion, and internationalization and media mobilization on the Tibet issue. While nonviolent resistance inside Tibet conveys the Tibetan people's genuine grievances to the PRC and the outside world, the dialogue through peace initiatives has formed the basis for negotiations with Beijing. The Constructive Programme of the TGE is aimed at protecting and promoting Tibetan religion and culture and actualizing a democratic free Tibet in exile. Lastly, the internationalization of the Tibet issue mobilizes international public, political and media support to put pressure on China for a peaceful resolution.

While scholars belonging to the realist or positivist school condemn the internationalization strategy, the second group of scholars who are in line with political idealism and pluralism appreciate the internationalization of the Tibet issue. Though both groups agree that Tibet is a strategic concern for China and the cultural survival of Tibetans is in peril, they offer quite different solutions. The realists recommend active third-party governmental (particularly US) involvement in the reconciliation and the return of the Dalai Lama to protect the lives of Tibetans without making any structural changes to the Tibetan political position vis-à-vis China. Barring international economic and social boycott as a means to pressure China into negotiation, the idealists propose an active Tibetan nonviolent engagement with China to save the Tibetan people and culture from destruction. However, both groups, in their obvious quest to handle the conflict in a way that can meet both parties' needs, have missed the crucial element in resolving asymmetric conflicts, that is, balancing the power relationship between the TGE and PRC for long-term, sustainable peace. Their ideas highlight the efficacy of nonviolent action and third-party involvement as crucial factors to alter the power balance and impact a peaceful change in the Sino-Tibetan socio-political relationship. Theoretically, these two activities contribute a great deal towards managing any asymmetric conflict: nonviolent action will raise the conflict to overt levels and third-party support can help to balance the power relationship of parties. Fittingly, these two elements form the core of the Dalai Lama's middlepath policy. Therefore, middlepath is more than a religious or moral principle. It is political and practical as well.

Though this four-dimensional strategy has not brought the PRC to the negotiating table, when considering the political success of garnering international support and solidarity and the costs involved, it can be said that this nonviolent political strategy has achieved as much as some of the other contemporary violent conflicts in Asia. It has been particularly successful in forestalling the conflict taking a violent turn within Tibet. Undoubtedly, violence in Tibet will kick-start a spiral of violence at immense human and material costs to all the parties when one considers the enduring resistance in Tibet and other ethnic minority nationalities within the PRC. Violence in Tibet in the globalized context will also affect the present status quo of the conflict and provoke intervention at the regional level, particularly from India where nearly 80,000 Tibetan refugees live, and at the international level, mainly from the United States, where the Tibetan lobby is very active.

Nonetheless, the asymmetric conflict situation which is knotted in the unbalanced social and political relationship between the powerful PRC and the powerless TGE poses tremendous challenges to conflict resolution. Since the structure helps the dominant and powerful to win and the minority or the powerless to lose, the conflict can be resolved only by changing the structure and raising the conflict to manifest level. Nonviolent actions are the only effective method to do this, and although Tibetan nonviolent action has so far not been successful in resolving the existing latent violence in Tibet and has kept the conflict at the latent level, with minor exceptions like the protests of 1959, 1987 and 1989, it is the only key to increasing the conflict to manifest level, bringing in structural changes, preventing future violence in Tibet, and leading the Tibetan conflict towards a peaceful settlement.

Conclusion

As demonstrated, the purpose of this essay is not to challenge or deconstruct the Dalai Lama who shares the Gandhian view on the inseparable nature of religion and politics. Rather, it is a humble attempt to highlight the realistic aspects of his politics that are driven by Buddhist spiritual values. This critical analysis of the Dalai Lama's middlepath policy is of importance to the ongoing nonviolent movement and evolving democratic politics. On the other hand, the Tibetan case offers a new, effective and nonviolent means of conflict resolution that can be tailored to meet similar or different situations against dictatorship or authoritarian governments. Thus, following the traditions set by peace philosophers like Tolstoy, Gandhi and King, the Dalai Lama, too, has challenged Machiavellian notions of violence and voiced and worked for improving the peaceful conditions of the world. Though he is utopian in his desire to break conventions for idealized politics, he is also pragmatic since he has actualized his vision in 'this world' by peacefully handling the conflict with China and democratizing the Tibetan polity. Though his policies have a penchant for optimism, he draws inspiration from hope, not traumas, and develops alternatives, not assumptions. His handling of the Tibetan issue and revolutionizing of Tibetan politics clearly reflects his motivation to improve the system as a whole, where Tibetans, Chinese and their neighbours benefit together. Hence his political philosophy, particularly the middlepath policy, rooted in Buddhism, Gandhian satyagraha and realistic understanding of international politics becomes sound material for peace research.

A Monarch or a Socialist?

Ela Gandhi

Since his exile, His Holiness has been trying to negotiate a peaceful settlement with China. He continues to struggle for his country and his people on the Gandhian path of nonviolent resistance, bearing all suffering while continuing to love and pray for his adversaries that some day they may see light. India, a leading member of the non-aligned movement, gave asylum to His Holiness. But in addition it also gave a place to the thousands of Tibetan exiles who have now built a Tibetan village in exile at Dharmasala. The western bloc has in many ways supported the struggle for freedom of the Tibetan people. How much of the support is for the Tibetan cause and how much of it is against the last post of the communist world is a moot point. His Holiness is as yet breaking ground in getting the support of the Third World. The introduction of the debate on the Tibet issue has been out-voted at the United Nations.

This lack of support from the emerging nations of the world raises the issue of the dilemma that has been created by the historic roots of systems of monarchical governance which have been overthrown through popular revolutions in many parts of the world. Did Tibet also have a monarchical rule by a person who is believed to be the reincarnation of the Buddha?

The idea of reincarnation of the Buddha is not acceptable to modern scientists, to populist culture, to non-believers and to those who do not believe in reincarnation. Such people would, therefore, feel that this is just another cult, another exploitative regime, and would have no sympathy with the people.

By no means are the opponents of the Dalai Lama a homogeneous group. By the same token, by no means are those who support the struggle of the Tibetans a homogeneous group. The supporters of the Tibetan cause range from Chinese scholars to ordinary Chinese workers, from people belonging to the leftist movements in various countries to those belonging to the ultra-right. Within this, diverse groups lay various motivations for supporting this struggle, as also for not supporting it.

While there is a vast body of people who are deeply concerned about the blatant human rights abuses and feel strongly about the repression suffered by the people of Tibet, there are also those who are driven by their own motives. These could range from preserving capitalism to preserving some narrow self-interest to a much wider interest in maintaining a hold over a strategic position. The globalization and anti-globalization movements have revealed to us one truth: that such self-interests have very strong links and although driven by a small group they often wield power in many ways.

We live in a modern world. A world that has become a neighbourhood. Yet, it is a world divided by diversities of many kinds—religious differences, ideological differences, wealth and poverty, black and white and a million shades in between, rural and urban, modern and traditional, the list can go on. But instead of enriching the world with the rich mosaic of this diversity, man is killing man, nations are killing nations, and in the midst of all this there are millions who desire peace. They are desperately seeking peace. His Holiness is one among the leaders who are trying desperately to alter the course mankind has set for itself. Will he succeed?

Tracing the history of China one sees the oppressive,

monastic feudal social order in China replaced by a socialist movement. The merits and demerits of this movement are not the subject of this book, and so suffice it to say that a popular movement deposed the wealthy barons of China.

The story is that the peasants in China rose up under the leadership of successive socialist leaders and eventually deposed the Chinese empire under the leadership of Mao Zedong. The empire was replaced by the people's republic. A new social order was established. The story goes on to maintain that for the first time the poverty-stricken and oppressed peasants were able to live with self-respect. On the whole, therefore, the story is that the stark poverty that confronted millions of Chinese had come to an end.

Yet history records that time and again those who have faced repression of the most terrible kind have little compunction in repressing other people. How this happens is difficult to fathom. But there are millions of examples throughout the ages of people who continue to repress and forget their own oppression at the hands of others. So the Chinese did not hesitate to conquer Tibet. Ostensibly they were bringing a better life to the Tibetan people who, they argue, were living under a feudal system. They were bringing in a new socialist, communist order to replace the feudal system that the people of Tibet were living under. In reality, they wanted to occupy Tibet. His Holiness recognizes this but has never condemned the Chinese. Therein lies his magnanimity and humility.

When one begins to read the many books written on him, the story of his life and the story of his people, a picture emerges of a visionary, a compassionate spirit and a totally liberated soul. He said in *Essential Teachings*, for instance, 'Look around us at this world that we call "civilized" and that for more than 2000 years has searched to obtain happiness and avoid suffering by false means, trickery, corruption, hate, abuse of power, and exploitation of others.'

His Holiness is a simple, smiling monk who is not

affected by the inhumanity of the Chinese aggression. One sees the deep pain and hurt when he talks about the destruction of his beloved land, the deaths of almost a million of his people, and continued imprisonment and torture of hundreds of Tibetans. His concern, nevertheless, is not based on narrow self-interest or just the interests of his people; for him the world and the universe are issues of concern. The pollution of the pure mountain water, the degradation of the environment through the clearing of indigenous forests, the flattening of mountains by dynamite, and the killing, the torture and incarceration, all these have an effect not only on him and his people, he constantly reminds us, but also on the world's ecosystem. Although his ever-smiling face and jovial nature may hide the pain and deep hurt of this continued destruction, there are times when one can see in the deep-set lines of his face his cry for help, his cry to the world to heed the warnings of nature.

For some he is but a monk, to others he is the head of a feudal society, and for many he is a unique personality who could indeed be a reincarnation of the Buddha, although he himself dismisses this possibility. In this essay I want to dispel the myth of him as a feudal lord. He has said in *Essential Teachings*, 'If in India, Africa and other countries misery and famine rule, it is not because natural resources are lacking, nor that the means of bringing about lasting well-being are flawed. It is because each person has looked only for his own profit without fear of oppressing others for selfish goals . . .'

His Holiness, with the kind of power he wields, chose to use his power to begin a process of reform of his order. In 1963 he shed his power in favour of democracy. One person, one vote was introduced. A democratic parliament was elected in exile. The Tibetan people at his instigation drafted a constitution which reflects democratic principles. He declared that once free, an interim government would be set up with the specific purpose of putting in place a constitutional assembly to draft a new constitution. He has further declared that after accomplishing this task he will retire and live as an ordinary monk, transferring all his power to the newly-elected government.

His Five-point Peace Plan is as follows:

1. Transformation of the whole of Tibet into a zone of peace.
2. Abandonment of China's population transfer policy which threatens the very existence of the Tibetan people.
3. Respect for the Tibetan people's fundamental human rights and democratic freedoms.
4. Restoration of Tibet's natural environment and the abandonment of China's use of Tibet for the production of nuclear weapons and dumping of nuclear waste.
5. Commencement of earnest negotiations on the future status of Tibet and of relations between the Tibetan and Chinese people.

He has now added to this the stoppage of the excavations for oil and mineral wealth.

This plan reflects the reasonable nature of his offer to bring an end to this long and brutal aggression of his people. He is in fact extending a hand of friendship to the Chinese whom he refers to as his brothers and sisters. He recognizes that they share a common religion, a common history and are neighbours dependent on each other. Many Chinese deeply admire him and feel great reverence towards His Holiness. Despite the repression suffered by his people he believes that the two nations can live in peace as neighbours.

His Holiness in his writings advocates compassion, sharing simplicity, living close to the earth, conserving the environment and leading a wholesome life. While retaining his traditional beliefs, he has a deep understanding of the modern age. Like Mahatma Gandhi, His Holiness advocates adhering to good traditional values and discarding those customs and traditions which are oppressive and inhibit development.

In his book *The Art of Happiness*, His Holiness says of human beings,

> Generally speaking, you can have two different types of individuals. On the one hand, you have a wealthy successful person, surrounded by relatives and so on. If that person's source of dignity and sense of worth is only material, then so long as his fortune remains, maybe that person can sustain a sense of security. But the moment the fortune wanes, the person will suffer because there is no other refuge. On the other hand, you can have another person enjoying similar economic status and financial success, but at the same time that person is warm and affectionate and has a feeling of compassion. Because that person has another source of worth, another source that gives him or her a sense of dignity, another anchor, there is less chance of that person becoming depressed if his or her fortune happens to disappear. Through this type of reasoning you can see the very practical value of human warmth and affection in developing an inner sense of worth.

His Holiness clearly sees modern materialism as a source of destruction. He has said that real happiness comes from within, from satisfaction and reconciliation with oneself, and not by acquiring material objects. Clearly he expounds socialist and not feudal ideals, and it must be remembered that despite belonging to a traditional society, His Holiness has spoken about the rights of women, something that the Tibetan constitution upholds.

Moves are being made to involve women at all levels of society and to accord them equal status. Tibetan women play a prominent role in international women's organizations and locally within Tibetan society. They are also taking leadership positions in the liberation movement and many have been imprisoned for their participation in the struggle. Yet, in trying to come to terms with why the Chinese have occupied Tibet, why some people support the struggle of the Tibetans and others do not, and what is it that draws people to His Holiness even as people were drawn to Mahatma Gandhi, one needs to develop a deeper understanding of Buddhism. His Holiness is an excellent scholar of Buddhist philosophy and in his works he explains in simple terms the very essence of it. It is when we begin to understand this philosophy that we get a glimpse into a mind that is so sharp and yet full of compassion, that is so concerned about the future and yet content in the present, that is so active and yet still. Such a being can never fit the cloak of a monarch. His ideas are socialist in nature and his life and work will live on to inspire generations to come.

The Dalai Lama and India

Dalip Mehta

For the past forty-four years India has had the good fortune of the Dalai Lama's presence on its soil. India has long enjoyed renown as a land where great spiritual leaders flourished; a land where persecuted people found refuge and eventually made their home, adding one more piece to the rich mosaic that is India's pluralistic, multicultural society. The arrival of the Dalai Lama in March 1959 followed by thousands of his people provided welcome proof that these cherished traditions were still alive.

In his own country, the Dalai Lama was revered as a god–king, but little known outside it. During his long years of exile in India, he has grown into one of the world's most loved and respected leaders. Equally remarkably, he has succeeded in keeping alive the aspirations and hopes of the Tibetan people and in preserving Tibet's unique culture. He has achieved the delicate task of adhering to his principles and at the same time not jeopardizing the interests of his adopted homeland. And he has ensured that the Tibetan diaspora, not just in India, but elsewhere in the world, has developed and progressed in the modern world, even while remaining rooted in their traditions. In his quest for 'freedom in exile' in India, the Dalai Lama has perhaps achieved far more than he would have if destiny had not forced him to flee Tibet.

China's invasion and occupation of Tibet in 1950, and its brutal suppression of the Tibetan national uprising in Lhasa in 1959 finally persuaded the Dalai Lama to seek political asylum in India. In the turbulent years that followed, the Chinese systematically destroyed Tibet's culture and civilization in the hope that it would become just another indistinguishable region of the People's Republic, losing its distinct and separate identity.

Differing views exist on the legal status of Tibet, but it has been convincingly argued, by the Dalai Lama among others, that throughout its history Tibet has remained an independent country and that it was never a part of any other, though like many it had been subjected to invasions and had in turn occupied territories that belonged to other countries. It therefore came as a bitter disappointment to the Tibetans when in 1954 India signed an agreement with China which recognized Tibet as a part of China. In so doing India, in a sense, changed the political and historical identity of Tibet. By describing Tibet in an official agreement as the 'Tibet region of China', Chinese sovereignty over Tibet was given legitimacy.

Nevertheless, the Dalai Lama's request for asylum was immediately granted by Nehru's government which received him with honour when he arrived at the end of March 1959, and it is in India that he has continued to live ever since, inspiring his people, both inside Tibet and outside, and keeping their spirit of freedom alive. Nehru's decision was indeed a courageous one, for he fully realized that the already difficult relations with China would be further complicated at a time when he believed that friendship between India and China was essential for peace in Asia. While granting asylum to the Dalai Lama was not the sole reason for the souring relations between the two countries, it has continued to be a source of friction over the years and something for which the Chinese have never forgiven India.

The Dalai Lama left his homeland with the greatest reluctance and much debate among his advisors, for it was not an easy decision to leave behind his six million compatriots who regarded him as their god and king, and in their difficult times their saviour and only hope. However, it was the Dalai Lama's belief that he could do more for his people and country from the freedom that he would enjoy in India than the suffocating constraints placed on him by the Chinese in Lhasa that finally persuaded him to leave his country.

At the early age of twenty-four the Dalai Lama found himself far removed from the cloistered, mediaeval world he left behind in Tibet, and thrust into the hurly-burly of the complex relations between nations at the highest levels, where the players were towering personalities like Nehru, Mao Zedong, Chou En-lai among others. In this world the inexperienced Dalai Lama sought to achieve his twin goals of independence for Tibet, and the preservation and continuance of his country's religious and cultural traditions. He realized early in his political career that violence and force could never defeat the might of the Chinese. He learned from Mahatma Gandhi, whom he greatly admires, that nonviolence is the only way to conduct politics and far from being a passive response, it is one of great moral courage and far more effective than the use of force.

Soon after arriving in India the Dalai Lama established his Government in Exile, and though never formally recognized by the Indian government, it has throughout been allowed to function unimpeded. As the Dalai Lama himself has said, the Indian government often vehemently opposed his point of view but never did anything to prevent him from holding it, much less from expressing it. There was no interference from Delhi over how he and the Tibetans should conduct their lives. As Nehru told him, India was a free country so he had 'complete freedom to follow his own conscience'. Today the Dalai Lama's government, known as the Central Tibetan Administration, functions for all purposes as a body that guides the destiny of the over-100,000 Tibetan diaspora scattered in a dozen countries.

Over the years the Dalai Lama has interacted with every prime minister of independent India. Relations with some have been close, while with others formal and correct. Yet, without exception, they have all held him in high regard. Among Indian political figures the Dalai Lama recalls with special warmth his association with Rajagopalachari, Rajendra Prasad, Jaya Prakash Narayan and Acharya Kripalani. He regarded Lal Bahadur Shastri as an outstanding leader who left a powerful impression on him. His relations with Nehru, often complicated by differing political compulsions, sometimes led to frustration and disappointment, but did not detract from his admiration of a man of great humanity, liberalism and magnanimity. He also enjoyed a close personal rapport with Indira Gandhi who often confided in him, even regarding matters of state.

In all his dealings with the Indian leadership the Dalai Lama has always kept India's sensitivities and national interests in mind, even while pursuing his own objectives, and has unfailingly expressed his immense appreciation for the warmth and hospitality he has received from the Indian people and government. It was in his early interactions with Nehru that the Dalai Lama had his first experience of the harsh world of realpolitik, where moral and ethical considerations often had to bend to the more pragmatic imperatives such as national security. While he greatly appreciated Nehru's humanism and his genuine concern for the welfare of the Tibetan people, the Dalai Lama realized that for Nehru relations with China had higher priority. Yet the Dalai Lama has never forgotten that it was Nehru who took the crucial and, in a sense, life-saving decision to grant him asylum in India, fully sensitive to its consequences, and to rehabilitate over 80,000 Tibetan refugees who crossed into India.

Over the years the Dalai Lama has made various overtures to the Chinese leadership in the hope of securing his country's legitimate interests within parameters he thinks are realistic and acceptable to the Chinese. For example, in his address to the United States Congress in September 1987, he outlined his Five-point Peace Plan which he continues to believe could be the basis for a permanent solution to the Tibetan question. It calls for making Tibet a zone of peace and nonviolence, the abandonment of population transfers that are changing the demographic character of Tibet, respect for the Tibetan people's fundamental human rights and democratic freedoms, the protection of Tibet's environment, putting a stop to using Tibet for all nuclear activities and, finally, the commencement of earnest negotiations on the future status of Tibet and the relations between the Tibetan and Chinese peoples. All reasonable suggestions, but to which the Chinese have reacted by accusing the Dalai Lama of attempting to split the country.

Chinese intransigence led to a complete breakdown of contacts for a decade, until the visit in September 2002 of the Dalai Lama's envoys to Beijing. From the Tibetan point of view the visit served to explain to the Chinese leadership what has since come to be known as the Dalai Lama's Middle Way Approach, which in essence calls for Tibetan self-rule within the People's Republic of China. The Dalai Lama has drawn a distinction between freedom and independence for, with his characteristic pragmatism, he realizes that complete independence is no longer feasible. According to the Middle Way Approach, China would control Tibet's foreign and defence policies while internal administration, culture, religious affairs and the economy would be left to the Tibetans. In other words, the Dalai Lama no longer calls for the independence and separation of Tibet from China, but his Middle Way Approach does provide for genuine autonomy for the entire Tibetan region and its six million people, to enable them to preserve their distinctive culture, religion and way of life.

In his annual 10 March statement, the Dalai Lama has spoken of the necessity for dialogue as the 'only sensible, intelligent and human way to resolve differences' and 'to put behind decades of bitterness, distrust and resentment and to form a new relationship based on equality, friendship and mutual benefit.' As he has pointed out, 'looking around the world we cannot fail to notice how unattended conflicts with ethnic roots can erupt in ways that make them extremely difficult to solve.' He hopes that China's new leadership will take a ·more humane and accommodating view of Tibet's aspirations as embodied in the Middle Way Approach. China, however, remains inscrutable. There are those who believe that China is merely biding its time and willing to wait till the present Dalai Lama passes away so that they can then install a successor of their choice who will do their bidding.

The Dalai Lama has been extraordinarily successful in arousing the conscience of the world to the plight of his people and country. The Tibetan question is very much on the world's agenda though governments still baulk at outright support. Non-governmental organizations espousing Tibet's cause have mushroomed, such as the International Campaign for Tibet, which seeks to influence various governments' policies to support the 'legitimate aspirations of the Tibetan people'. The Dalai Lama's quiet, sustained effort, without polemics or provocation, has won the Tibetans friends and supporters around the world. His indefatigable energy has taken him to countries across the globe, patiently explaining, seeking understanding and support for his cause, without the slightest trace of rancour or recrimination. His peaceful and nonviolent approach in trying to resolve even this most intractable problem won him the Nobel Prize for Peace in 1989, which also symbolized international recognition of all the profound spiritual values he stands for. The citation says, 'the Dalai Lama has developed his philosophy of peace from a great reverence of all things living and upon the concept of universal responsibility, embracing all mankind as well as nature.'

The Dalai Lama has often said that his ideas about universal responsibility have evolved from ancient Indian traditions, and that as a Buddhist monk his entire training has its roots in the culture of India. For him India is in many ways his spiritual home. As he points out, Buddhism went to Tibet from India along with many other important cultural influences. He has even gone to the extent of saying that in his opinion India had a better claim to Tibet than China, 'whose influence at best was only slight'. The Dalai Lama has likened the relationship between India and Tibet to that between a teacher and a pupil.

Fundamental to the Dalai Lama's political philosophy is the belief that love, compassion and forgiveness can lead to peaceful change, and that a nonviolent revolution which may seem unrealistic to some is indeed possible. He is aware that many Tibetans feel that the time has come to resort to more militant ways to deal with the Chinese. The Dalai Lama has, however, been steadfast in his belief in ahimsa, and has said that if the movement for freedom turns violent he would abdicate.

Exile in India has provided the Dalai Lama the opportunity to overhaul and modernize various archaic Tibetan practices and institutions, in a manner both pragmatic and far-sighted. The rigours of protocol surrounding his person have been reduced and simplified, making him more accessible to his people. The age-old theocracy has been transformed into a functioning democracy with, most remarkably, the Dalai Lama voluntarily abdicating his temporal powers to institutions that now determine the destiny of the Tibetan people, to the extent that the elected assembly, by a two-thirds majority vote, can remove the Dalai Lama from office. This indeed was revolutionary and unprecedented at the time of its enactment in the early 1960s. The Dalai Lama has since stated that when Tibet eventually regains its freedom, he would have no political or administrative role in the government, as without such responsibilities he would be better placed to serve his people as an elder statesman who when called upon would advise and assist. It is his firm belief that if Tibet is to survive in the modern world it must reflect the collective will of its people rather than just that of an individual.

Today the Tibetan Government in Exile functions from Dharamsala and has all the necessary departments to run its affairs. The executive is headed by a council of ministers, elected by and responsible to the assembly. An independent judiciary exists. The constitution, known as the Charter of the Tibetans in Exile, adopted in 1991, adheres closely to the Universal Declaration of Human Rights and provides all Tibetans equality before the law and the enjoyment of rights and freedoms without discrimination on the basis of sex, religion, race, language or social origin.

Throughout his many years in exile, an abiding concern of the Dalai Lama has been the welfare and rehabilitation of the refugees from Tibet. Apart from the obvious humanitarian aspect, the Dalai Lama has all along believed that the only way to preserve Tibet's culture, religion and way of life is by building strong and vibrant communities abroad. With the support and assistance of the Indian government the refugees have been resettled in several centres around the country, where they have been able to reorganize their lives and preserve and continue their traditions. Today in India Tibetan civilization remains alive having been largely destroyed on its own soil. The initiatives taken by Pandit Nehru and followed by successive governments in Delhi have produced a multitude of schemes for the rehabilitation of the refugees. In a typical manifestation of his enlightened and liberal approach, Nehru had said that in order to preserve Tibetan culture it would be necessary to have separate schools for the refugees, and for this purpose he created the independent Society for Tibetan Education within the Indian Ministry of Education. Nehru also advised that while Tibetan children should have a thorough knowledge of their own history and culture, it was vital that they should be fully familiar with the ways of the modern world, and for this it was essential to know English and to use it as the medium of instruction as it is the international language of the future. This advice, well taken, has helped the scattered Tibetan community to make its presence felt internationally, far out of proportion to its small size.

Agriculture, carpet weaving, the manufacture of garments, the food and restaurant business and the service sector have been the mainstay of the Tibetan community in India. Today there exist over eighty schools with close on 30,000 students in India and Nepal, fifty-four settlements and welfare offices, a dozen missions in various countries apart from cultural institutes, libraries, archives, publishing houses and charitable trusts. Religious establishments include more than 200 monasteries and nunneries, with around 20,000 inmates representing all the sects of Tibetan Buddhism. Tibet's rich and unique arts and crafts, its medical and philosophical traditions are alive and flourishing.

Last but not the least is the Foundation for Universal Responsibility, established by the Dalai Lama from the money he received with the Nobel Prize. According to its charter, it seeks to benefit people everywhere, regardless of nationality, race or creed; to cultivate the common ground between different faiths; to assist nonviolent methods; foster communication between science and religion; and secure human rights and democratic freedoms. The Foundation recognizes the interdependence not only of nations and communities but of all living things, and in fact represents the Dalai Lama's moral and political thinking in action. Among the programmes the Foundation currently supports are those of Women in Security, Conflict Management and Peace (WISCOMP), which has done courageous work among the victims of militant violence in Kashmir, has awarded scholarships to enhance the professional efficacy of Asian women in international relations, and projects for environmental regeneration. Other programmes run by the Foundation enable students to spend time in Tibetan monasteries and religious leaders to visit places of worship of each others' faiths.

The Dalai Lama believes that people all over the world are basically the same; they seek happiness and the avoidance of suffering. Suffering is caused by ignorance, selfishness and greed. True happiness comes from a sense of peace and contentment which in turn is achieved through compassion, empathy and love, and by the elimination of anger, hatred and greed. The problems that the world faces today are all man-made: violent conflicts, poverty, hunger, the destruction of the environment and many others. They can all be resolved by human effort, understanding and the development of a universal brotherhood. The Dalai Lama has spoken out time and again against religious intolerance, which inevitably sows mistrust and divides communities.

The Dalai Lama embodies the very qualities that he preaches: love and compassion and goodness, forgiveness and charity, and universal responsibility. His teachings are simple and lucid, devoid of jargon and metaphysical tangles, and delivered with directness, charm and an unfailing sense of humour. His joie de vivre and his easy manner of delivery immediately establish a close personal rapport with all those who come to hear him speak or who are fortunate to meet him. He is completely free of pomposity and a person of true humility. I recall an occasion when the Dalai Lama called on President Venkataraman to seek his advice on the eve of a trip abroad on how he should respond to various issues that could be raised. 'Who am I, a mere mortal,' replied the President, 'to advise a god incarnate on earth!' The Dalai Lama's response, after a moment of complete surprise, was to break into loud, infectious laughter.

When once asked how he wished to be remembered by posterity, the Dalai Lama replied, 'Just as a human being; perhaps as a human being who often smiles.' That remark sums up the essence of the Dalai Lama's personality: deep wisdom, deep love and compassion, deep humility.

The Dalai Lama and the
Tibetan Monastic Academia

Thupten Jinpa

In the early 1960s His Holiness the Dalai Lama once paid a brief visit to the Tibetan refugee community in Dalhousie, formerly a summer retreat for the officers of the British imperial raj, located in the hills of what is today the state of Himachal Pradesh in northern India. A part of the community was a small group of monks from Sera, Drepung and Ganden, the three great monastic universities of Tibet, known for their tradition of logic and philosophical scholarship. A few hours after his arrival, so the story goes, His Holiness convened a session of debate.

As all the scholars gathered inside the hall, the Dalai Lama sat down comfortably, prepared for a long session of intellectual feast. He selected two monks at random and asked one to sit down to defend and the other, who was standing, to open a debate. Unfortunately, the two selected turned out not to be the best of the scholars in the group. Nevertheless they began their debate. Quite soon, it became obvious that they were at their wit's end. As the exchanges between the debaters progressed, the two monks' eastern Tibetan dialect became heavier and heavier, and soon no one could understand what was being said. Needless to say, the Dalai Lama politely asked them to stop and called for two other monks to take their place.

This is a well-known anecdote amongst the scholars of the Tibetan monastic colleges now re-established in India. The story, though amusing, tells us the depth of the Dalai Lama's passion for Tibet's thousand-year-old intellectual tradition of logic and philosophical debates. It also serves as a warning to the students in the monastic colleges for the story reminds us that anyone could easily be in a similar situation as those two monks when His Holiness visits the monastic universities.

I first had the privilege to participate in a debate in the presence of His Holiness in 1980. This was during one of his visits to Drepung and Ganden monastic universities in Karnataka, south India. I was then a young student at the Shartse College of Ganden monastic university. Apart from my own nervousness, what I remember most of this event is His Holiness's single-pointed—I could say almost the meditation-like absorption—attention to the exchanges. Since then, I have had the privilege to experience this deeply inspiring sight on many occasions.

What follows in this brief essay is a glimpse into one aspect of the Dalai Lama's intellectual life, of which, despite its critical importance, very little is known outside Tibetan circles. I am referring to the role and influence of the Tibetan monastic academia on the life and thought of the Dalai Lama. Thanks to his two successful autobiographies,[1] and more recently Hollywood's two films, *Kundun* and *Seven Years in Tibet*, many people outside the Tibetan community have a sense that monks and scholars played an important role in the Dalai Lama's upbringing. But few are aware of the exact nature of this role, for how can they be expected to know the scope and nature of the unique education the Dalai Lama received in his youth.

My approach here is more impressionistic than systematic, weaving personal observations with anecdotes I have heard as a young student at Ganden. I shall make no attempt to present any comprehensive account of the Dalai Lama's intellectual life, a task better left in the hands of professional biographers and historians. Furthermore, there are other important aspects of the Dalai Lama's intellectual life such as the development of his social and political thought, his extensive engagement with modern science, his interaction with theologians and so on, which must remain outside the scope of this essay.

Today, there are many important matters competing for the Dalai Lama's time and attention. Needless to say, the plight of the Tibetan nation and its six million people must weigh heavily on his shoulders. On any given day, when he is in residence in Dharamsala, one can see a stream of new Tibetan refugees coming to see him with obviously distressing news about his people back home. Within India, the Dalai Lama and his Government in Exile not only coordinate the campaign for the freedom of the Tibetan people, they also oversee the welfare of the thousands of Tibetan refugees scattered all over the world today. The cause of Tibet is undoubtedly the Dalai Lama's primary responsibility and he seems to have a deep, historical sense of this duty. In addition, the Dalai Lama has shouldered upon himself the responsibility to promote closer understanding between the world's major faiths.[2] As part of this effort, he has, in addition to participating in countless numbers of inter-faith services, initiated several high-profile joint pilgrimages to the holy sites of the different traditions, such as Jerusalem and Lourdes in France.

There is, however, a third area of concern that also makes a strong demand on the Dalai Lama's time. This is what His Holiness calls the 'promotion of basic human values'. At the core of this mission lies the belief that fundamental ethical values such as love, compassion and tolerance are indispensable for basic human happiness and must therefore be accepted as universally binding moral principles. The Dalai Lama sees this mission as an important personal responsibility as a human being living in an increasingly complex and evermore interconnected world.[3] Ever since he won the Nobel Prize for Peace in 1989, the demands on his time with matters relating to this third mission have increased exponentially. Today, the Dalai Lama is increasingly seen by millions as a powerful symbol of peace, justice, compassion and environmental awareness. All of these three 'missions' take him away, and often far, from his exiled Tibetan community.

Despite demands on his time, and more importantly, despite his emergence as a tremendously respected international figure, the Dalai Lama has continued to retain his traditionally close ties with the Tibetan scholastic monasteries. He visits them regularly, lectures on important classical texts, keeps close contact with senior scholars and follows the progress of young emerging scholars. The Dalai Lama's relation to the Tibetan monastic academia in general and the three Geluk[4] scholastic monasteries—Sera, Drepung and Ganden—in particular is an intriguing one. One could say that the large monastic universities, especially the well-known trio, form a special constituency for the Dalai Lama. On the one hand, the Dalai Lama is a former student whose formal accreditation of education is conferred by the authorities of these institutions. Thanks to the archival instincts of some individuals, modern television audiences all over the world can still witness the formal ceremony of the Dalai Lama's final examination in Lhasa in the presence of several thousand monks. Prior to this event, he had visited each of the three monastic universities to sit for separate debate examinations.

On the other hand, the Dalai Lama is not on the rolls of any of these colleges. Moreover, the appointment of the abbots of the individual colleges of the three monastic universities, though based on the selection of candidates by the members of the monasteries, is still finalized by the Dalai Lama.

Historically speaking, up until the time of the Great Fifth, formally, the Dalai Lamas were one, though very high, reincarnate lamas of the Loseling college of Drepung monastic university. In fact, the name of the Dalai Lama's government in Tibet, *Ganden Phodrang*, previously belonged to the Dalai Lama institution at Drepung. Since the Great Fifth's assumption of temporal power in the mid-17th century, the Dalai Lama's institution became the Tibetan government.[5] Nevertheless, the Dalai Lamas have continued to be educated in strict accordance with the curriculum of the Geluk scholastic monasteries, and the tutors have been graduates of these universities. For example, of the two main tutors of the Dalai Lama, Kyabje Ling Rinpoche was a scholar of formidable reputation from Drepung, while Kyabje Trijhang Rinpoche was one of Ganden's most renowned personalities of the 20th century. In addition, the present Dalai Lama had several scholastic assistants (*tshen shap*) such as the Mongolian scholar Ngodup Tsoknyi and the late Serkong Tsenshap Rinpoche, all of whom were graduates of the Geluk monasteries.

The core of the Tibetan monastic academic curriculum entails a highly systematic training in logic and epistemology, philosophical investigation into the nature of reality, a detailed investigation into the nature and varieties of religious experience, psychological and phenomenological enquiry into the nature of the mind and its modalities and, of course, a detailed study of ethics. Together, these five fields of knowledge are known as the study of the Five Great Treatises (*shung chen ka pö nga*). Of these, study of the first discipline, logic and epistemology, is based primarily on the works of the Indian thinkers Dignaga (c. 400–485 CE)[6] and Dharmakirti (c. 650 CE) and their subsequent Indian and Tibetan commentators.

The study of the second discipline, which is perhaps best characterized in contemporary language as metaphysics and ontology, is based principally on the works of the highly influential Indian philosopher Nagarjuna (c. 150–250 CE) and his main interpreters such as Buddhapalita (c. 470–540 CE) and Chandrakirti (c. 650 CE). In the third field of study, the writings of Indian masters such as Maitreyanatha (c. 270–350 CE), Asanga (c. 310–390 CE) and Haribhadra

(c. 8th century CE) form the core texts. For the study of psychology and phenomenology, the principal works that constitute the basis of enquiry are by Asanga and his brother Vasubhandu (c. 320–400 CE). Finally, for the study of ethics, the central texts are those that pertain primarily to the detailed analysis of the precepts of monastic discipline. Mastery over these five fields of study is necessary if the candidate is to qualify for the title of Geshe Lharam, which is the Tibetan equivalent of a doctorate in divinity. Incidentally, this is the formal higher education degree the present Dalai Lama holds.

The principal medium of the Tibetan monastic academic training is debate, a highly systematic, Socratic style of disputation which operates through drawing out a series of consequences, often unacceptable to the defender, based on the premises of the opponent's stated theses. This system of debate employs extensively principles of identity, contradiction, and the law of the excluded middle, which lie at the heart of the logics of deduction and induction. Tibetan historians accredit Chapa Chökyi Senge (1109–1169) with the development of this sophisticated system of enquiry. Chapa is believed to have authored several short texts that were together entitled Collected Topics (*Dü dön*), which presented in an ingenious instructional manner a critical treatment of many logical and epistemological themes from Dharmakirti's seminal work *A Thorough Exposition of Valid Cognition (Pramanavarttika)*.[7] Chapa's brilliance lies in illustrating the logical principles in a series of structured debates using the example of common, everyday objects. Today an entire genre of literature exists within Tibetan monastic academic studies which carries the label Collected Topics. These texts are written in such a way that they can be used effectively, which is the case today, as manuals for training young students in the art of debate and familiarizing them with the operation of the key logical principles.

It is this kind of rigorous intellectual training that the

Dalai Lama received in his student years. The Tibetan education theorists speak of three aspects of intelligence that must be cultivated and developed. First, there is the 'clear intelligence', which refers to an ability to perceive questions with an unconfused mind. Second is the 'sharp intelligence', which refers to the ability to swiftly grasp an issue without much difficulty. Finally, there is the 'penetrating intelligence', which refers to the ability to view a problem with greater depth and comprehensiveness.

Debate is believed to help enhance all these three aspects of intelligence in the individual, which are critical for the development of a learned mind. It is said that those who excel in the first type of intelligence are often highly gifted in their power of articulation, while those who excel in the second become seasoned debaters, capable of dismantling the solidity of the opponent's positions. Finally, those who excel in the third type of intelligence are said to become great defenders, capable of adopting a panoramic perspective on any chosen subject under enquiry. Those who have heard the Dalai Lama would recall all these three aspects of intelligence at play.

If there is one thing the Dalai Lama feels he lost in his youth it is perhaps not to have had the freedom which an average monk normally enjoys as a student in the monastic colleges. He occasionally idealizes what is called the life of a *drapa drakyang*, which is best translated as the life of an ordinary monk, simple and unattached. In fact, he once told me when I was a student at Ganden that I was fortunate to have, unlike him, this unique opportunity to be a student as a simple, ordinary monk. I must admit I was a bit surprised at the time.

Perhaps, from the point of view of contemporary education, one of the most admirable features of Tibet's scholastic debate training is that it underlines the critical importance of openness. The debating courtyards in the scholastic monasteries are one of the best places for the teaching of humility. On any given day, students and seasoned scholars are constantly exposed to the humbling experience of having to modify their standpoints, some of which they may have held for long with a high degree of confidence. In fact, when this occurs the individual is said to gain greater maturity as he or she obtains what is called a 'burst of growth in understanding' (*lo kye*). When this happens, there is often a palpable sense of collective acknowledgement on the part of everyone participating in the discussion.

This burst of growth in understanding arises in the context of one's exchanges with debating colleagues. It is, therefore, often said that one's debating colleagues are as much teachers as one's professors. It is this kind of academic training that conditions the individual to have the preparedness to modify his or her position in the light of new insights. Such training also teaches students not to take themselves too seriously. Anyone who has witnessed a live performance of this monastic art of critical enquiry would recall the laughter and liveliness of the atmosphere that unmistakably accompanies the exchanges between the various parties in the debate. There is also something very scientific about this method of critical enquiry.

The Dalai Lama's classical academic training appears to have left a lasting impact both on his personality and his thought. Despite his extensive exposure to modernity and contemporary western thought, his appreciation of the scholastic tradition of Tibet remains as strong as ever. In fact, his world view remains deeply rooted in the ancient teachings of the Buddha and the philosophical tradition that developed on the basis of these for over a period of more than two millennia in India and Tibet. Belief in ethical-religious ideas such karma, the possibility of rebirth, the natural potential for perfection that is thought to exist in human beings and so on, form the bedrock of the Buddhist world view, and these still retain their cogency and vitality for the Dalai Lama.

On the philosophical level, it is Nagarjuna's anti-essentialist metaphysics and his rejection of any reified notions of substantial reality that inform the Dalai Lama's understanding of the nature of reality. As he often points out, almost in the fashion of a motto, everything is a 'dependent origination' and exists within a nexus of 'interrelationships', with no independently existing discreet entities 'relating' with each other. It is this basic philosophy of the world's interconnectedness that underlies the Dalai Lama's perspectives on the natural world.

One of the most memorable experiences of my monastic years was catching a glimpse of the Dalai Lama's heavily annotated personal copy of Nagarjuna's philosophical classic *Fundamentals of the Middle Way (Mulamadhyamakarika)*.[8] I was travelling with His Holiness as his interpreter and we were waiting in the airport lounge in Mumbai for our Indian Airlines flight which had been delayed by several hours. As soon as the official protocol business of being received by the airport authorities was completed, the Dalai Lama delved into his small shoulder bag and took out his copy of Nagarjuna's book and launched into a deep study. To see His Holiness approach this text almost as a student was a truly humbling yet most inspiring experience, particularly since I was then 'lecturing' on this text at Ganden monastery.

Amongst Tibetan thinkers, undoubtedly Tibet's great reformer and philosopher Tsong Khapa (1357–1419) appeared to exert the greatest influence on the Dalai Lama's philosophical views. There are some unmistakable strands of Tsong Khapa's thought that constantly resonate in the Dalai Lama's more philosophical writings. For example, the Dalai Lama often invokes an important methodological principle, first developed fully as a crucial principle by Tsong Khapa, which underlines the need to distinguish between what is negated through a particular method of enquiry and what has not been observed through such a method. In other words, he reminds us not to conflate the two processes of 'not finding something' and 'finding its non-existence'. So, as for Tsong Khapa, so for the Dalai Lama, not seeing something is not equal to seeing its non-existence. This is a crucial methodological principle the Dalai Lama brings to bear when he engages in dialogues with contemporary thought, especially modern science. Furthermore, in his unshakable belief in the liberating potential of critical thinking, which he calls 'analytic meditation', one can also see the unmistakable influence of Tsong Khapa's writings.[9]

Similarly, the Dalai Lama's understanding of the human psyche—the nature of emotions, the relation between reason and emotion, the connection between certain emotions and behaviour, how to deal with the destructive tendencies of certain emotions and so on—derive from the long history of Buddhist psychological and phenomenological thinking, rather than contemporary western thought. This latter includes, amongst others, the influential psychoanalytic theories of Sigmund Freud and, of course, many aspects of cognitive scientific disciplines. This is not to suggest that there exist no convergences between the two intellectual traditions. For example, parallel to the psychoanalytic notion of the unconscious, there is in Buddhist psychology a notion of what are called 'propensities' for specific emotions.[10] Unlike the emotions themselves, these propensities are thought not to be actual, manifest, felt states of cognition. Rather, they exist more as 'subconscious' forces.

In dealing with the cognitive aspects of the human psyche, the Dalai Lama's understanding of the nature of perception and experience, the cognitive processes involved in generating inference, the definitions of knowledge, and so on are based, again, on the writings of Buddhist philosophers and not on the works of contemporary cognitive science. I remember once, at a dialogue with some cognitive scientists, the Dalai Lama, after listening to a scientific understanding of how a moment of perception occurs, immediately attempted to translate this into the language of Tibetan epistemology. At the heart of this Tibetan system is a sevenfold typology of cognitions: (1) perception, (2) inference, (3) correct assumption, (4) inattentive perception, (5) subsequent cognition, (6) doubt, and (7) false cognition. The nature, causation and the interrelation of these seven classes of cognitions constitute a major focus of Tibetan epistemological thinking to this day.

The point I am trying to make is this. The Dalai Lama's intellectual and ethical world view remains firmly rooted in the classical Tibetan heritage. His advocacy of compassion as a universal spiritual principle, his belief in the basic goodness of human nature, his persistent belief in the power of nonviolence as a means of resolving human conflicts, his passionate advocacy of altruism as an effective means of achieving individual happiness, all have their roots in the teachings of the Buddha.

Here again, two classical Indian thinkers stand out in terms of their influence on the Dalai Lama. They are Nagarjuna and Shantideva, the author of the well-known 7th century Buddhist classic, *Guide to the Bodhisattva's Way of Life* (*Bodhicharyavatara*).[11] Those who are familiar with the Dalai Lama's writings will note the frequency with which he cites Shantideva in his lectures. In fact, the Dalai Lama has repeatedly stated that his greatest source of inspiration is the following verse from Shantideva:

> For as long as space remains,
> For as long as sentient beings remain,
> Until then, may I too remain
> And dispel the miseries of beings.[12]

One area where the Dalai Lama's views are firmly grounded in modern science rather than his own inherited classical Buddhist thought is cosmology. Here, the Dalai Lama appears to have abandoned the entire cosmological system derived from the highly influential Buddhist classic entitled *Treasury of Knowledge* (*Abhidharmakoshakarika*), written by Vasubhandu in the 4th century. Like many cosmological theories current in ancient Indian thought, in

Vasubhandu's cosmology, known as the 'Abhidharma cosmology', the sun and the moon revolve around the earth, and the latter is thought to be supported by forces of the four elements, which are stacked upon each other in an ascending order. Judging by his comments on classical Abhidharma cosmology, it seems that the Dalai Lama was never convinced of the cogency of the system. There is also the simple coincidence that before the young Dalai Lama was exposed to the intricacies of the classical Abhidharma cosmology, which traditionally happens much later in one's academic scholarship, he had already been introduced to some powerful symbols of modern cosmology, such as the globe atlas and photographs of the volcanic craters on the surface of the moon. He was also aware of the scientific, as opposed to the classical, Buddhist explanations of the occurrence of solar and lunar eclipses.

His Holiness once lamented that he does not understand why many of the senior Tibetan scholars in the monastic colleges are so reluctant to let go of the ancient cosmological theories. To his mind, most of this cosmology has been falsified by the weight of empirical evidence gathered by modern scientists. And given that the scholastic monks trained in the system of philosophical debates are conditioned to modify their views in the light of new insights, His Holiness feels that it is only emotional attachment to old theories that comes in the way of the scholars accepting the new cosmology. I sensed a rare note of impatience in him. I was then a graduate at Ganden and felt that I should at least try to present the case of these senior Tibetan scholars.

Politely I reminded His Holiness that regardless of its lack of modern scientific foundation the Abhidharma system 'works' so far as the proponents of the system are concerned. For example, based on this system, almanacs are produced, highly accurate predictions of solar and lunar eclipses are made, the changing lengths of daylight are predicted and accurate calculations of stellar positions are developed. In other words, the Abhidharma system makes predictions of events that are observable and highly relevant to the everyday life of the people. It will be unrealistic, I opined, for the monks to abandon this model until they are explained how each of these facts are also supported in the alternative, new cosmology, which, in addition, has solid empirical foundation. Ever since, I have noticed that His Holiness has been much more appreciative of the perspectives of his senior colleagues on cosmology.

It is this kind of complex background that often brings the Dalai Lama back into the folds of the classical Tibetan academic monasteries. Not only is the Dalai Lama there to observe the progress of the emerging scholars, he is there also to stimulate his intellectual development. This becomes all the more necessary as he ventures deeper and deeper into dialogues with scientists and thinkers from various contemporary disciplines.[13] In this context, it may be worth noting the special relationship that the Dalai Lama has had for a long time with a unique Tibetan scholar. I am referring here to the late Shakor Gen Nyima-la from Drepung Loseling monastic college, who was one of the 20th century's greatest interpreters of Nagarjuna's and Tsong Khapa's philosophical writings. Once, in a conversation, His Holiness told me that he felt that in Gen Nyima-la he had found someone who had not only penetrated the depths of Nagarjuna's insights, but someone who had also been able to bring them to life. He then lamented the fact that hardly any of Gen Nyima-la's lectures were ever recorded! I have myself had the privilege of attending one series of lectures this great scholar gave on an influential work of Tsong Khapa at Drepung.

It must be truly refreshing for the Dalai Lama to intellectually engage with a senior scholar such as Gen Nyima-la who was able to relate to His Holiness as a genuine colleague. Unlike most Tibetan scholars in the exiled community in India and Nepal, Gen Nyima-la was not overwhelmed by the Dalai Lama's presence. This is partly because, like the Dalai Lama's two late tutors, Gen

Nyima-la has seen his intellectual development since His Holiness was a young student.

It is also conceivable that the Dalai Lama finds the atmosphere of the monastic academia a rather sobering counterpoint to the many other areas of his very public life. It is one sphere where he is not expected to be the 'great' authority. Furthermore, exchanging diverse and often opposing views is a part of the intellectual culture of the monastic academia. Every now and then, the Dalai Lama gives a series of formal lectures on an important philosophical treatise at one of the three monastic universities. These lectures would, on an average, last for two to three weeks. During these occasions, formal debate sessions are held in the evenings, where top scholars of the monastic academia debate on the issues addressed in the text the Dalai Lama is lecturing on, while he listens with total absorption. Needless to say, these are truly stimulating events.

It is perhaps too early to judge what would be the lasting intellectual legacy of the Dalai Lama in so far as the Tibetan monastic academia is concerned. Unlike many of his predecessors, the present Dalai Lama has so far not chosen to pen any major scholarly treatises in Tibetan. Yet, amongst all Tibetans who have had a truly classical education, the Dalai Lama has engaged most with the various scholarly disciplines of contemporary western thought, especially science. No doubt historians would take particular note of this fact and come to realize that in many ways the Dalai Lama's life mirrors the wider picture of classical Tibetan culture's encounter with modernity.

An Unconventional Tibetan Perspective

Bhuchung Tsering

What does His Holiness the Dalai Lama mean to young Tibetans? On the face of it, this question may seem to be an unnecessary one. Don't all Tibetans have the same approach towards His Holiness?

Prior to 1959, an average Tibetan could only hope to meet someone who may have been fortunate to get a glimpse of His Holiness from a distance. At best this glimpse may have been at a religious teaching or when the Dalai Lama undertook his irregular travels in Tibet. It would be rare to meet someone who had had an audience with His Holiness.

The structure of Tibetan society in independent Tibet was such that there was very limited access to His Holiness as also to the senior officials of the Tibetan government. Elaborate protocol was the rule of the game. Therefore, ordinary Tibetans did not have the opportunity of interacting with His Holiness at close quarters. To them, he was their Gyalwa Rinpoche, the Victorious One, who was the focus of their daily prayers. Nobody even dreamt of any close encounters with him.

But in the post-1959 period, following the flight into exile, the institution of the Dalai Lama has undergone a dramatic transformation, much to the delight of His Holiness. Aided by circumstances, the institution has become less protocol-heavy, more accessible to the public and more practical. Over a period of time, this has led to a close interaction between His Holiness and the Tibetan people, a historical development of sorts.

The most obvious indication of this metamorphosis is the increase in the number of Tibetans with the first name Tenzin. Almost every other Tibetan who is born in exile and under the age of twenty may have this first name. As Tibetans know, Tenzin is the name that His Holiness gives when Tibetans resort to the convention of approaching a lama to name their child. Prior to 1959 only a privileged few Tibetan children may have had the opportunity of getting their names from His Holiness.

Life in exile has also led to His Holiness's interaction with the outside world, mainly through his visits across the world. This has shown the Tibetans a new side of the Dalai Lama, particularly those who are fortunate to be growing up in a free society. While most young Tibetans still hold strong to their Buddhist faith, and thus subscribe to the traditional perspective of the Dalai Lama, they have also been able to see his human side and to appreciate it as such. His Holiness has become a role model for young Tibetans.

I belong to the generation of Tibetans who grew up in exile, a generation which has to be the spokesperson for our people without having direct experience of life in Tibet. This change in our situation, however, has given me a fresh insight into the Dalai Lama and has provided people like me with an opportunity unimaginable in my parent's generation.

Growing up in the Tibetan settlement in south India in the 1970s or attending high school in Darjeeling or college in New Delhi in the beginning of the 1980s, I did not dream even for a minute that one day I would be in the same room as Kundun, leave alone being able to strike a conversation with him. But that day arrived in the late 1980s and is fresh in my memory even to this day.

I was accompanying an Indian photojournalist to the residence of His Holiness in Dharamsala as part of my work at the Department of Information and International

Relations. Between photo sessions, His Holiness looked towards me, just a newcomer to the Tibetan civil service, and asked me from which part of Tibet I was. That one ordinary-sounding question altered the course of Tibetan social history, for me at least. Kundun had spoken to me, an ordinary Tibetan, and acknowledged my presence. Since then I have been privileged to interact with His Holiness on quite a few occasions in the course of my work.

My interaction with His Holiness is in a way symbolic of the transformation of the institution of the Dalai Lama that Tenzin Gyatso has brought about. The significance of the transformation can be comprehended only when one has looked at the history of modern Tibet, as well as that of the Fourteenth Dalai Lama. To be objective, the course of modern Tibetan history dictated certain changes in the institution as well as in Tibetan society as a whole.

However, things may not have changed as rapidly as they did had the Fourteenth Dalai Lama not complemented historical development with his own liberal outlook and foresight. My fascination (if I even dare use this term) with His Holiness has more to do with his social activism and less with his religious role. While His Holiness's outreach to the international community, in the field of religion and spiritualism as well as in drawing attention to the plight of the Tibetan people, is acknowledged internationally, not many know much about his influence on the social thinking of the Tibetan people as well as his other followers.

The most important factor in changing the Tibetan society in exile has been the establishment, mainly with the assistance of the Indian government, of a system of universal modern education for young Tibetans. That one act by the Dalai Lama has not only provided a level playing field for all Tibetans in terms of educational opportunity, but the blend of modern and traditional education that is part of the curriculum results in a new generation of Tibetans modern in outlook yet also knowledgeable of their cultural heritage.

His Holiness is a social reformer and an iconoclast. Relying on his moral authority and the well-founded justification of Buddhism as a rational religion, His Holiness has altered the theological perceptions of Tibetan Buddhists when these did not conform to scientific reality. This ranges from asking monks to accept the earth as round instead of flat, as is found in Buddhist scriptures, to removing the mystery behind the institution of the Dalai Lama, and thereby forcing the very many Tulku institutions to follow suit. He has encouraged the doing away of irrelevant monastic rituals and political protocols. He has transformed Tibetan Buddhism from being ritualistic to a practice relevant to any individual interested in it.

His Holiness has been able to make effective use of his coveted position to change the social system not only of the Tibetans but also of communities that share the same cultural values. For example, although people living in the Tibetan cultural environment do not have a caste system, people following certain professions are looked down upon.

One issue that has personally affected me is His Holiness's contribution in changing the dietary habits of Tibetans. Tibetan Buddhists traditionally eat meat and the reason is that Tibet in the past did not have adequate non-meat products. Since 1959, Tibetan society has changed greatly. Today, Tibetans whether living in exile or inside Tibet do have access to vegetarian food, although meat continues to be an integral part of the diet—much to the consternation and confusion of outside observers who tend to equate Buddhism with vegetarianism.

Many people do not comprehend the significant role His Holiness has been playing in promoting vegetarianism. Through his personal example (he turned vegetarian for some years, but then had to resume a non-vegetarian diet on the advice of his physicians) and consistent advocacy, using his coveted position, His Holiness has started leading the meat-eating Tibetan society along the path of vegetarianism. He has encouraged food workshops towards this end. This is a significant development and there are now increasing numbers of Tibetans like myself who have become vegetarians.

His Holiness is also a role model for a balanced approach to life. He can adjust easily with royalty and heads of state as well as with a simple monk in a meditation cave. I once overheard a Swiss tourist exclaiming *Sehr einfach*! ('Very simple') when he found that he was travelling in the same tram car as His Holiness. He can be very solemn in a ritual Buddhist ceremony or jovial among schoolchildren in a Tibetan settlement.

Generally, Tibetans believe in the ability of His Holiness to liberate them from the suffering of this material world. This is a spiritual and subjective belief that only people subscribing to Tibetan Buddhist principles can comprehend. But the new perspective of His Holiness as a role model is one which is shared by Tibetans and non-Tibetans alike.

A Journey through Bylakuppe

Anees Jung

I never did see Tibet when it was Tibet. Now that I would like to, it is no longer Tibet. The Potala Palace, that overwhelming symbol which is indelible in the imagination of every Tibetan, is today 'a sombre shipwreck beached on the shores of an alien city' in the words of Sonam Tenzin, a returning Tibetan native. Its mythical outlines loom ghost-like, empty of life, empty without the presence of the man who lived in it and lent it the magic of his being. I have no desire to go to Tibet and join the hordes of men and women who buy tickets to visit the apartments where the Dalai Lama once lived. To see Potala Palace as a tourist seems a sacrilege. It would seem as if one were visiting a monument abandoned and disgraced.

What seems grounded in Lhasa is the skeleton of the wrecked ship. What it contained has sailed on, invisibly, finding a mooring, miles away, in a land without an imposing palace, without majestic hills, without the snows shimmering down. But the presence that once prevailed in Lhasa now reigns over Bylakuppe in a distant corner of south India where it never snows but rains. Bylakuppe by its very name means 'a place of rains'. In the presence of the Dalai Lama even the rains, it seems, decide to step back.

Bigger than the rains is the Dalai Lama's yearly visit to Bylakuppe. I am fortunate to be among the thousands of Tibetans who have travelled distances for his darshan. They line the routes he travels, standing in single file—hundreds of men, women and children, with heads bowed, fervently clutching white scarves of peace, bunches of wild flowers, offerings so finely wrapped in devotion. Their eyes are lit, their faces wreathed in anticipation. They present a picture not of ebullience but of quiet animation. To see such quietude in a mass is a rare sight. Looking at the Tibetans always gives me a good feeling. I find in their faces a peace unfazed by the rigours of the hardships they have borne so heroically, so stoically. I have been a witness to crowds before, the kind that gather or are gathered to cheer political leaders. They are more in the nature of a spectacle, disorganized, frenzied, more curious than expectant. But to see a crowd of Tibetans standing hours in the rains is to witness a picture of serenity, of humility and patience born of an unyielding faith. It is a moving sight to see the old, the dying and the disabled being brought out, lying on their beds, with tears in their eyes, clutching a flower or two in trembling hands, their last offerings. It is as if the Buddha has returned.

As indeed he has. But this Buddha it seems belongs to another time. He carries his mantle lightly, is less like a god, more like a friend. Pomp and grandeur reminiscent of the shades of the Last Emperor circle Sera-je monastery, a replica of what existed in Tibet. But the one who is seated on the throne-like chair is a humble monk, like those assembled around him. The air is charged with vapours of ritual, resonant with sounds that remind one of Gregorian chants. Mixed with mournful strains of the Tibetan clarinet, and cymbals crashing like thunder, they strike an eerie contrast with the quietude of the still red sea that the presence of the lamas evokes. Robed in maroon is the Dalai Lama, smiling, waving a hand, gazing indulgently at the long line of devotees who walk past him carrying offerings from flowers to white scarves to bags of rice and maize, the fruits of their new earth. Watching their faces, I choke.

When he speaks to the crowd that has gathered through

the night (some had brought their bedding and slept in the drizzle) he again seems to talk to each one. He even recognizes in the melee faces that he has met, smiles at them, waves now and then a hand of affirmation, watches with glee a child pursuing a yellow balloon. While waiting for the microphones to begin working, he gazes into the eye of the crowd that is not restless. Nor is His Holiness. The wait is indefinite but does not seem long because of the serenity that prevails. The microphones refuse to work. 'Why not go and have your lunch, stretch your legs and return,' suggests His Holiness with a laugh. 'By the time you return the microphones may start working.' The crowd bursts into laughter echoing his short laugh. There is not a trace of protest from a crowd that has waited a whole night to hear him.

Dutifully and in good humour they are back again, sitting patiently between intermittent sun and rain. A sea of people, their faces darkened in the strong Karnataka sun, old men and women turning prayer wheels, counting beads, many of whom have probably braved the journey from Tibet. Across from them are children in a disciplined crowd dressed in crisp blue uniforms. And as happy as the children are the lamas dressed in maroon and saffron robes gathered in another mass. Hundreds of colourful umbrellas unfurl when the Dalai Lama gently advises that they protect their heads against the glare. They hang on to each word he utters. When he talks, the tone is not of a man espousing a sermon but of a person who is reflecting and searching for answers himself. He constantly seems to question the changing realities of his time and seeks new answers and solutions. Buddha did it in his own time, leaving behind a path that the Dalai Lama now walks on. It has been for him, as for his people, a long, arduous road that together they have travelled finding a freedom that is charged with sunshine and laughter.

Bigger than a place are the people who give that place a definition, fill it with the aura born out of a collective racial memory and nostalgia. I have not seen the mythical grandeur of Tibet but have been fortunate to witness the miracle of how a people, so visibly doomed, can re-build not only their lives but a place which is bound to their destiny and their very existence. That's what the Tibetans have done, turning Bylakuppe into the Tibet of their dreams and imagination. When the first batch of them arrived in this desolate corner of Karnataka, so generously given to them by the state government, they bowed, as Tibetans so naturally do, in deep gratitude. It was an alien landscape, a wilderness where elephants lived and roamed, animals they had never seen in their native Tibet. Some succumbed to the wild animals but many did not. They learnt how to challenge the great animal by gathering in groups and beating tins. Soon the elephants receded. But not the snakes and the scorpions. Some of them died when bitten, some became wary and cautious, slowly learning to fend them. The men cleared the jungles, the women gathered wood to burn.

Soon there were clearings where fields could be ploughed and planted with unfamiliar grains—maize, tobacco, cotton and ginger. Around the fields rose homesteads, small houses with red-tile roofs, the kind their Indian neighbours lived in. Like them, the Tibetans learnt to harness the bullocks. Gone was the familiar yak, that beast of their burden, whose meat gave them the strength and heat. In this distant land, green with the perennial rains, they made vegetable gardens, got acquainted with their colour and taste, and without realizing it slowly became vegetarians. It suited the climate and way of life. It was less violent, as the Dalai Lama told them. Having once watched a chicken being killed and been turned into a meal for him he gave up eating chicken. He advised Tibetans not to raise poultry and piggery but grow less violent foods. Today the poultry farm in Bylakuppe is an old-age home. His Holiness makes it a point to visit the elderly each time he comes to Bylakuppe. He never fails to stop at the pond on the way to feed the fish that sweep up in shoals to eat out of his hand. He makes an unexpected stop on the road to lay a white scarf on the grave of a Chinese man who left Tibet to make his home here. These are gestures that speak broadly and loudly. They speak of his compassion for animate and inanimate beings, for friends and so-called enemies.

I am reminded of a story which Sonam Tenzin quotes of how a lady from Lhasa dressed in the traditional striped apron and *chuba* travelling in a bus asked him if he had ever seen Kundun, referring to the Dalai Lama by the name he was called as a child. 'You are fortunate,' she told him. 'We have no freedom at all . . . It's as if we are lying on a bed of thorns—we never know when things might change for the worse.' This sad reality has escaped the 10,000 Tibetans who have lost a home but gained another—a home that radiates in the presence of Kundun who lives among them. Unlike the woman in Lhasa, they deem themselves fortunate to get a glimpse of him and be blessed by his presence. He remains not only a spiritual light but a leader in the true sense who has been shepherding their journey, watching over each stop of their growth, development and progress, and as a friend giving them advice, care and concern, not the way a leader does when he is elected, but as one who loves them as much as they revere and trust him. Their well-being is his victory.

In Praise of His Holiness

Lama Thubten Zopa Rinpoche

His Holiness the Dalai Lama is the great treasure of infinite compassion embracing all sentient beings, the sole source of benefit and happiness, and the sole refuge. His Holiness is incomparably kinder to us, the fortunate disciples in many countries who are able to see his holy body and hear his holy speech, than all the past, present and future Buddhas.

The kind Shakyamuni Buddha, out of his great compassion, descended to this world of Dzambu in the Arya land of India for the sole purpose of bringing benefit and happiness to migratory beings by leading us to liberation and full enlightenment.

It is said in *The White Lotus Sutra*:

At one time when the Buddha was residing in Milk-Plant Park, he turned to face the north and smiled. Five rays of light issued from the curled hair between his eyebrows. When the bodhisattva Meaningful to Behold asked why, the Buddha replied, 'O son of the Mahayana type, there is a land in the north known as the Land of Snow where the Buddhas of the three times have not yet put their holy feet. However, in the future, the holy Dharma will spread and flourish there like the rising sun and all the living beings there will be liberated by Lord Avalokiteshwara, who once made the following prayer:

May I liberate all sentient beings in the Land
of Snow, who are difficult to subdue. May I
subdue them. May I lead the sentient beings
in that outlying barbarous country [Tibet] on
the path to liberation and full enlightenment.
May even that barbarous country become a
field that is subdued by me. May all the holy
Dharma taught by all the tathagatas be spread
and flourish for a long time in that country.
May the sentient beings there enjoy the holy
Dharma by hearing the name of the Triple
Gem, going for refuge and achieving the
bodies of happy migratory beings.

The bodhisattva Meaningful to Behold, to whom Shakyamuni
Buddha predicted the spread of Dharma in Tibet, saying, 'In
the future when my teaching has degenerated in India, the
sentient beings in the Land of Snow in the north will be the
objects to be subdued by you, the bodhisattva,' and the
Compassion Buddha who has benefited all with the light of
Dharma, is none other than the present Dalai Lama.

Even ordinary people can realize that the incomparable
qualities and the holy actions of His Holiness's body, speech
and mind benefiting other sentient beings signify the infinitely
compassionate aspiration that he has made in the past. Not
only did His Holiness give prayers to extensively benefit
Tibet by subduing the sentient beings there, but nowadays
he shines the light of Dharma to eliminate the darkness of
ignorance and bring the sunshine of peace and happiness
even to the western world.

It is proven that His Holiness is the present living
Compassionate-eyed Looking Buddha, Avalokiteshwara, even
from the lineage of the incarnation, which starts from
Avalokiteshwara and, during Buddha's time, the bodhisattva
Meaningful to Behold, King Jigten Ngawang and the Brahmin
Khyeu Nan-che; then continues through Sangye Gyalwa;
Nyatri Tsenpo; the first king of Tibet, Chogyal Trisong

Duetsen; Chogyal Songsten Gampo; Lama Atisha's translator, the great Dromtonpa, who is the forty-fifth incarnation; the first Dalai Lama, Gendun Trupa, who founded Tashi Lhunpo monastery; Gendun Gyatso; Sonam Gyatso; Yonten Gyatso; the Fifth Dalai Lama; Tsangyang Gyatso; Kelsang Gyatso; Jampal Gyatso; Lungtok Gyatso; Tsultrim Gyatso; Khedrup Gyatso; Trinley Gyatso; Thubten Gyatso; and the present Dalai Lama, Tenzin Gyatso, the sixty-fourth incarnation.

His Holiness Serkong Dorje Chang, who passed away in Tibet, had a dream in which a spontaneously arisen statue of Avalokiteshwara with five faces predicted that he would see the Compassion Buddha the following day. The next day he saw His Holiness.

One day the great scholar–yogi Tehor Kyoerpen Rinpoche, renowned in Sera, Gaden and Drepung monasteries, told all his disciples that they were going to meet Dromtonpa, an incarnation of Compassion Buddha. They then went to see His Holiness.

His Holiness preserves the complete teaching of the Buddha, the three higher trainings of morality, meditation and wisdom in the three basket teachings, which is the essence of the Hinayana teaching and the foundation of the causal Mahayana Paramitayana path and the resultant secret vajrayana. Because of that, His Holiness is able to continuously produce many hundreds of thousands of holy scholars and highly attained yogis, like stars in the sky. Today, in the west and in several other countries of the world, people receive teachings from highly qualified practitioners—teachers from the monasteries of Sera, Gaden and Drepung, and also from the monasteries of the other traditions—and are able to study in depth with them. By putting these teachings into practice, they are able to make their lives meaningful and find fulfilment. They have so much opportunity to enjoy peace and happiness and are able to direct their lives towards liberation and enlightenment, and this is increasing every year. This is solely due to His Holiness's kindness.

Without His Holiness Buddhism would suffer, and it would be extremely difficult to continue to preserve the entire Buddhadharma. Without the teaching of the Buddha, sentient beings suffer because it is the only medicine to cure all diseases, delusions, negative karma and their imprints. His Holiness is completely liberated from all the fears of samsara—the circling aggregates which are suffering in nature—and is highly skilled in liberating others from all suffering. Therefore, from the bottom of our hearts, we should always pray for His Holiness to have a stable life until samsara ends.

His Holiness's holy body, speech and mind are the source of peace for all living beings. He is ultimate among those who are learned, ultimate among those who are pure in morality, and ultimate among those who are warm-hearted. He is unstained by delusion and ego-seeking happiness for self. He is unstained by even the subtlest obscurations.

For us sentient beings, both human and animal, just seeing or touching his holy body purifies our minds and makes our lives meaningful. It brings unforgettable peace and happiness and plants the seeds of liberation and enlightenment in our mental continuum. It gives incredible inspiration and the hope for a better life.

The ever-loving smile and compassionate face of His Holiness radiates warm rays of light that pacify all fears and anxieties, all the karma and delusions of sentient beings. No matter how much one looks at the holy body of the Compassion Buddha, one never feels satiated. There is no limit to the qualities of the stainless holy body and to the extensive benefit that sentient beings receive from it.

One hour, or even a few minutes, of the gentle, soothing nectar of his holy speech is enough for people to understand immediately the very essence of Buddhism and to make their lives more beneficial and meaningful. His holy words, which come solely from egoless, compassionate, loving thought, present everything in a very simple, clear, logical way and suit exactly the mind of each person who hears them. Even if a hundred thousand people listen to His Holiness, every single person is uplifted with unbelievable joy and finds the answers to his questions. The problems in their lives are immediately solved.

In the very short time it takes to hear a few of his holy words, they receive a profound wisdom that illuminates the darkness of ignorance obscuring the clear nature of their minds. They develop the wisdom to know what is right and to be practised, and what is wrong and to be abandoned. They are able to practise the Dharma and benefit others, as well as obtain the ultimate happiness of liberation from samsara and full enlightenment.

Although western countries are highly developed in the fields of science, technology, psychology and so forth, they are unable to find answers to many of the complicated issues of life, especially relating to birth and death, and also economic, legal and social problems. Each of His Holiness's words is a sword that immediately cuts through these problems. He gives simple solutions, none of which is separate from Dharma, not only to problems related to religious practice but also to business, family relationships and other aspects of our daily lives. All his advice is based on not harming others and on benefiting them. There is no contradiction between the spiritual and political because his advice comes not only from a pure motivation of compassion but from wisdom as well.

His Holiness's speech takes care of the earth and the living beings inhabiting the earth. If people were to put his speech into practice, it would protect even the environment from destruction. He gives so much love and compassion that each person's mind is transformed. Each person who hears His Holiness and then puts these words into practice transforms his mind into the qualities His Holiness speaks about, thus bringing peace and happiness to the world. Millions of people have been inspired in this way. They have become more sensitive to others, with the loving compassionate thought of caring for others' rights and needs. It is enough if one person in an audience stops causing harm to others—for example, refrains from killing or getting angry. It brings peace to all other living beings. Therefore, it is easy to understand how His Holiness is the source of all the temporary and ultimate joy and peace for all sentient beings.

As to the qualities of the holy mind, His Holiness has infinite qualities, such as the ten powers, the four fearlessnesses, the eighteen qualities of unmixed Dharma and so forth, which cannot be comprehended by even a tenth-level bodhisattva let alone by an ordinary being. Each pore of his body is able to perform the function of his mind and directly see all existence and benefit all sentient beings. His holy wisdom manifests and works for each sentient being exactly in accordance with their karma.

A special quality of His Holiness that every ordinary person can see is that he seeks to benefit even those who harm him. He feels even greater compassion for them and cherishes them most in his heart. He praises their qualities and prays only for their well-being, for their temporary and ultimate happiness, up to enlightenment. This leaves us in no doubt that His Holiness is a bodhisattva, the Compassion Buddha.

When the Chinese communists invaded Tibet they caused unbelievable destruction of buildings, especially monasteries, and of the environment, and tortured and killed not only ordinary people but lamas and highly educated monks and nuns as well. They even prevented monks and nuns from teaching Buddhism, especially the higher training of morality.

In such a situation an ordinary world leader would hold a grudge and regard the Chinese as enemies. His Holiness, however, is solely concerned about the freedom, peace and happiness of six million Tibetan people and the future of the most precious, profound culture in the world which preserves the teaching of the Buddha. He cherishes the Chinese deeply and is greatly concerned about their sufferings.

He prays for their freedom, peace and happiness, and feels a special concern and unbearable compassion for Mao Zedong.

If the Chinese are unable to open their hearts to His Holiness and accept his wishes, it will be a great pity and a great loss of opportunity. If they can open their hearts it will mean not only freedom, peace and happiness for six million Tibetan people, but also the opportunity to continue to preserve and strengthen the whole of Buddhism. It will also mean that the rest of the world will be able to deepen their understanding of the cause of happiness and suffering, and gain the opportunity to attain enlightenment, which is the ultimate source of peace and happiness for all.

In addition, millions of Chinese will receive unbelievable peace and happiness from His Holiness. If the key figures in the Chinese government use His Holiness to communicate with and help their people, there will be incredible benefit in terms of peace and happiness, which non-religious officials cannot offer because they lack his qualities. In the past, the emperors of Chinese dynasties invited prominent Tibetan lamas to China to learn from them. They received teachings and initiations and studied the path to enlightenment in order to bring the greatest benefit to their lives.

The present Dalai Lama has benefited the west, where he has opened the hearts of millions. He shows his understanding about the western world and culture and is able to deal with issues in a down-to-earth manner with humour that uplifts the spirit. People who are religious benefit from his essential and practical advice about how to make their lives most profitable and enjoyable. He also shows the non-religious practical ways to make their lives meaningful.

Such extensive benefit was not characteristic of previous Dalai Lamas. His Holiness has accomplished much more in the world than merely working for the independence of Tibet. This aspect is extremely important for us sentient beings, who are in danger of nuclear war, in danger of dying from new diseases, and who suffer from desire, violence, anger and the gloom of ignorance.

Most precious is the Buddha's psychology, the Buddha's way of pacifying suffering and achieving happiness. There is no way by which we can repay the kindness of His Holiness, the preserver of the doctrine, even if we offer him the whole world filled with wish-fulfilling jewels for eons. From His Holiness's teaching we are able to prepare our mental continuum for every happiness, including liberation and enlightenment. Thus, we should practise his essential advice of loving kindness and compassion, caring more for others and serving them. We should put into practice his holy teachings and fulfil his holy wishes, particularly his wish to free the Tibetans from the misery and fear they are now facing and help them towards the freedom they once enjoyed.

With palms joined, we should constantly pray for His Holiness to guide us in all our lifetimes until we achieve enlightenment.

When we see His Holiness the Dalai Lama, what we are actually seeing is the holy body of the Compassion Buddha in human form. So besides hearing his speech, just seeing his body is great purification—it prepares our minds for liberation from the oceans of samsaric suffering and plants the seed of enlightenment.

Even a yogi who is not enlightened is unbelievably meaningful for us sentient beings. Besides a yogi, an unenlightened being who has those realizations, or even a practitioner of the Heruka deity, become meaningful to behold for sentient beings. There is no question then about the benefit of seeing an enlightened being or Avalokiteshwara like His Holiness.

Not just seeing his body, but with each hour that we hear his holy speech we are closer to attaining liberation and enlightenment. His Holiness's speech is simplified and easy to understand, but it contains the depth and extensiveness of everything that is explained in Buddha's holy texts.

Each word is like an atomic bomb that destroys our inner enemy, our delusions, and defeats the strong, selfish mind. His Holiness's words also destroy the creator of not only human problems, but all samsaric sufferings, which creates death and rebirth, old age and sickness, dissatisfaction, emotional pain and other sufferings.

As amrit nectar is the purest drink, His Holiness's speech is the supreme nectar for our minds. And even though at any moment we might not be able to see His Holiness's infinite qualities, we are aware that His Holiness is filled with wisdom, offering solutions to every difficulty in every aspect of life, and showing all those who think their life has no meaning and no hope how to make their lives most meaningful. We can also see that His Holiness is filled with loving-kindness, compassion and respect for everyone, whether they praise him or criticize him, whether they are rich or poor.

By seeing His Holiness, especially by hearing his speech, and by seeing all his qualities, the hearts of many millions in the world have been filled with hope, joy and peace. Of course, we *should* see His Holiness in the pure aspect of Buddha Avalokiteshwara, but as is mentioned in the teachings, 'Even if all the Buddhas actually descend in front of us, one does not have the fortune to see the holy body with the holy signs and exemplifications except the present appearance (the ordinary impure appearance projected by the ordinary impure mind) until one is free from karmic obscuration.' Since ordinary beings like myself only have the karma to see the Buddha in a human form, His Holiness is the manifestation in this inspiring human form exactly in accordance with our karma, giving us the opportunity to directly hear and see this aspect. This kindness of His Holiness is without limit or measure, like the limitless sky. By being able to see His Holiness and hear his holy speech we can awaken or enlighten our minds—this is the best gift we can receive in this life.

By showing the Four Noble Truths His Holiness

introduces true suffering and where it comes from—the true cause of suffering. How is this possible? Because there is the true path, and by showing us the Four Noble Truths, His Holiness liberates sentient beings from the oceans of samsaric suffering and brings us to liberation. This is the most important education a teacher can give.

Many of us have no idea what the I is, what the mind is; we have no idea of ultimate truth and conventional truth. Our minds are totally dark. Even though everything—including the I, the Self—exists by being merely labelled by the mind and because of that is totally empty, we are constantly overwhelmed by an erroneous belief in apparently true appearances projected by ignorance. All that we see as real His Holiness sees as empty; His Holiness sees all phenomena as existing because they are merely labelled so by the mind. All the sense objects appear most pure to His Holiness. We constantly suffer, overwhelmed by negative emotional thoughts, if not by anger then by ignorance or desire, like a city covered by the ocean's waves. But His Holiness's holy mind is totally free from obscuration, from disturbing emotional thoughts such as desire.

We are like oil spilt on paper. Whatever we do, we are totally overwhelmed by self-cherishing thought. But many eons ago His Holiness became free from self-cherishing thought, with no thought, even for a second, of seeking happiness for the self.

His Holiness has even made his role as the political leader of Tibet total Dharma, that is, benefiting others. In this world the best politician, the one who causes no harm to any being but only benefits them, is Shakyamuni Buddha and Avalokiteshwara—His Holiness. His Holiness is also purest in morality, or ethics, and is the Omniscient One whose compassion embraces innumerable sentient beings, never giving them up even for one second.

There is no way to repay the kindness of each word of advice or teaching. To put into practice whatever advice we are given, to pray for the freedom of the Tibetan people, one of His Holiness's main wishes, and do what we can to help this cause and, finally, to constantly request His Holiness to live until samsara ends and guide us all the time—these are the best ways to repay his kindness.

Musings

Jeffrey Hopkins

When the Chinese communist government in Beijing hears that the Dalai Lama has been invited to visit a country, it immediately registers a protest with that country. Often, as a result, his visit becomes inconvenient, is downsized in importance, becomes a 'personal' visit. What do these countries fear? The Dalai Lama has no army, no economic pressure, no political cards to play. He advocates nonviolence and compassion. What do they fear?

The Chinese communist government in Beijing offered to negotiate anywhere at anytime if the Dalai Lama would not bring up the topic of independence. He agreed, but the response has been refusal to talk. What do they fear?

He has inspired the re-building of Tibetan cultural institutions outside of Tibet. He has asked the religious and political leaders of the world to look beyond narrow interests for the greater good. He has advocated attention to the basic needs of society regardless of religion or politics. Is this what is feared?

His power comes from a life of ethics, the force of truth. In Tibetan, he speaks with a range, depth, inspiration, humour and sincerity that inspire insight and motivate dedication to others' welfare. I have often wished that all the world could hear this marvel in his own tongue.

The Dalai Lama's longer name is *rJe btsun 'jam dpal ngag dbang blo bzang ye shes bstan 'dzin rgya mtsho srid gsum dbang bsgyur mtshungs pa med pa'I sde dpal bzang po.*

In English, syllable-by-syllable, it means 'leader, holiness, gentleness, renown, speech, dominion, mind, goodness, primordial, wisdom, teaching, hold, vastness, ocean, being, triad, controlling, unparalleled, glory, integrity.'

Leader of the world recognized for true *holiness,*
Gentleness personified in persuasive *renown,*
Speech of compassion pervading the planet in its *dominion,*
Mind of altruistic endeavour reaching all in its *goodness,*
Primordial in the depth and range of profound wisdom,
Teaching encompassing all phenomena in its *hold,*
Vastness of love's deeds rippling throughout life's *ocean,*
Being so merciful is played in suffering's *triad,*
Controlling the unruly through kindness *unparalleled,*
Glory in forms of endeavour sealed in total *integrity,*
May the teacher of the world bearing compassion
And wisdom indissoluble see all obstacles dissolve.

*

Middling Exposition of the Stages of the Path*

At lectures by the holy
Misconceptions are removed,
Previous realizations increase,
And the unrealized newly dawns to the mind.

At your lectures on the *Stages of the Path,*
Twenty-two new dawnings occurred for me.

Just as the past was quick,
So one should consider the future will be.

*Written in 1972 on the occasion of His Holiness the Dalai Lama's discourse on Dzong-ka-ba.

The purpose of meditating on impermanence
Is to realize that suffering quickly comes.

Like being deceived by a small present,
All compounded things are deceptive phenomena.

The body is an anode of afflictive emotions,
Assisting the generation of afflictive emotions.

That afflictive emotions are difficult to abandon
Is because they seem to act like protectors to oneself.

At birth one is alone
Without helpers and friends, a pathetic time.

If one remembered one's birth,
One would think, 'May this not be needed!'

Contaminated pleasures
Are not at all unfabricated pleasures.

The function of ethical behaviour
Is to stop coarse ill-deeds.

The doctrine is the actual object of refuge,
Realized by taking it to practice.

When going for refuge it is necessary
For true cessation to dawn well to the mind.

Nagarjuna and Asanga relied on the Perfection of Wisdom
    Sutras
As sources for the profound and vast.

All sentient beings filling space
Are equal in wanting happiness and not wanting suffering.

One should think that since others are so great in number
They are so much more important than oneself.

Because a consciousness knows something,
Although emptiness is difficult, it can be known.

The way things appear to exist inherently
Is that they appear to cover their bases of designation.

It is necessary to identify the root afflictive emotions
And secondary afflictive emotions that arise from ignorance.

Having a conception of one's own inherent existence,
One gets angry at a mouse that has eaten barley.

A sign of realizing just the non-existence of a self-sufficient
    person,
Is that upon searching for the mental and physical aggregates
    they still are found.

One should meditate on the person, the qualificant,
And the reality of emptiness as mutually dependent.

Although a Buddha's exalted body is supreme
It is incontrovertibly empty of inherent existence.

A Buddha's good qualities
Are a source of insatiable perception.

Since in that way religious awarenesses
Arose dependent upon your speech,
I respectfully bow to Your Holiness.
What teacher other than you is there!

*

Six Collections of Reasonings*

At the discourse on the Six Collections of Reasonings and
    Avalokiteshwara initiation,
Hearing mind-transforming words helped from the depths.
As before, twenty-two sets of meanings arose.
For the sake of remembering them, I will set them down
    here.

In this one short human life
It is difficult to find speech causing understanding of the
    profound.

The inherent nature refuted in the *Fundamental Wisdom*
Is with all whatsoever phenomena.

The mode of appearance as if covering the spot of the basis
    of designation
Is to appear as if existing concretely where the monastic is
    sitting.

If the sense of pointability dawns stably,
One will think, 'What is there more true than this!'

If something is other from its own side,
It must be other without reliance on another.

If one analyses, the mode of being exists right there.
One does not at all need to search elsewhere.

Though it is easy to experience the sign that is not to find
    the thing,
It is difficult to realize the boundary of the self-instituting
    status refuted by it.

*Written in 1972 on the occasion of the Dalai Lama's discourse
on Nagarjuna.*

Just as upon seeking a human appearing in a dream, it is
    not Foundation for Universal Responsibility but its
    appearance is not contradictory, so it is with a human.
Through reasoning analysing harmer and harmed
A consciousness conceiving their true existence is refuted
    but not the conventions.

Though the current conception of inherent existence is
    strong,
Cultivation of the mind of selflessness will make it limitless.

The clear light pervading the entire circle of objects of
    knowledge
Transcends anything fabricated by mind.

If Buddhahood is not attained quickly,
Opportunities to help others will be wasted.

Since sentient beings are a Buddha's special objects of
    intent,
One should not view them as lower than oneself.

Since sentient beings are the field for accumulating merit,
One should perforce view them as higher than oneself.

One should make use of each short moment
For the sake of helping others.

Among the many good qualities of a Buddha,
It is most difficult to attain the qualities of speech helpful
    to others.

In a palace whose 'substance' is exalted wisdom
A moon of compassion dawns at the heart.

The emptiness of that dawns as a vajra.
If so, one surely becomes definite in the Great Vehicle
    lineage.

Through the 'substances' of very subtle body, speech and
   mind
One becomes fully purified in Buddhahood.

The difference between sutra and mantra is made by
   meditative stabilization.
The difference in speed is that in mantra the realization of
   emptiness is stronger.

The meaning of the non-duality of the three exalted bodies
   and of the profound and the manifest
Is symbolized by *Om mani padme hum.*

Because such doctrine of the union of the profound and vast
Came to be heard in your presence,
It is difficult to express the benefit of encountering you.
I bow to Your Holiness from the depths.

The Dalai Lama and History

U.R. Ananthamurthy

It is only Truth that triumphs in history,
Believe the Dalai Lama's Tibetan Buddhists—
compassionate and mystical that they are.
Whatever triumphs will become Truth,
Believe the Chinese—
shrewd and cunning that they happen to be.

At Delhi, on some day,
the Dalai Lama noticed a black ant
on his saffron robe, even as he was speaking
with intense concentration and concern
about the plight of his unfortunate countrymen
trapped in the vicissitudes of modern history—
Gently smiling throughout.
The soft spoken sanyasi stopped speaking,
held the ant gently and carefully by the tips of his fingers,
let it out to move around safely on the table,
proceeding to talk, smilingly.

The Dalai Lama thus waits—
even though it appears for the moment
that the Chinese have triumphed in history—
in the countless moments and the infinity of time,
for Truth to triumph.

(Translated from the Kannada by
N. Manu Chakravarthy)

His Holiness in Conversation
with Rajiv Mehrotra

RM Your Holiness, you are regarded by millions of people as the incarnation of the Buddha. What is your experience of your divinity?

HHD I always describe myself as a Buddhist monk. Then of course there is the issue of reincarnation. There are different interpretations of reincarnation. For myself, it means deliberately taking birth in order to succeed in what was begun in the previous but not yet fulfilled. In that sense I feel I am a reincarnation.

RM What do you think is the incomplete work for your Holiness?

HHD I feel that the Thirteenth Dalai Lama began some work in both the spiritual as well as the temporal fields, and though he made some progress, the work could not be completed as he passed away in his late fifties. We believe he made a long-term plan, to be completed after his own lifetime. In my dream state, I have met the Thirteenth Dalai Lama thrice. While I am not necessarily the same being, I have a very strong karmic link with him.

RM Can you explain reincarnation? Obviously the physical body decays after death. Is it the mind or is it consciousness that gets reincarnated?

HHD   The basic question is 'What is self?' Certainly the body itself is not the central being, the mind alone is also not the central being. I am a human being called Tenzin Gyatso. There are many different Buddhist schools of thought, and each of them has a different central being. The *Prasangika* is one of the Madhyamika schools of thought, and in this system, they say that Tenzin Gyatso, the human being designated on the combination of this body and mind, is a central being.

This body comes from parents, from parents' parents, and thus has its own causes and conditions. According to certain Buddhist scriptures, the space particle that is the original cause of this body is also the cause of the previous whole universe. At the same time, the mind is momentary and changing. Anything that is changing is affected by causes and conditions. So the mind is also a product of similar causes and conditions. That is the basis of the rebirth theory.

The being is designated on the combination of the body and the mind, and also the subtler level of the body and grosser level of the mind. Therefore rebirth is the continuation of the mind or the continuation of being. Reincarnation is deliberate birth at a certain time and a certain place. This could be the same person or same being, or a different being come in his or her place to fulfil the previous unfulfilled work.

RM   Do you have any memories of your past life?

HHD   Sometimes it is difficult to remember what happened in the morning! However, when I was small, say two or three years old, my mother and some close friends noticed that I expressed clear memories of my past life. That is possible.

RM   How real is the meeting ground between science and spirituality?

HHD   Science is divided into what is called 'soft science' and 'hard science.' Scientists are generally sceptical about what they cannot definitely see. However, I believe that science itself has some limitations. It is limited to the field that you can measure. Life, consciousness, minds—these have not yet been explored fully. They are definitely connected with the brain. Today scientists are investigating the relationship between the mind and the brain and will gain more knowledge about the nature of the mind and mental function. There is interdependence—what we call Shunyata or emptiness. Shunyata means an object's absence from independent existence. The thing does not exist in itself; its existence is due to other factors—causes and conditions. This reality is also the point of modern physics, especially quantum theory. Some physicists, when they explain quantum theory, are even reluctant to use the word 'reality' as if it is independent. There is no such thing. Everything depends on another factor. Here, science and Buddhism say the same thing—that nothing exists in itself, and therefore there is impermanence, constant change.

Western psychology is very young compared to eastern psychology, eastern thought. But their way of investigation is quite different. Sometimes, their scientists introduce themselves saying, 'We are radicals, materialistic. We do not even accept the existence of the mind.' But once the discussions start, then some among them show more and more interest about Buddhist explanations, methods, about our account of the mind, and such things. We also learn and get many benefits from their research and findings, and the Buddhist perspective gives them a new way of looking at things, new ways to investigate. That has been my experience.

RM   The Tibetan tradition has very sophisticated mind-training techniques. Do you feel that the mind, like the body, can be trained?

HHD   From personal experience, I can tell you with confidence that the mind can be changed through training. When I was young, I was quite short-tempered. Although it never lasted long, I used to lose my temper very often. Now, with training, and perhaps age, I have changed. Now temper as well as attachment come and go, but without much effect on my basic monk mind. The mind is like an ocean: on the surface, waves come and go, but underneath the ocean always remains calm.

The elimination of negative emotions is rather difficult; it needs a lot of effort, a lot of meditation, and action. But it is possible to reduce the intensity of emotions. The ancient scriptures, their methods and techniques are very relevant in today's world, irrespective of whether a person is a believer or a non-believer.

We should have a clear awareness of the benefits as well as the negative, harmful effects of the mind. We should have clear recognition of the usefulness of compassion, love, contentment and forgiveness; and that on the other side there is hatred, discontentment, attachment—these lead to problems. Even from the point of view of physical health, the more compassionate mind becomes calmer because compassion brings us inner strength and self-confidence, and these bring calmness. On the other hand, anger and hatred are very, very harmful for developing calmness or self-confidence. Because your own mental attitude towards other people is negative, they automatically have the same kind of attitude towards you, which brings more fear, more doubt. So the result is uneasiness and unrest—a mental state that is very harmful for health.

The mind is like a successful life, or a happy family, where different kinds of emotions are involved. The more compassionate, the more open-minded bring more happiness to the home or the community. However, anger and attachment are also very important emotions. They are part of daily life, and without them, life would be colourless. With these extra emotions, your life becomes more colourful.

RM   Do you experience any of these emotions?

HHD   Sometimes. But when you experience these emotions less, your mind becomes steadier and as a result you physically also become much more stable. Too many up and downs in the mind are also very harmful for the body.

The demarcation between positive and negative emotions is very simple. Everybody wants happiness; the very purpose of our life, we can say, is happiness. Those emotions and actions that ultimately bring happiness, satisfaction, calmness and peace are positive. Those emotions and actions that ultimately bring suffering, either for others or for one's own self, are negative.

Many believe that money will solve all human problems. I believe that the answer to these problems is not external. While the western materialistic way of life or development is, of course, very important and very useful for humanity, at the same time traditional or spiritual values are equally or more important. We should not neglect our own traditional richness. This inner richness is a combination of material development, physical comfort as well as mental comfort through spiritual training. This should not be limited to Indians or Tibetans but should extend to humanity as a whole. For proper balance, material development and spiritual development must go together.

RM   You have written a book, *Art of Happiness*, a best-seller in the west. What is happiness?

HHD   Happiness, or nirvana or moksha, is freedom from suffering, from negative emotion, from the serfdom of ignorance. This is the concept of Dharma, especially in Indian philosophy, where liberation from ignorance—happiness—is the goal. All beings are equal in the sense that all, including animals, have a natural tendency to wish for happiness and freedom from suffering. Everyone has a right to be happy.

People believe that economic difficulties, illiteracy and ill-health lead to unhappiness, and pay a lot of attention to material development. However, even in the developed countries of the west, people are experiencing loneliness, anxiety and fear deep inside, often due to greed, discontent and mental unrest. Neither money nor technology can help to develop inner peace, which requires the right kind of mental attitude. The problems are caused by human intelligence, and we must find the answer also within human intelligence. Today scientists inform us that increased movements in certain parts of the brain are positive. Soon people will realize that inner tranquillity is based on a more open mind and a more open heart, a sense of caring, of concern towards others, a sense of entire humanity as one entity. In such a concept, to achieve our own happiness we have to respect the right of others to be happy. This may seem idealistic, but human history has shown us that many things that have looked unrealistic as a blueprint have worked out eventually.

RM   Buddhism has been essentially a system of personal practice and personal evolution. There is the notion of the bodhisattva which you embody. Now in contemporary society we have the idea of engaged Buddhism, which means Buddhism more engaged with social issues and social phenomena, and not just personal happiness. How does a system of philosophy that is basically geared to personal transformation translate into a social reality?

HHD   First, I never say that I am a bodhisattva. I am just a person who has a great desire to become a bodhisattva. But Buddhism was always actually engaged with society. The concepts of *dana* (generosity) and *shila* (ethical discipline) involve the other. The Mahayana way is heavily engaged with society. Dana means giving to others, not oneself. The three practices of shila—restraining from harmful action, cultivating, protecting and increasing virtue, and helping and benefiting living things—all involve being engaged with the other, without neglecting one's own improvement.

    I have always admired our Christian brothers and sisters who are very devoted to God but at the same time are heavily engaged in social service and social activity, especially in the fields of education and health. Sometimes we Buddhists, even those like myself who are practising to become bodhisattvas, are negligent about the practice of helping or serving others. The scriptures clearly mention giving one's own body, one's own organs; therefore, engaging in service to society should be the top priority.

RM   Buddhism emphasizes method and wisdom. In some ways intellectual wisdom can be acquired by listening, by reading, and by looking at the lives of great masters and people of service. Where method is concerned, the issue becomes a lot more complicated. I might know that compassion is very useful, that I must be gentle, calm, polite and so on, but it is difficult for me to transform myself to being in that state. Buddhism and the traditions that you embody have mastered the method. What practices could people who are not formally Buddhists follow to achieve this transformation, this change?

HHD   If the central motivation for all human activities is compassion, then all activities become humanized. Without compassion, our activities become too mechanical. If our activity in every field—education, economy, technology, scientific research—is motivated by sincere compassion and not just by how much profit is possible, or temporary benefits, then they will benefit others. Then our daily activities can become the actions of a bodhisattva.

RM   Your Holiness, in some ways you and your actions embody the culture of Tibet. There have been increasing images and reports that more and more of the disaffected elements of Chinese and western culture are coming into Tibet. How threatened, in the long term, do you feel is the civilization you represent?

HHD   If the present situation continues, then it is very difficult for Tibetan culture to survive. The majority of the Chinese now coming into Tibet are unskilled people who find it difficult to get work in China. They find more opportunities in Tibet, as Tibetans cannot compete with them. These unskilled Chinese are more interested in making money than in the Tibetan culture, even to the extent of learning the language, so local Tibetans are compelled to speak Chinese. As a result, the Tibetan language has become almost useless. Similarly, the local people's way of thinking, their lifestyles and food styles, are also changing. We notice this change in people who come from Tibet, especially the younger people. I think old people may not change but among the younger people, we have noticed a change in their attitudes.

I think the Chinese authorities, especially the local authority, have helped to cause this change in attitudes intentionally, out of fear. They look at every aspect of life politically. Their fear is that Tibet may one day separate, so they are very, very concerned. In everything related with Tibetan identity, including Tibetan language, or religion or culture, they see the seed of separation, the threat of separation. They have no intention of protecting Tibetan culture; instead they put a lot of restrictions on Tibetan study.

RM   But why is it important that Tibetan heritage and culture be preserved now, at a time when everywhere in the world it is the American, western globalized culture that is dominating, that is spreading and all the traditional cultures are declining. So while it is partly the impact of the Chinese, traditional cultures could be declining because of the effect of modernization, of westernization.

HHD   There are aspects of Tibetan tradition that are linked with the social system and the economic system and economic conditions; climatic conditions are also involved. These are not important; as times change, these also need to change. In these areas, Tibetans should have modernization.

Then there is another level, another aspect of Tibetan culture that is much influenced by the Buddhist Dharma. This influence is evident in the Tibetan's attitude towards oneself, towards other fellow human beings, towards animals, towards everything. I think, generally speaking, Tibetans are more compassionate, more peaceful than other people. I believe that this heritage is really worth preserving, because when we are passing through a difficult period in life, this heritage will be very helpful. I feel certain aspects of Tibetan culture are certainly useful for humanity as a whole, and therefore it is really worthwhile making an attempt to preserve them. But such preservation is not easy. I feel preservation of the Tibetan culture should be voluntary. Unless you see some benefit, some reasons for adopting a culture to preserve it, it is difficult to develop these aspects of the culture from within.

RM   After a long gap, your representatives visited China and there has been some dialogue. Is there a reason for you to feel that there is significant hope as a result of these processes?

HHD   At the first meeting the atmosphere seemed positive. We felt it was a good start. Right from the beginning we have believed that the best way to solve our problem is through talk. Therefore even as early as 1973 and 1974, when China was involved in the Cultural Revolution, we, here in Dharmasala, had already made up our minds that sooner or later we would have to talk with the Chinese government. The question of independence is irrelevant. We settled in our minds the idea of the middle way of approach—autonomy, self-rule—meaningful self-rule. *That* should be our goal. With that goal, we have held negotiations with the Chinese authorities. The Chinese still feel that I am involved in some kind of movement for independence; therefore there is still misunderstanding and lack of trust. Our views are different, and we need to find common ground. We must meet face to face and talk; I consider this to be extremely important. So we feel happy that the talks have been renewed.

It is a good start, even though we are not expecting too much. You see, the Tibetan issue is very complex. We are making efforts to achieve stability, unity and prosperity. The Chinese government also has the same aim. The methods are a little different. The Chinese government seems to try to achieve these things through sanitization, with less emphasis on Tibetan unity. My approach is to keep Tibetan unity at the centre, which will actually help to enrich the culture or spirituality of the Republic of China. We believe that this is the commonsense approach. Both Chinese and Tibetans are human beings. The unity must come from the heart and not be built on fear. At present there is some kind of stability, some kind of unity, but it is founded on fear. It is not genuine. Certainly Tibetans should get genuine satisfaction. But up to now, their lot has been suspicion, distress and so on. So I recently visited the Chinese prime minister and informed him about this. But inside Tibet there seems to be no improvement. I am a little concerned about this, because the goal of direct talk or dialogue is the improvement of Tibet or Tibetans—improvement inside Tibet—and not just the question of my return. Once the situation of Tibetans improves, once the Chinese government begins to think and behave realistically, then the time of my return would have arrived because only then would I be of some use there. Without such freedom, without a sort of improvement of present circumstances, even if I go there, it would be merely as a tourist; I would be able to achieve nothing there.

In fact, in the early 1980s the Chinese government—the Chinese leadership—made a proposal about my return. It was a five-point proposal: I would be allowed to retain the old privileges, status, and such things. I responded that this was not the issue; that the real issue was the Tibetan people's rights and their future. Since then, there has been no improvement inside Tibet.

RM   In recent history most conflicts have ceased because one side had something to negotiate with. Your approach is based on the logic of compassion. Though you have a lot of verbal support from political groups globally, there is no concrete pressure that might force the Chinese to act other than their sense of compassion and good nature. So what do you think would precipitate that change?

HHD   The bureaucracy of China is changing. More and more ordinary Chinese, intellectuals, artists and businessmen are now showing genuine interest in Tibet. Also, China's relations with India are improving. These changes will eventually force the Chinese government to think seriously and realistically about the situation inside Tibet.

RM   In the past you said that you felt you were confident that the issues would be resolved within your lifetime. Do you see any reason to change that point of view?

HHD   No, even though I am almost seventy years old. I think the new generation, the younger generation, is growing in quite a healthy way. I think the foundation of Tibetan spirit is very sound. The Tibetan spirit, both inside Tibet and outside, is very strong. We also have an elected leadership since two or three years, so even if I am sort of semi-retired, the Tibet issue still remains strong. And the people of China have also started considering things with a global perspective. Things are changing in a positive way. So I am optimistic about Tibet.

RM   You have often described India as the guru and Tibetans as the chela. India has been very remarkable and generous to the Tibetan community, hosting 150,000-odd people in exile, providing education, and doing lot to preserve Tibetan culture. But you have frequently said it has not done enough politically. Now, when there seems to be a softening of relations between India and China, what do you think India's role might be?

HHD   I have felt right from the beginning that China should not be isolated; it must be brought into the mainstream of the world community. The best and most logical way of persuasion is through friendship and not hostility. I have already made this clear in Washington, in Europe and in India. Therefore I welcome the improvement of relations between these two giant Asian nations, the two most populous nations. I don't think the improving relations with China will affect India's attitude towards the Tibetan community. Speaking politically, I sometimes describe India's attitude towards Tibet as over-cautious. Tibet has not been part of India's China policy for many decades, and this will continue. But in practice, India has done much regarding the preservation of Tibetan culture, education and so on.

China is changing, approaching democracy and openness, though with great caution, especially with regard to free elections and free media. And this is understandable, as China is a huge country. There have been great upheavals in the past; if the central authority collapses suddenly, there could be a lot of chaos and even bloodshed. That is in nobody's interest, not even the Tibetans'. The transition should be peaceful and smooth.

India gains economically as well as becomes stronger through improved relations with the Chinese government. I think India can influence the Chinese leadership, convince them that eventually a realistic policy regarding Tibet would be more beneficial to Chinese unity, the Chinese image, and also bring meaningful economic development to Tibet.

RM   To what degree do you think that Tibetan Buddhism, with the values that it embodies, would survive and grow outside Tibet? Do you think Tibetan heritage and culture can thrive in a different environment?

HHD   In certain fields like medical science and psychology, some top scientists are now showing interest in the Tibetan or the Buddhist view or explanation. Buddhist psychology is based on knowledge and not religion. And, as I have said earlier, it is much older than western psychology. Now there are a lot of people outside Tibet who are taking an interest in Tibetan perceptions. The culture is not limited to Tibet. Northern India, northern Nepal, Bhutan also have the same culture and heritage. And so do Mongolia and some other republics from the Russian Federation. Now, with freedom, there is a real chance to study Buddha Dharma in these areas.

RM   You have been engaged in a great deal of inter-faith dialogue. We commonly say that all religions have the same goal but that is not entirely true. There tend to be different areas and emphasis. What do you think is the common ground between various religions?

HHD   All major world religions bring the same message of love, compassion and forgiveness. But it would not be correct to say that all of them have the same objective or beliefs; there are substantial differences. For example, some religions believe in a Creator, and others do not—that represents a fundamental difference.

However, I believe there is a good purpose for these different views. Within humanity, there are so many different dispositions that one philosophy, one belief simply cannot satisfy all. Therefore, the great ancient masters had to demonstrate different philosophies and traditions. For example, some may like malted food, others may not. Similarly, spirituality is food for the mind, and different religions are very necessary for different problems and issues, different mental dispositions. Once you understand this, you can appreciate and respect the differences in religion. The purpose of different religions remains the same—it is for the betterment of humanity, to bring about a more compassionate and harmonious humanity.

RM   You frequently use the words 'love' and 'compassion'. What is the difference between them?

HHD   I do not know the exact difference between 'love' and 'compassion'. In Sanskrit there is one word, Karuna and in Tibetan there are two words, *inji* and *chamba*. Chamba means a desire to have happiness, while karuna and inji mean the desire to overcome suffering. Genuine compassion does not depend upon whether the other is nice to me; it is based on the realization and acceptance that the other is also a central being and has the right to be happy and to overcome suffering irrespective of his or her attitude towards me. Even an enemy who is harming me is a central being, and has every right to overcome suffering, to achieve happiness. So genuine compassion is a sense of concern towards everyone. Also, compassion is not like a feeling of pity; it is based on respect for another's rights and a recognition that the other is just like myself.

RM   Compassion is, in a sense, virtuous; it is desirable. In what way does compassion make me happier, or a better human being?

HHD   I will answer this with an example. When I meet someone on the street, I am reassured of my human feelings. Regardless of whether I know him or not, I smile at him. Sometimes there is no response; sometimes there is suspicion. But I get the benefit of smiling. Whether the other person gets any benefit or not depends upon his own thinking as well as on the circumstances. So the results of practising compassion go first to the practitioner. I believe it is very important to understand this, otherwise we will believe that compassion benefits the other, and has nothing for us. Compassionate attitude helps us to communicate easily with fellow human beings and other central beings. As a result, you make more genuine friendships, the atmosphere is more positive, which also gives you inner strength. This inner strength helps you to voluntarily concern yourself with others, instead of just thinking about yourself. Scientific research has shown that those individuals who often use words like 'me', 'I', 'mine' face a greater risk of heart attack. If one thinks of oneself always, one's thinking becomes very narrow; even a small problem appears very significant and unbearable. When we think of others, our mind widens, and within that width, some big personal problems also appear insignificant, and this, according to me, makes all the difference.

RM   Your Holiness, you mentioned the motivation of compassion. There is a distinction, in philosophy, between motivation and method. For example, Gandhi has distinguished between the method and the goal: the means and the end. You do not emphasize much on what the means are. How do you draw this distinction?

HHD   Take, for example, violence and nonviolence. Ultimately the demarcation is based upon motivation. If sincere compassion is the motivation, then a harsh word or action, such as that of parents towards children, or a teacher towards the student, cannot be called violence. Even if it appears outwardly harsh, it is ultimately nonviolence. In the same way, if there is negative emotion or negative motivation, for example, if one wants to cheat another, or to take advantage of another, and uses kind words, it is actually a kind of violence. So motivation is the most important demarcation. But again, if the method is a kind of dramatic or drastic violence, we cannot simply justify it using motivation. But generally, motivation is most important. Even harsh methods can be justified with sincere, positive motivation.

RM   Your Holiness, you have said that the secret of your happiness must remain a secret. Could you reveal the secret?

HHD   Good sleep, good food. I don't think it is one particular thing, but the attitude towards oneself, towards others. Life is not easy from the Buddhist point of view. This body is a hindrance; negative karma or samsarik karma can create problems; you also sometimes see unfortunate things happen. But unfortunate things can be transformed into a positive event; you can use them to gain experience.

Therefore they are helpful in daily life. Of course, right from the beginning you should avoid negative consequences. But once something happens, try and look at it from different directions. For example, we have lost our country. But the situation also presents new opportunities; if you look at things from a positive aspect frustrations become less.

Notes and References

The Ocean of Wisdom

1. William M. Johnson, ed. *Encyclopedia of Monasticism*, 2 vols. (Chicago: Fitzroy Dearborn, 2000).
2. I have explored this relationship and its possible fruit in my book *The Mystic Heart: Discovering a Universal Spirituality in the World's Religions* (Novato, CA: New World Library, 1999).
3. The Dalai Lama, *The Good Heart: A Buddhist Perspective on the Teachings of Jesus* (Boston: Wisdom Publications, 1997).
4. For the text of this document see, *A Source Book for Earth's Community of Religions*, edited by Joel Beversluis (Ada, MI: CoNexus Press, 1995), p.171.
5. Tenzin Gyatso, *Ethics for a New Millennium* (New York: Riverhead, 1999).

A Buddha of Compassion

The Dalai Lama, *The Thirty-seven Practices of the Bodhisattva* (audiotape), translated by Jeffrey Hopkins. (Los Angeles: Thubten Dhargye Ling, 1989).

Dudjom Rinpoche and Jikdrel Yeshe Dorje, *The Nyingma School of Tibetan Buddhism* (Boston: Wisdom Publications, 1991).

Lama Zopa Rinpoche, 'The Compassion Buddha is No Other than Your Holiness', from the praise and request offered to His Holiness after the Kalachakra initiation in Sydney, Australia, September 1996. Reprinted in *Mandala Magazine*, November–December 1996.

Universal Responsibility in the Dalai Lama's World View

1. Damien Keown, *Contemporary Buddhist Ethics* (Richmond, Surrey: Curzon Press, 2000, p.63).
2. Richard Dagger, 'Rights', in Terence Bull et al. (eds.), *Political Innovation and Conceptual Change* (Cambridge: Cambridge University Press, 1989, p.297) as cited in Damien Keown, *Contemporary Buddhist Ethics* (Richmond, Surrey: Curzon Press, 2000, pp.59-60).
3. Peter Harvey, *An Introduction to Buddhist Ethics* (Cambridge: Cambridge University Press, 2000, p.119). Also see, *The Dalai Lama, A Policy of Kindness: An Anthology of Writings by and About the Dalai Lama*, edited and compiled by Sidney Piburn (Ithaca, NY: Snow Lion, 1990, pp.111-15).
4. S.S. Barlingay, 'Responsibility, Universality and Religion', in Ramesh Chandra Tewari and Krishna Nath (eds.), *Universal Responsibility: A Collection of Essays to Honour Tenzin Gyatso the XIVth Dalai Lama* (New Delhi: Foundation for Universal Responsibility of His Holiness the Dalai Lama and A'N'B Publishers Pvt. Ltd., 1996, p.121).
5. Ibid., pp.122, 123.
6. Ibid., p.121.
7. Christopher Queen (ed.), 'Introduction: A New Buddhism', *Engaged Buddhism in the West* (Boston: Wisdom Publications, 2000, p.3).
8. Ramesh Chandra Tewari and Krishna Nath (eds.), *Universal Responsibility: A Collection of Essays to Honour Tenzin Gyatso the XIVth Dalai Lama* (New Delhi: Foundation for Universal Responsibility of His Holiness the Dalai Lama and A'N'B Publishers Pvt. Ltd., 1996, p.xvii).
9. Mathew Kapstein, 'Three Questions About Universal Responsibility', in Tewari and Nath, *Universal Responsibility*, note 4 above, p.213.
10. Tewari and Nath, *Universal Responsibility*, note 4 above, p.xii.
11. Ibid., p.xxiii. An example can be given of The Foundation for Universal Responsibility of His Holiness the Dalai Lama at New Delhi: 'The Foundation is not there to promote any one individual, political ideology or cause. It is rather to build bridges of cooperation and understanding.' Geeti Sen and

Rajiv Mehrotra, 'Laughter and Compassion: His Holiness Tenzin Gyatso the XIVth Dalai Lama of Tibet in Conversation with Geeti Sen and Rajiv Mehrotra', *India International Centre Quarterly* (New Delhi), vol. 18, no. 4, p.127.

12. 'Importance of Compassion in Human Life', in A.A. Shiromany (ed.), *The Spirit of Tibet: Universal Heritage, Selected Speeches of HH the XIV Dalai Lama* (New Delhi: Tibetan Parliamentary and Policy Research Centre and Allied Publishers Ltd., 1995, p.253).

13. The Dalai Lama, 'Universal Responsibility', in *Ancient Wisdom, Modern World: Ethics for the New Millennium* (London: Abacus, 1999, 2000, p.168).

14. Speech at Parliamentary Earth Summit, in Shiromany, *The Spirit of Tibet*, note 12 above, p.299.

15. Ibid., p.299.

16. Eleanor Rosch, 'Portraits of the Mind in Cognitive Science and Meditation', in Tewari and Nath, *Universal Responsibility*, note 4 above, p.163.

17. The Dalai Lama, 'Asian Values and Democracy', *Tibetan Bulletin* (Dharamsala: Department of Information and International Relations, Central Tibetan Administration), vol. 3, no. 1, January-February 1999, p.19.

18. L.P.N. Pereira, *Buddhism and Human Rights: A Buddhist Commentary on the Universal Declaration of Human Rights* (Colombo: Karunaratne and Sons, 1991, p.24).

19. 'Asian countries' have propagated ten points justifying why human rights should not be raised or linked with trade and aid: sovereignty and human rights; internal matters; development; food; individual vs. society; order; historical and religious background; socio-genic and cultural specific; higher morality; and trade and aid. Lopsang Sengay Taksham, 'Human Rights and Universality: Asian Excuses and Contradictions', *Tibetan Review* (Delhi), vol. XXX, no. 2, February 1995, pp.12-16.

20. Samuel P. Huntington, 'The Clash of Civilizations?', *Foreign Affairs*, vol. 72, 1993, pp.40-41. The argument was explored further in Samuel P. Huntington, *The Clash of Civilizations and the Remaking of the World Order* (New Delhi: Penguin, 1997, pp.40-41); also see from pp.22-49.

21. 'Controversies and Cultures', *The Economist* (London), 5 December 1998, p.10.

22. Advocates of 'Asian values' sometimes say that the Asian places the 'common good' before the individual, whereas the west accords priority to the individual. Mahathir Mohammad has listed the six most important societal values of the East Asians on the basis of a survey by David Hitchcock. They are (1) an orderly society, (2) societal harmony, (3) the accountability of public officials, (4) openness to new ideas, (5) freedom of expression, and (6) respect for authority. Mahathir Mohammad, 'Let's Have Mutual Cultural Enrichment', *New Straits Times*, 16 March 1995, pp.10-11. Also see, Michael Freeman, 'Human Rights, Asian Values, and the Clash of Civilization', *Issues and Studies* (Taipei: Institute of International Relations, National Chengchi University), vol. 34, no. 10, October 1998, p.62. Michael Freeman suggests that the comparable values held by the Americans are: (1) freedom of expression, (2) personal freedom, (3) the right of the individual, (4) open debate, (5) thinking for oneself, and (6) the accountability of pubic officials. Mahathir conclusively says that this makes it apparent that East Asians give priority to order-supporting values whereas Americans privilege rights-related values. Michael Freeman, 'Human Rights, Democracy and "Asian Values"', *The Pacific Review*, vol. 9, no. 3, 1996, pp.352-66. Also see, David I. Hitchcock, *Asian Values and the United States: How Much Conflict* (Washington, D.C.: Centre for Strategic and International Studies, 1994).

23. The Dalai Lama, *Speeches, Statements, Articles, Interviews: 1987 to June 1995* (Dharamsala: The Department of Information and International Relations, Gangchen Kyishong, 1995, p.205); The Dalai Lama, 'Asian Values and Democracy', note 17 above, p.20; The Dalai Lama, Speech Delivered to New York Lawyers Alliance for World Security and Council of Foreign Relations, New York City, 27 April 1994.

24. 'Human Rights and Universal Responsibility', in A.A. Shiromany (ed.), *The Political Philosophy of His Holiness the XIV Dalai Lama: Selected Speeches and Writings* (New Delhi: Tibetan Parliamentary and Policy Research Centre and Friedrich-Naumann-Stiftung, 1998, p.89).

25. Ibid., p.90; The Dalai Lama, *Speeches, Statements*, note 23 above, p.205.

26. Dawa Norbu, 'Tibetan Buffer Good for Both India and China', *Demilitarization of the Tibetan Plateau* (Dharamsala: The Department of Information and International Relations, 2000, p.23).
27. 'Interview to *The Economic Times*', in Shiromany, *The Political Philosophy of His Holiness*, note 24 above, p.195.
28. The Dalai Lama, *Speeches, Statements*, note 23 above, p.206.
29. Ibid, p.204.
30. Chandradhar Sharma, *A Critical Survey of Indian Philosophy* (Delhi: Motilal Banarsidass Publishers, 1987, pp.72-75).
31. The Dalai Lama and Jean-Claude Carrière, *The Power of Buddhism* (Dublin: Newleaf, 1994, 1996, p.35).
32. *Encyclopedia of Applied Ethics*, Vol. I (San Diego: Academic Press, 1998, p.394).
33. There is a category of natural suffering which includes phenomena like war, poverty, crime, into which the Dalai Lama has incorporated contemporary issues like illiteracy and certain diseases also. The second category is of natural suffering like old age, sickness and death. See, The Dalai Lama, *Ethics for the New Millennium*, note 13 above, pp.138, 141.
34. Ibidi., p.141.
35. Ibid., pp.141-42.
36. Fredrick R. Hyde-Chambers, 'Buddhism in Action: The Dalai Lama and the People of Tibet', in *The Middle Way* (London), May 1996, vol. 71, no. 1, p.9.
37. The Dalai Lama, 'Asian Values and Democracy', note 17 above, p.19.
38. Mrinal Miri, 'A Note on the Idea of Human Rights', *Journal of Indian Council of Philosophical Research* (New Delhi), vol. XVII, no. 2, January-April 2000, p.160.
39. The Dalai Lama, 'Asian Values and Democracy', note 17 above, p.19.
40. Ibid., p.19.
41. Shiromany, *The Political Philosophy of His Holiness*, note 24 above, p.xxvi.
42. Peter Harvey, *An Introduction to Buddhist Ethics* (Cambridge: Cambridge University Press, 2000, p.239).
43. Ibid., pp.185-86.
44. Some scholars have attempted to explain environmental issues from the Buddhist perspective by drawing a parallel from the

Buddhist concept of impermanence. Impermanence of phenomenon is a tenet of Buddha's teaching. While teaching that we must accept transitoriness, he forbade willful killing. It was Buddha's injunction that in order to retain our environment, we must not kill and destroy beyond the capacity of Mother Earth. Doboom Tulku Lama, *The Buddhist Path to Enlightenment: Tibetan Buddhist Philosophy and Practice* (California: Point Loma Publications, 1996, pp.162–63).

45. Ibid., p.163.

46. The Dalai Lama, *The Four Noble Truths* (New Delhi: HarperCollins Publishers India, 1997, 1998, pp.130-50).

47. 'No Substitute for Love', in Shiromany, *The Political Philosophy of His Holiness*, note 24 above, p.79.

48. The Dalai Lama, 'Asian Values and Democracy', note 17 above, p.19.

49. 'Speech on India's Role on Tibet', in Shiromany, *The Political Philosophy of His Holiness*, note 24 above, p.89.

50. 'Human Rights and Universal Responsibility', in Shiromany, *The Political Philosophy of His Holiness*, note 24 above, p.93.

51. 'Importance of Compassion in Human Life', in Shiromany, *The Spirit of Tibet*, note 12 above, p.252.

52. 'Address to the US Congress, US Capitol Rotunda, 18 April 1999', in Shiromany, *The Political Philosophy of His Holiness*, note 24 above, p.64.

53. Jay L. Garfield, 'Human Rights and Compassion: Towards a Unified Moral Framework', in Tewari and Nath, *Universal Responsibility*, note 4 above, p.197; The Dalai Lama, *The Global Community and the Need for Universal Responsibility* (Boston: Wisdom Publications, 1992); The Dalai Lama, *Kindness, Clarity and Insight*, Jeffrey Hopkins and Elizabeth Napper (eds.), translated by Jeffrey Hopkins (New York, Ithaca: Snow Lion Publishers, 1984).

54. A. Baier, *Moral Prejudices* (Cambridge: Harvard University Press, 1964, p.25), and J. Tronto, *Moral Boundaries: A Political Argument for an Ethic of Care* (New York: Routledge, 1993).

55. The Dalai Lama, *The Global Community and the Need for Universal Responsibility*. It has been acknowledged that there is a similarity in the arguments proposed by Baier (1964) and Tronto (1993). For reference of both Baier (1964) and Tronto

(1993) (note 54 above). See Jay L. Garfield, 'Human Rights and Compassion: Towards a Unified Moral Framework', in Tewari and Nath, *Universal Responsibility*, note 4 above, p.184.

56. A. Wayman, *The Ethics of Tibet* (Albany: State University of New York Press, 1991, p.26).

57. A. Schopenhauer, *On the Basis of Morality*, translated by E.F.J. Payne (Indianapolis: Bobbs-Merrill, 1965, p.144).

58. Ibid., p.205.

59. Ibid., p.210.

60. The Dalai Lama, *The Power of Compassion: A Collection of Lectures by His Holiness The XIV Dalai Lama*, translated by Geshe Thupten Jinpa (New Delhi: HarperCollins Publishers India, 1994, pp.62-63).

61. Ibid., p.67.

62. Henry J. Steiner and Philip Alston, *International Human Rights in Context: Law, Politics, Morals* (Oxford: Clarendon Press, 1996, p.208).

63. Ibid., p.208.

64. Ibid., p.208.

65. Pannikar as cited in Steiner and Alston, *International Human Rights*, note 62 above, p.209.

66. Ibid., p.207.

67. *Gemeinsam* in German means together, mutual, joint, common. Therefore, Gemeinschaft means community. Gemeinschaften is the plural of community. See, 'The Langenscheidt', *Langenscheidt's German-English, English-German Dictionary* (New York: Pocket Books, 1952, 1970, p.120).

68. Pannikar, note 65 above, p.205.

69. The Dalai Lama, 'Universal Responsibility: Key to Human Survival', Asian Human Rights Commission, <*http.//www.ahrck.net/solidarity/199903/v93-16.htm*>.

The Dalai Lama and the Tibetan Monastic Academia

1. The Dalai Lama, *My Land and My People* (New York: McGraw-Hill, 1962) and *Freedom in Exile* (New York: HarperCollins, 1991).

2. For an informative account of this aspect of the Dalai Lama's stated mission, see the Dalai Lama, et al. *The Good Heart:*

The Dalai Lama Explores the Heart of Christianity (London: Rider Books, 1996).

3. The Dalai Lama has devoted an entire book to the promotion of what he calls secular ethics in *Ethics for the New Millennium* (New York: Riverhead Books, 1999).

4. The latest of the four main schools of Tibetan Buddhism (the other three being Nyingma, Sakya and Kagyü), founded by Tibet's great reformer and philosopher Tsong Khapa (1357–1419).

5. For a concise history of Tibet and, in particular, the emergence of the Dalai Lama's rule, see Lee Feigon, *Demystifying Tibet: Unlocking the Secrets of the Land of Snows* (Chicago: Ivan R. Dee, 1996).

6. All dates of the classical Indian thinkers are from Hajme Nakamura, *Indian Buddhism: A Survey with Bibliographical Notes* (New Delhi: Motilal Banarsidass, 1987).

7. Dharmakirti's thought is today a major area of focus in contemporary academic scholarship on Sanskrit and Buddhist studies. To date, four international conferences on Dharmakirti have taken place, attended by scholars from Europe, Asia and North America.

8. For an accessible translation and study of this important Buddhist philosophical classic, see Jay Garfield, *Fundamental Wisdom of the Middle Way* (New York: Oxford University Press, 1995).

9. Various aspects of Tsong Khapa's thought have received extensive attention in contemporary scholarship. See, for example, Robert Thurman, *Tsongkhapa's Speech of Gold in the Essence of True Eloquence* (Princeton: Princeton University Press, 1984) and Thupten Jinpa, *Tsongkhapa's Philosophy of Emptiness: Self, Reality and Reason in Tibetan Thought* (Richmond: Curzon Press, forthcoming).

10. For a concise study of the key parallels between Buddhist psychology and contemporary psychoanalytic thought, see Mark Epstein, *Thoughts Without a Thinker* (New York: Basic Books, HarperCollins, 1995).

11. For a lucid translation of this influential Buddhist classic, see Shantideva, *The Bodhicaryavatra* (New York: Oxford University Press, 1996), translated by Kate Crosby and Andrew Skilton.

12. This translation is mine. For Oxford World's Classics version, see Shantideva, note 11 above, p.143.
13. The Dalai Lama has had close friendships with several influential contemporary thinkers, in particular the late British philosopher of science Sir Karl Popper, physicists David Bohm and Von Weisecker, and the late Chilean neurobiologist Francisco Varela. Especially since 1987, the Dalai Lama has been engaged in ongoing conversations with scientists and philosophers on the interface between Buddhist thought and contemporary science. Entitled Mind and Life conferences, they take place once every two years at his residence in Dharamsala. The proceedings of some of these meetings have been published under the following titles: *Gentle Bridges* (Boston: Shambhala, 1992), *Sleeping, Dreaming and Dying* (Boston: Wisdom, 1997), *Healing Emotions* (Boston: Shambhala, 1997) and *Consciousness at the Crossroads* (Ithaca: Snow Lion, 1999).

Notes on Contributors

U.R. Ananthamurthy is a prominent Indian poet and writer of novels such as *Samskara* and *Bharatiputra* whose writing emphasizes his existential approach to life. He is an activist and academic. He has been the president of the Sahitya Akademi, New Delhi and is presently the Chairman of the Film and Television Institute of India, Pune.

Swati Chopra is a Delhi-based journalist who writes on spirituality and religion. Her interview with His Holiness, the Seventeenth Karmapa has appeared in *Tricycle: The Buddhist Review* and her writing has featured in *Resurgence* magazine. She has written a soon-to-be-published book on Buddhism and has edited *The Best of Speaking Tree*. Swati is editor of Life Positive Plus.

Mary Craig is a former broadcasting journalist and author of fourteen books including a trilogy on Tibet. Her book, *Kundun*, looks at His Holiness's family. The other books in the trilogy are *Tears of Blood* and *Waiting for the Sun*. She lives in England.

Ela Gandhi is the granddaughter of Mahatma Gandhi and a revered social worker and political activist based in South Africa. She is a member of the African National Congress and works closely with international organizations on peace issues and with Tibet support groups.

Daniel Goleman is a psychologist and journalist who has authored several international bestsellers including *Emotional Intelligence* and *Working with Emotional Intelligence*. He is the founder and CEO of Emotional Intelligence Services allied with a global consulting firm. He recently authored *Destructive Emotions: How Can We Overcome Them? A Scientific Dialogue with the Dalai Lama*.

Isabel Hilton is a staff writer of the *New Yorker* magazine and a London-based writer and broadcaster. She is an expert in Chinese affairs. Her last book was *The Search for the Panchen Lama* as a follow-up to her documentary film *Kingdom of the Lost Boy*, an account of the search.

Jeffrey Hopkins is Professor of Tibetan Buddhist Studies at the University of Virginia. Eight of his twenty-eight books have been collaborations with His Holiness for whom he served as chief interpreter on lecture tours from 1979 to 1989.

Pico Iyer is a well-known journalist, author and essayist who has written extensively on a range of issues including Tibet for the world's leading publications ranging from *Time* to the *International Herald Tribune*. He first visited His Holiness in Dharamsala in 1974. He is a contributing editor to *Tricycle: The Buddhist Review*.

Thupten Jinpa is a monk based in Canada, who is principal English interpreter to His Holiness and has translated and edited more than ten books by him including *The World of Tibetan Buddhism, The Good Heart: The Dalai Lama Explores the Heart of Christianity*, and bestseller *Ethics for the New Millennium*.

Anees Jung is a Delhi-based writer and journalist who has authored several books, many of which have chronicled the concerns and predicaments of South Asian women. She was educated in Hyderabad and the United States. Her books include *Unveiling India: A Women's Journey, Beyond the Courtyard: A Sequel to Unveiling India* and *Peace in Winter Gardens: Ordinary People, Extraordinary Lives*.

Dalip Mehta served in the Indian Foreign Service till 2002. During his career he was closely involved in India's relations with her immediate neighbours. He served as ambassador in Central Asia, based in Tashkent, and Bhutan, and was dean of the Foreign Service Institute in New Delhi. He serves as a trustee of the New Delhi-based Foundation for Universal Responsibility of His Holiness the Dalai Lama.

Alexander Norman worked closely with His Holiness in the writing of his autobiography *Freedom in Exile* and *Ethics for the*

New Millennium. He has also contributed numerous articles on Tibet to publications such as *Financial Times*.

Raimon Panikkar is a philosopher, theologian and expert in inter-religious dialogue. Professor emeritus, religious studies department, University of California, he is also the president of the Spanish Association for the Science of Religions. He was raised in Spain by a Catholic mother.and a Hindu father and was ordained a Roman Catholic priest in 1946.

Bharati Puri is a journalist and scholar who is a post-doctoral fellow working on 'Deconstructing Engaged Buddhist Ethics' with the New Delhi-based Centre for the Study of Developing Societies. She completed her Ph.D. on 'Engaged Buddhism in the Modern World: A Study of the Dalai Lama's Worldview' from Jawaharlal Nehru University, New Delhi in 2001.

Senthil Ram completed a Ph.D. in Central Asian Studies from Jawaharlal Nehru University, New Delhi. He is currently a visiting researcher at the Department of Peace and Development Research at Gothenborg University, Sweden and is working on a monograph, 'Nonviolent Approaches to Conflict Resolution: The Case of Tibet', for the Centre for Peace Studies, University of Tromso, Norway.

Nicholas Ribush is a medical doctor who first encountered Buddhism at Kopan monastery in 1972, when he became a student of Lamas Yeshe and Zopa Rinpoche. He is the founder of the Tushita Mahayana meditation centres in New Delhi and Boston as well as the Lama Yeshe Wisdom Archive in Boston.

Matthieu Ricard is a former scientist who chose to become a Tibetan Buddhist monk. He is His Holiness's interpreter in French, has translated numerous Buddhist texts, is a noted photographer, and co-author of *The Quantum and the Lotus* and *The Monk and the Philosopher*.

Lama Thubten Zopa Rinpoche was born in Nepal and was recognized as the reincarnation of the Lawudo Lama at the age of three. A disciple of Lama Yeshe, he currently serves as spiritual director of the Foundation for the Preservation of Mahayana Tradition and has travelled the world with his teacher, establishing centres of Dharma.

Sulak Sivaraksa is a prominent and outspoken Thai intellectual and social activist. He is a teacher, a scholar, a publisher, an activist, the founder of many organizations, and the author of more than a hundred books and monographs in both Thai and English.

Brother Wayne Teasdale is a Benedictine and monastic in the Sannyasa tradition. He is based in Chicago and serves on the board of trustees of the Parliament of the World's Religions. He has worked with His Holiness on the 1991 Universal Declaration on Nonviolence and the interdisciplinary symposium Synthesis Dialogues.

Robert A.F. Thurman is the director of Tibet House in New York City that he co-founded. He is a scholar, author, former Tibetan Buddhist monk and friend of His Holiness. Currently, he is the Jey Tsong Khapa Professor of Indo-Tibetan Buddhist Studies at Columbia University.

Bhuchung Tsering came to India with his family from Tibet in 1960 and joined the Tibetan Government in Exile in Dharamsala in the 1980s. He worked as editor of the official journal of the Tibetan government, apart from writing for several journals and newspapers. Currently, he is director of the Washington, D.C.-based, International Campaign for Tibet.

Acknowledgements

The Foundation for Universal Responsibility and I owe our deep gratitude to all the contributors to this book for their generous and spontaneous response to our request for these essays. It is a truly collective effort towards cultivating a deeper appreciation of the many facets of a great master and to provide contemporary commentaries on him for posterity.

At Penguin, David Davidar and V.K. Karthika have been wonderful—a constant source of encouragement as I still nervously take my steps into authorship—and my editor Krishan Chopra has been truly indulgent and gently supportive. I would also like to thank Sumitra Srinivasan for her editorial work on the book.

My gratitude to Tulika Srivastava, Simmi Bali, Nandita Surendran and R. Lalitha for their continuing help in putting the manuscript together.

HAY HOUSE PUBLISHERS

We hope you enjoyed this Hay House book.
If you would like to receive a free catalogue featuring additional
Hay House books and products, or if you would like information
about the Hay Foundation, please contact:

Hay House UK Ltd
292B Kensal Rd • London W10 5BE
Tel: (44) 20 8962 1230; Fax: (44) 20 8962 1239
www.hayhouse.co.uk

***

Published and distributed in the United States of America by:
Hay House, Inc. • PO Box 5100 • Carlsbad, CA 92018-5100
Tel.: (1) 760 431 7695 or (1) 800 654 5126;
Fax: (1) 760 431 6948 or (1) 800 650 5115
www.hayhouse.com

Published and distributed in Australia by:
Hay House Australia Ltd • 18/36 Ralph St • Alexandria NSW 2015
Tel.: (61) 2 9669 4299; Fax: (61) 2 9669 4144
www.hayhouse.com.au

Published and distributed in the Republic of South Africa by:
Hay House SA (Pty) Ltd • PO Box 990 • Witkoppen 2068
Tel./Fax: (27) 11 467 8904 • www.hayhouse.co.za

Published and distributed in India by:
Hay House Publishers India • Muskaan Complex • Plot No.3
B-2 • Vasant Kunj • New Delhi – 110 070.
Tel.: (91) 11 41761620; Fax: (91) 11 41761630.
www.hayhouse.co.in

Distributed in Canada by:
Raincoast • 9050 Shaughnessy St • Vancouver, BC V6P 6E5
Tel.: (1) 604 323 7100; Fax: (1) 604 323 2600

***

Sign up via the Hay House UK website to receive the Hay House
online newsletter and stay informed about what's going on with
your favourite authors. You'll receive bimonthly announcements
about discounts and offers, special events, product highlights,
free excerpts, giveaways, and more!
www.hayhouse.co.uk